# Political Campaigns

This book is an interpretive analysis of political campaigns in America: instead of focusing on how campaigns are designed and run, it investigates the role that campaigns play in our American politics, and the close symbiosis between campaigns and those politics. The text examines how campaigns are an important manifestation of how we "do" politics in this country.

Hallmarks of this text include:

- showing how campaigns can undermine our democracy and asking how democratic they—and by extension, our politics—really are;
- demonstrating that the ability of the media to accurately, fairly, and deeply report on campaigns has been severely compromised, both because of the growing "distance" between campaigns and media outlets and because of the structure of "Big Media" corporate ownership and its tight relationship to "Big Money." It asks important questions about the media including:
  1. How do the media, reporters in particular, cover campaigns? What pressures and forces shape what and how they present campaigns?
  2. What is the impact of the ever-increasing chasm separating campaigns and the media?
  3. How does the close tie between corporate mainstream media and SuperPac money affect campaign coverage?
  4. How does the ability of campaigns and media to segment voters into ever-smaller slices influence how campaigns are covered?
- tracking the continuing growth of unregulated, private, unaccountable "dark money" in campaigns as a threat to our democratic elections and politics. Democracy rests fundamentally on transparency and accountability—sunlight—and our campaign laws and norms now allow and encourage exactly the opposite, largely because of decisions by the United States Supreme Court.

**Richard K. Scher** is Professor of Political Science at the University of Florida, Gainesville.

Professor Richard K. Scher takes a deep dive into the campaigns that drive our politics, and he asks fundamental questions about the electioneering process. Students and readers of all stripes will find the book fascinating —and good preparation for interpreting what candidates and the news media say and do each political season.

Larry J. Sabato, University of Virginia Center for Politics

As we strive to meet the permanent need to govern in a time of the permanent campaign, Professor Richard K. Scher's book provides important insights into the politics of campaigns.

Mark R. Kennedy, George Washington University

Richard K. Scher does a superb job of demystifying the American political campaign process for the reader. He provides a comprehensive and keen analysis of modern politics and the prominent role that political consultants, media outlets, and big money play in campaigns and elections.

John Allen Hendricks, Stephen F. Austin State University

*Political Campaigns in the United States* is an excellent introduction to how American political campaigns work and how they have evolved with the increased role money, media, and an expanded professionalized campaign industry. Scher argues that contemporary campaigns are undermining American democracy by turning over them over to a campaign industry that is closely allied with 'big money' and corporate interests, thus undermining the role of everyday voters. He calls for reforms in campaigns, which will bring more transparency, accountability, fairness, and responsiveness which will bring back more vitality and trust in our democracy.

James A. Thurber, American University

# Political Campaigns in the United States

## Richard K. Scher

Routledge
Taylor & Francis Group

NEW YORK AND LONDON

Published 2016
by Routledge
711 Third Avenue, New York, NY 10017

and by Routledge
2 Park Square, Milton Park, Abingdon, Oxon, OX14 4RN

*Routledge is an imprint of the Taylor & Francis Group, an informa business*

© 2016 Taylor & Francis

*Library of Congress Cataloging in Publication Data*
Names: Scher, Richard K.
Title: Political campaigns in the United States / Richard K. Scher, University of Florida.
Description: First edition. | New York ; Milton Park, Abingdon, Oxon : Routledge, 2016.
Identifiers: LCCN 2015035172| ISBN 9781138181830 (hardback) | ISBN 9781138181861 (pbk.) | ISBN 9781315646732 (ebook)
Subjects: LCSH: Political campaigns—United States—History.
Classification: LCC JK2281 .S345 2016 | DDC 323.70973—dc23
LC record available at http://lccn.loc.gov/2015035172

ISBN: 978-1-138-18183-0 (hbk)
ISBN: 978-1-138-18186-1 (pbk)
ISBN: 978-1-315-64673-2 (ebk)

Typeset in Sabon
by FiSH Books Ltd, Enfield

Printed and bound in the United States of America by Publishers Graphics, LLC on sustainably sourced paper.

For Aida, Nada, and AH, whom I never had the pleasure of meeting

For Nick and Catherine and Greg, wherever and however he is

For Coby and Amy, and Eric and Danny

And for my late parents, who awakened my interest in politics and campaigns (Eisenhower/Stevenson, 1952) and who always encouraged me to learn

# Contents

# Illustrations

## Figures

## Tables

# Preface

This is a unique book. It is not about how to "do" campaigns, although readers will learn a good deal about how campaigns are structured and how they go about their business of getting candidates elected to office, or ballot initiatives passed (or defeated). It is not a case study of any particular campaign, presidential or otherwise, although many examples and anecdotes from past campaigns will be cited to help illustrate points or strengthen arguments. Nor is it a history of campaigns, although the author firmly believes that looking backwards can help illuminate the present and, perhaps, the future.

Rather, this book is about the politics of campaigns. It explores how campaigns have become part and parcel of our "regular," "everyday" politics. The book asks how and why our political campaigns take the shapes and forms they do and how they illustrate broader themes in American politics. In short, it argues that our campaigns are an important manifestation of how we "do" politics in America. It looks at who are the candidates, how they emerge, and what are the consequences of the forces through which they do so. It further examines the players—especially the Campaign Industry, media, and money—that strongly determine how campaigns go forward, and their impact on the interested (and voting) public. And finally it asks how our political campaigns may be undermining the quality and health of democratic elections in America, and thus our politics more broadly writ.

\* \* \* \*

At the outset, perhaps it is important to state what this book does *not* deal with. It does not, for example, ask why political campaigns even exist. We know that something like campaigns go back at least to Roman times, and probably before then.

But do democratic elections actually require the existence of political campaigns? Given the sophistication of modern marketing techniques, and the increasing universality of digital media, why go through all the hoopla and tumult and expense of political campaigns? After all, they rely on very sophisticated statistical models (which we will meet in a later chapter) that

---

### Political Campaigns in Ancient Times

Classics scholar Professor Philip Freeman a few years ago published an amusing and insightful op-ed piece on a nasty political campaign in ancient Pompeii. It seems that an up-and-coming young man named Marcus Cerrinius Vatia was running for *aedile*, a sort of local magistrate, from which he hoped to launch a career in politics. But the campaign quickly turned ugly, complete with dirty tricks, negative attack ads, questionable money from trade guilds, and endorsements from dubious characters. It all sounds very familiar, and modern. Alas! The election was never held, because fate intervened in the form of Mt. Vesuvius' blowing up and smothering Pompeii and all of its inhabitants, including the candidates, under ash and lava.[1]

For additional insights into ancient Roman politics and campaigns, readers are urged to read Robert Graves's classic *I, Claudius* (New York: Vintage, 1989) and to watch the superb PBS dramatized version with the estimable Derek Jacobi (1977), available on DVD and through Internet streaming.

---

can very accurately identify and cull out individuals and groups likely to vote for a given candidate, but not for another. Could not these high-end marketing techniques render campaigns irrelevant and obsolete? Couldn't we do something else and still have elections that could be called democratic? These are interesting questions, but we shall leave them to other students of elections, journalists, pundits, and the like.

There is another side to the question of why we have political campaigns that we will only briefly touch on: nobody likes them, so why have them? We know the public finds them distasteful, demeaning, too long, wasteful, too expensive, and not informative. Other than political junkies, and maybe a few souls who somehow find meaning and fulfillment in their lives by living vicariously through campaigns, are there people who actually look forward to the next round of political campaigns?[2]

Candidates, of necessity, put on happy faces and tell the public how much fun campaigning is, but it is all bunkum. Anyone who has ever talked to a candidate in the middle of a tough campaign, privately and honestly and off the record, knows that candidates, even those destined to win, find campaigns anything but fun. The Campaign Industry loves campaigns, because they are the Industry's bread and butter. The media, both print and electronic, probably like campaigns but only because they give self-important media outlets a chance to throw their political weight around in an effort not so much to inform readers/viewers but to define the "real" candidates, establish a campaign agenda (euphemistically called "issues"), and influence the outcome. Campaigns also give reporters something to do and ownership a chance to sell (expensive) advertising. Billionaires might like campaigns, because they offer a chance to buy elections and shape future policy. But the views of the Campaign Industry and the media and billionaires simply underscore the question posed: are their wishes and desires sufficient reason to continue to have campaigns, given that nobody else likes them? The question answers itself.

Do political campaigns do any good? Do they inform voters about issues and candidates, and the kind of choices citizens/voters have to make in order to select those who will govern our nation, states, and communities? Our grade school teachers told us: campaigns are essential so that voters can make informed choices and vote intelligently. Does that really happen? Is that what campaigns actually do?

As it turns out, there are long shelves in libraries dealing with these and related questions. They are important questions. We won't go there, but will instead invite readers to look further and think about these questions on their own.[3] Indeed, it is the position of this book that, regardless of whether campaigns actually "do any good," or influence voters' views of the candidates, as noted above they are very much part and parcel of our political environment, and are not going away. So it is our task to understand why they take the form that they do and how they are yet another way in which we Americans engage in political activity.

There is a related question: Do campaigns motivate people to vote? Indeed, which segments of the population are inclined to vote, which might vote if a candidate/campaign captures their imagination and/or engages their attention, and which segments of the population refuse to vote, or would not vote unless they are bribed? These are important questions dealing with the fields of voting behavior and political participation, about which there are also huge literatures.[4] But they are ancillary to the focus of this book: What drives our campaigns?; Why do they take the form they do?; What forces influence the direction they take?

Instead of addressing the previous (and similar) questions, this book starts with a very particular premise: political campaigns are very much a part of our culture, including our popular culture, are imbedded in it, reflective of it, and, in spite of the generally negative public view of them, they will, like death and taxes, remain with us. Rather, campaigns are part and parcel of how we as Americans, not especially interested in or receptive to "politics," carry out the essential task of making collective decisions about who we are and what we collectively want to do—an unavoidably and fundamentally political task.

Instead of taking politics seriously, and engaging in public discussions about public matters, we create campaigns as a sort of secular ritual and entertainment ranging from low comedy to high drama, a smokescreen or diversion really, a way to make decisions about what happens "next" by electing this person or that one, approving or disapproving this ballot initiative or amendment but not that one, without an individual having to spend a lot of time or energy worrying about what we should do or not do. Instead, we let candidates jabber away in something called a campaign, choose one of them to occupy a seat of public office (which has the legitimacy and authority, granted by Constitutions and laws, to act), and decide for us so we don't have to be bothered, but can go about our daily lives instead.

In short, campaigns are how Americans signal one another that it is time to elect our leaders and representatives, and decide on amendments and referenda. The fact that for presidential elections only a little more than half of age-eligible voters participate in the process and, for "off-presidential" midterm elections and purely state and local ones, the drop-off can be 20 percent and more, probably speaks to the low level of involvement, interest, and engagement that many Americans have for politics generally, and campaigns in particular.[5]

These considerations reinforce the view that the distinction between "campaigns" and "politics" probably never existed but, even if it did, it is one that dissolved a number of years ago. It is thus our task in this book to show how campaigns are part and parcel of our politics, how they are manifestations of how we collectively make decisions about ourselves, and that there is no incongruity or dissonance between how we "do" our campaigns and how we "do" our politics.

\* \* \* \*

Who is the audience for this book? Students of course, both undergraduate and graduate, for the latter primarily those in programs in American Politics, Political Campaigning, or Practical Politics. But students in Comparative Politics, especially those looking cross-nationally at electoral systems and voting behavior, and those in American Foreign Policy classes, will find the book helpful as they try to grasp what future American foreign policy makers have to go through before they enter public (especially elective) office and "govern."

But the book has an audience beyond the academy as well. The interested lay public who involve themselves in civic and political life— members of the League of Women Voters come to mind, and those participating in Good Government and Watchdog groups—might find much to learn in its pages. So will journalists—print, electronic, and blogosphere—who write about political campaigns. Those interested in the nexus between technology and politics will be engaged, especially in those portions that deal with the increasing importance of digital campaigning. Lawyers and judges who deal with election laws, and state and local officials (such as Supervisors of Elections or administrators of

State Elections Offices) who must implement them, will find much to ponder in these pages. And finally, perhaps candidates, or wannabe candidates, should read the book, in order to grasp what will shape and influence their next campaigns.

The text is specifically written to be accessible to a wide audience. It assumes a sophisticated readership, but the second criterion for writing sentences and paragraphs, after accuracy, is clarity and comprehensibility. To the extent that the text engages, even challenges, a wide readership, so will the author have met his goal.

\* \* \* \*

The section of the Preface where the author makes acknowledgements and expresses thanks is very treacherous, like a slippery slope or pond with too-thin ice. Missteps are not only possible, but likely, each with disastrous results. One can easily overlook the contribution made by someone; or one can make the fatal mistake of too many Academy Award-winning acceptance speeches, of turning acknowledgements into an insincere laundry list.

Rather than following either of these paths to unhappiness, embarrassment, and hurt feelings, I ask the readers' indulgence in taking a minimalist approach, limiting specific names but making clear the universe of persons and experiences to whom and to which I am indebted: the many candidates over the years (some victorious, some not, but with one exception all winners as human beings) who have invited me to help them with their campaigns and provided me with a wealth of street-level experience (rare for academicians) and knowledge about campaigns; the hundreds and hundreds of students who have flooded my Modern Political Campaigns class in the Department of Political Science at the University of Florida (UF; Gainesville), who helped shape an earlier book and this one by their insightful comments and penetrating questions; the journalists who in interviewing me have raised important questions, challenged my knowledge, and piqued my curiosity; esteemed colleagues who provided intellectual, academic, moral, and even physical support, especially M. Margaret "Peggy" Conway, Distinguished Emerita Professor of Political Science at UF; Professor Ido Oren, Chair, Department of Political Science at UF, whose support and encouragement have been unflagging; Professor Michael Martinez, former Chair, Department of Political Science, UF, whose valuable suggestions for references and further reading in the behavior literature were inestimable; Mr. Roger Austin, attorney, senior Ph.D. student in the UF Department of Political Science and long-time active political consultant, who repeatedly reminded me of the mores and ways of political campaigns, as well as their craziness, as they unfold out on the street, on TV, in the print media, and increasingly in the blogosphere; Mr. Jose Castaneda and Mr. Jose Lavergne, both advanced undergraduates at UF, whose research contributions to this manuscript cannot be overstated; and to Jennifer Knerr, my editor at Routledge, who took me on because she believed in this project.

But a special shout-out and *ruf-auf* is in order to members of my family who amaze me by continually supporting me even though they undoubtedly think my professional interests lie somewhere between the obscure and the zany; and most importantly my wife Aida, who came to this country not knowing anything about our campaigns, became a citizen and voter, watches and thinks and talks about them, and now after well more than two decades still finds them wacky and cause for rolling her eyes in disbelief. No argument there! Deepest thanks to her, and to all of the others who have been so patient and helpful over the years.

Gainesville, Florida
Summer, 2015

## Notes

1   See Philip Freeman, "The Attack Ad, Pompeii Style," *New York Times*, August 30, 2012, viewed online at http://campaignstops.blogs.nytimes.com/2012/08/30/the-attack-ad-pompeii-style, June 8, 2015.

2   See, for example, Arthur C. Brooks, "The Thrill of Political Hating," *New York Times*, June 8, 2015, viewed online at www.nytimes.com/2015/06/08/opinion/the-thrill-of-political-hating.html?action=click&pgtype=Homepage&module=opinion-c-col-right-region&region=opinion-c-col-right-region&WT.nav=opinion-c-col-right-region&_r=0, June 8, 2015.

3   The question of whether, or to what extent, political campaigns have an impact on the electorate is one that occupies considerable attention by journalists and pundits, and one that enters sometimes vigorous discussions around office water coolers and in lunchrooms and barber shops, and at backyard barbeques. Political scientists have also explored this question. Readers wishing to investigate what they have to say about it should start with John Sides, Daron Shaw, Matt Grossman, and Keena Lipsitz, *Campaigns and Elections: Rules, Strategy, Choice* (2012 Election Update Edition) (New York: W.W. Norton, 2013). See also Paul Farhi, "Do Campaigns Really Change Voters' Minds?," *The Washington Post*, July 6, 2012, viewed online at www.washingtonpost.com/opinions/do-campaigns-really-change-voters-minds/2012/07/06/gJQAEljyRW_story.html; Alan Abramowitz, "Do Presidential Campaigns Matter? Evidence from the 2008 Election," University of Virginia Center for Politics, August 2, 2012, viewed online at www.center-forpolitics.org/crystalball/articles/do-presidential-campaigns-matter-evidence-from-the-2008-election; WW, "Campaigns Still Don't Matter (Much)," *The Economist*, October 5, 2012, viewed online at www.economist.com/blogs/democracyinamerica/2012/10/presidential-election; June 28, 2015.

4   Readers who wish to enter the subjects of political participation and electoral behavior in America can do no better than to consult the following sources, which will in turn lead them to further literature:
    General Literature—
    Angus Campbell, Philip E. Converse, Warren E. Miller, and Donald E. Stokes, *The American Voter* (New York: John Wiley and Sons, 1960); D. Sunshine

Hillygus, and Todd G. Shields, *The Persuadable Voter: Wedge Issues in Presidential Campaigns* (Princeton, NJ: Princeton University Press, 2008); Michael S. Lewis-Beck, William G. Jacoby, Helmut Norpoth, and Herbert F. Weisberg, *The American Voter Revisited* (Ann Arbor: University of Michigan Press, 2008); Jan E. Leighley (ed.), *The Oxford Handbook of American Elections and Political Behavior* (New York: Oxford University Press, 2010). Political Participation— Raymond E. Wolfinger and Steven J. Rosenstone, *Who Votes?* (New Haven, CT: Yale University Press, 1980); Steven J. Rosenstone and John Mark Hansen, *Mobilization, Participation, and Democracy in America* (New York: Macmillan, 1993); Sidney Verba, Kay Lehman Schlozman, and Henry E. Brady, *Voice and Equality: Civic Voluntarism in American Politics* (Cambridge, MA: Harvard University Press 1995); Jan E. Leighley and Jonathan Nagler, *Who Votes Now?: Demographics, Issues, Inequality and Turnout in the United States* (Princeton NJ: Princeton University Press, 2013). The author is indebted to Professor Michael Martinez for suggesting these sources.

5  See University of California, Santa Barbara, "Voter Turnout in Presidential Elections, 1828–2012," 2015, viewed online at www.presidency.ucsb.edu/data/turnout.php; *New York Times* Editorial Board, "The Worst Voter Turnout in 72 Years," *New York Times*, November 11, 2014, viewed online at www.nytimes.com/2014/11/12/opinion/the-worst-voter-turnout-in-72-years.html?_r=0; FairVote, The Center for Voting and Democracy, "Voter Turnout," 2012, viewed online at www.fairvote.org/research-and-analysis/voter-turnout; and Drew Desilver, "Voter Turnout Always Drops Off for Midterm Elections, but Why," Pew Research Center, July 24, 2014, viewed online at www.pewresearch.org/fact-tank/2014/07/24/voter-turnout-always-drops-off-for-midterm-elections-but-why; all viewed June 29, 2015.

# 1 Political Campaigns in the United States

The onset of the second decade of the twenty-first century brought the culmination of what had been happening for about two decades in our campaign politics: there was no longer something called the "campaign season" of limited duration—perhaps like the baseball season, or the opera season, or the Christmas season—during which candidates campaigned, and the rest of the time office holders governed, and losing candidates went back to whatever they were doing before.

By the campaign cycles of 2010 and 2012 this distinction had disappeared, because campaigns had become perpetual, never ending. In contrast to politics and campaigns in earlier years, now it is often hard to tell the one from the other. "Campaigning" seems to take roughly 363 days of every calendar year, it seems to go on continuously, except possibly for Yom Kippur and Christmas Day. It is not always clear, for example, whether a politician, glaring into TV cameras in Washington, D.C., or haranguing in the state capitol or county administration building or on the steps of city hall, or posting a high-octane message on his/her blog, or sending out tweets and Facebook and Tumblr messages to his/her social networks, is staking out a position for a possible vote on an issue or firing salvos as part of an ongoing election campaign. Probably, it's both.

In earlier days of politics, good or bad depending on one's point of view, it was common to make a distinction between "campaigning" and "governing." Those who followed politics often heard phrases such as "campaign season," or "campaign mode," to describe how office holders and office holder wannabe's morphed into something other than public officials or private citizens to engage in "campaigning," as opposed to doing whatever they did as public officials involved in "governing," or would-be public officials who were engaged in some other kind of activity. And, when the elections were concluded and the campaigns mercifully finished, there would often be editorials or other commentary to the effect that the campaign season was over, time to get back to the business of governing.[1]

But while the distinction was a common one, many scholars and pundits began to suspect that by the 1980s and 1990s it was no longer real, nor necessarily an accurate way of portraying how American electoral politics played out.[2] Professor Lyn Ragsdale of Rice University was one of the first to see that the effectiveness of Ronald Reagan's presidency was based on the fact that he never stopped campaigning even when he moved into the White House.[3] Presidential scholar George C. Edwards III noted that, following the disastrous (at least for Democrats) 1994 midterm elections, President Bill Clinton realized that his ability to govern was intimately tied to his remarkable capacity to wage a perpetual campaign.[4] Any number of pundits have commented, positively and negatively, that much of President Barack Obama's standing among the public rests more on his effectiveness as a campaigner than as a "chief executive" who governs.[5]

Thus the point should be clear. The distinction between "political campaigning" and "governing," in this country had, by the end of the first decade of the twenty-first century, been blurred beyond recognition. They had become not two sides of the same coin, but the very coin itself. How could it be any other way? With the need for politicians/candidates to raise money 363 days a year; with the 24-hour news cycle which foists new rhetoric, new "crises," new "issues," new scandals, new anything-to-get-the-public's-attention virtually hour by hour; with the blogosphere and twittering and instant messaging in fifth gear 24/7/363, all directed at digital speed towards the public, offering "infomation" that may bear no relationship to facts, or sense, or decency—the distinction between "campaigning" on the one hand and the business of "governing" on the other, vanished some time ago.[6]

## Does It Matter?

Does it matter? What difference does it make that the separation of "governing" and "campaigning" has narrowed to the point that they are indistinguishable?

Able journalists such as Elizabeth Drew along with a host of others, and scholars of American politics such as those mentioned in the Preface, have thought and written extensively about the consequences of the breakdown between campaigning and governing, and we need not plow again over ground they have broken. But three consequences are of such importance that they bear at least a brief mention.

## The Money Machine in Fifth Gear

Because there is no respite in campaigning, campaign money machines operate 24/7/363. Campaigns have become incredibly expensive. They suck up money not just like vacuum cleaners but like black holes. To feed their insatiable demands, candidates—especially those for major statewide or national offices—are forced to "dial for dollars" continually; and their finance committees—arguably the most important component of a political campaign—have to operate around the clock.

---

### Raising Campaign Money Non-Stop[7]

Consider the following eye-popping examples. The following shows the cost of gubernatorial elections in four states during the 2014 cycle.

*Cost of Gubernatorial Elections, 2014*

**Florida—$150 M**
**Wisconsin—$82 M**
**Pennsylvania—$54 M**
**Connecticut—$30 M**

Consider further that money for these races mentioned above is raised over a 4-year period. Table 1.1 shows, for each state, how much money needed to be raised per year, per month over 48 months, per day (363 days/year over 4 years, 1,452 days), and per hour (12-hour day, 1,452 days, 17,424 hours). Calculations in Table 1.1 were made by the author from the above data, cited in Note 7.

*Table 1.1* Raising Money over Time for Gubernatorial Elections, 2014

|         | *Florida* | *Wisconsin* | *Pennsylvania* | *Connecticut* |
|---------|-----------|-------------|----------------|---------------|
| Yearly  | $37.5 M   | $20.5 M     | $13.5 M        | $7.5 M        |
| Monthly | $3.1 M    | $1.7 M      | $1.1 M         | $625,000      |
| Daily   | $103,000  | $56,500     | $37,200        | $20,700       |
| Hourly  | $8,609    | $4,706      | $3,099         | $1,722        |

---

Why is this important? Because time spent raising money is not time spent on policy questions, or resolving disputes, or creating a consensus around which to move forward. It is not time meeting with people (even non-voters), listening to their concerns and views. It is not time spent mobilizing support across a range of constituents and groups. It is not time spent with the public as a whole, but only that part of the public willing to donate money. And we leave until a later chapter the impact that raising money has in creating the relationship of obligation and dependence between candidate and donor, a relationship that may exclude consideration of the public interest in favor of narrow, private ones.

## Compromising the Politics of Compromise and Accommodation

Rhetoric in American political campaigns, as we will see in the next chapter, has often gotten ugly, nasty, *ad hominem*, and caustic to the point of toxicity. And so it does today, as well.

But in years past, once campaigns were concluded and the business of governing took over, rhetoric usually—but not always—changed. Because hammering out public policy required some degree of respect for opponents, and because the American political tradition of compromise and accommodation rested heavily on interpersonal relations in Congress, state legislatures, city councils, and executive branches at all levels, rhetoric needed to be tempered, and levels of vitriol lowered. Of course there were always broadsides and verbal shellings across party lines—and sometimes geographic and cultural lines as well—but this was mainly for public consumption and fodder for media stories. The actual behind-the-scenes negotiating over language in legislative bills and executive rules could get testy, but in the end it had to proceed in a reasonably seemly manner or nothing would happen.

But one of the consequences of the merging of campaigning and governing is that the old language and rhetorical rules no longer apply. As our boxed anecdote below will illustrate, interpersonal relations are no longer important to fostering public policy. Posturing, posing, attempting to seize the moral and political high ground, painting opponents as naysayers, persons of bad faith, and worse, has become all too common. This is precisely because the linguistic style of campaigning has replaced the verbal requirements of negotiating and consensus building. The effect of course is to undermine, even compromise, our traditional politics of accommodation and compromise, and to create gridlock and ill-feeling in the arenas of politics.

## Losing Respect for Political Institutions

The final consequence that we will mention of the merging of campaigning and governing is a bit more speculative, but highly likely. It is that office holders, constantly campaigning, and wannabes trying to get into the office, seem to have less of a sense of respect for the institutions to which they belong, or seek to join, than was the case years and decades ago.

True, office holders seeking re-election have always had to have one eye, at least, on the next election. But the other eye would have been on "governing," and playing a role in, even contributing to, the functioning of the institution to which they belonged. But that distinction has now largely vanished.

If office holders and candidates need to think mainly about their campaigns and elections (or re-elections) 24/7/363, then their orientation

## A Sea Change in Our Political Environment

The author had the occasion a few years ago in Tallahassee to be sitting with a small group of officials and academics one afternoon in the Capitol office of a senior member of Florida's executive branch. Suddenly the receptionist ushered in a very distinguished gentleman, long-time Republican lawyer and lobbyist, much respected and trusted on both sides of the aisle. He looked old, exhausted, thin, grey, completely worn out. Immediately a restorative beverage was placed in his hands, and he began to relax. When prompted, he said, he could not take it anymore, he could no longer do his job. Lobbying in Tallahassee, he said, used to be based on personal relationships and friendships across party lines; a commitment was a commitment, a promise a promise; and it was in everyone's interest to find a way past seeming impasses. No longer, he said. Partisanship and ideology trumped everything else; friendship meant nothing; and the word of an opponent was not to be trusted, indeed, your opponent could not be your friend. It was a disheartening and discouraging moment for everyone in the room.[8]

is far more heavily geared toward firing up their electoral base than to maintaining the integrity and strength of governing institutions, or working to ensure that they carry out their Constitutional functions. Why care about the traditions or mores and historical stature of Congress, or a state legislature, or the Mayor's Office, if what its members or aspirants really are concerned about is grandstanding and posturing and preaching to the choir for success in the next election?[9]

The point should not be overstated; most office holders show at least a modicum of respect for the offices they hold and the institutions of which they are members. But recent electoral results suggest that there are increasing numbers who do not, or not to the same degree that has been shown in the past. The effect, in the short run, is to increase governmental "gridlock," because there is very little incentive to make the wheels of government turn. Over the long term, the effect will be to erode support for governmental institutions, and to increase the gap between the public and the agencies of government that are supposed to serve their interests.

## New Developments in our Politics and in Our Campaigns

But the discussion thus far is really the beginning of the matter, not the end. What has also happened is that, just as campaign politics and "everyday" politics have merged, from a stylistic standpoint it is no longer possible to differentiate them. Not so long ago campaign politics could well be down and dirty; but "everyday" politics usually—not always—maintained a veneer of civility and respect for opponents. No longer. Ideological purity and partisan rigidity have become the norm in our politics and campaigns.[10]

Many other scholars, pundits, and politicians themselves have noted that, beginning in the 1980s, when the Republican party was taken over by right-wing conservatives and the Democratic party lost its identity, coherence, sense of direction, even moxie, politics in this country became increasingly rigid, ideological, and partisan. Political discourse, in campaigns and elsewhere, has become much more characterized by polarization, fulminations and vitriol than the traditional American style of accommodation, compromise, and bargaining.

What has assuredly changed in our politics, and our campaigns, is the intensity, the vehemence and viciousness, the finality with which political ideology and partisanship shove everything else off the table. Nowadays, promptly after the last ballot is cast and counted, and immediately after the last TV talking head has "analyzed" the results of the just-completed campaign, the savagery and blood-letting begin anew. Indeed, there is very little let-up, because the next campaign cycle literally begins the nano-second after the previous one stops, even before its detritus is cleared away.

## Political Scientists and Political Polarization

While journalists, pundits, and other observers of the political scene like to talk about increasing polarization in American politics generally, and in particular institutions (such as Congress, or state legislatures) more specifically, political scientists have also investigated the extent of polarization, if any, in our politics. As might be expected, they present a more complex picture than the more facile ones offered by journalists.

To oversimplify a bit, there are two schools of thought about polarization in American politics. On the one hand there is the view of Alan Abromowitz and his colleagues. They argue that in fact polarization in America has increased since the 1970s and that it is across the board, meaning that it includes both elites and the politically "engaged" population. While recognizing that this phenomenon increases tensions and even gridlock in our politics, it can also serve to increase political involvement and participation, especially by actively committed citizens.

Interested readers might want to consult the following as representative of the Abromowitz point of view:

Alan I. Abramowitz and Kyle L. Saunders, 2008. "Is Polarization a Myth?" *Journal of Politics* 70: 542–555.

Alan Abramowitz, 2010. *The Disappearing Center: Engaged Citizens, Polarization, and American Democracy.* New Haven, CT: Yale University Press.

The other major view on political polarization is represented by Morris Fiorina and his associates. Fiorina argues that polarization has not increased, but what has happened is that parties, and especially voters, increasingly sort themselves out based on particular issues, at particular times and circumstances. In fact, he states, public views on basic political issues have not significantly changed over the past few decades. And, he argues, the classification of states, or counties, or voters into "red" or "blue" aggregations is both exaggerated and misleading, because the political views of the public are not as starkly divided as these labels suggest.

Readers wishing to examine Fiorina's writings might well consult the following:

M. P. Fiorina, S. A. Abrams, and J. C. Pope, 2008. "Polarization in the American Public: Misconceptions and Misreadings." *Journal of Politics* 70: 556–560.

Morris P. Fiorina and Samuel J. Abrams, 2008. "Political Polarization in the American Public." *Annual Review of Political Science* 11: 563–588.

Readers might also wish to digest the following important article, which sheds light on the question of political polarization by using data to point out that increasingly those who identify with one of the major parties (Republican or Democrat) have less favorable, and even more hostile, views of the other party than previously:

S. Iyengar, G. Sood, and Y. Lelkes, 2012. "Affect, Not Ideology: A Social Identity Perspective on Polarization." *Public Opinion Quarterly* 76: 819–819.

For a scholarly but accessible overview of the professional debate over political polarization in the United States, readers are urged to examine John Sides and Daniel J. Hopkins (eds.), *Political Polarization in the United States* (London and New York: Bloomsbury Publishing, 2013).

Finally, readers wishing to follow the debates over political polarization in the scholarly literature might wish to consult regularly a blog by the political scientist Keith Poole, who provides links to interesting articles and pieces: http://voteview.com/political_polarization_2014.htm.

And there have been other important new developments in campaigning as well. One of course is money, to which we shall devote an entire chapter later. For now, we need only note that the issue is not the amount of money, but its sources (thanks to *Citizens United vs. FEC*[11] and subsequent decisions such as *SpeechNow.org vs. FEC*[12] and *McCutcheon vs. FEC*[13]), and how it is spent, specifically the avalanche of "soft money" campaigns that allow messages, including intensely negative ones, to be disseminated, often anonymously, while legally—if not politically, and certainly not ethically—separated from the candidate's campaign.

The role of the media in campaigns has also changed significantly in the past two decades. There is an entire chapter in the book which will discuss this point. But for now we can make two brief points: the impact of corporate ownership of major media outlets that sets sharp limits on who are the legitimate candidates, and on the boundaries of campaign discourse; and, because of the way campaigns are structured, designed, strategized, and carried out, the traditional media, at least, has very little knowledge of them, and "coverage" is largely limited to trivia and sideshows and superficial descriptions of the "horserace."

What is also different now is the impact of the digital media, especially social networking. Through its incredible speed and intensity it is possible for campaigns and candidates to reach like-minded voters to reinforce what they already believe or think they know, to raise considerable sums of money even from small donors, and to mobilize their voters to volunteer, to talk up the candidate, and to show up at the polls. These and similar messages go out continually, 24/7/363; the campaign messages never end, all traveling at light speed and in staggering numbers. Nothing like this has ever been seen before in American political campaigning.

---

### The Campaigning Never Stops

In a recent iteration of the Modern Political Campaigns class offered by the author in the Department of Political Science, University of Florida, one of the students remarked that, while she was visiting her Grandmother on Christmas Day in a recent year, late in the afternoon they both began receiving tweets from a local candidate, seeking their support and money.

---

### Political Campaigns and the Public

An entire book could be written that simply lists public criticisms of political campaigns. They are too long. They are too expensive. They are distasteful. They are too negative. They don't deal enough with issues but are too dominated by personal attacks and character assassinations. Campaign ads interrupt favorite TV shows. The stuff they send out clogs up mailboxes. They insult the intelligence of voters. They insult the public. They demean the candidates. They cause acrimony at home and in the workplace. They are nothing but lies after lies after lies. They deliberately deceive the public because candidates make promises even they know they cannot keep. They are all hot air and no substance. Even when they are over no one knows anything substantive about the candidates, or why this candidate or that one is the better choice. Etc., etc., etc.

And so it has been for a long time. As the second chapter of this book will show, criticisms of campaigns in this country have been around ever since they started. Where do these views come from? Probably from Americans' long-standing indifference, antipathy, suspicion, and/or hostility towards politics generally. Part of the great American mythology is that the nation was founded on principles, not politics. Grade school teachers for generations have pounded into students' heads the belief (one that approaches dogma) that the Founding Fathers were above politics and did not descend to the pettiness and ugliness that "politics" involves. Indeed, our patriotic iconography of the Founding Fathers virtually always portrays them as stalwart, dignified, high-minded statesmen. The very phrase "Founding Fathers" even implies that they should be afforded the status of patriots, demi-gods, even secular saints.

## Portrayals of the Nation's Founders

Viewers are invited to look at any of the famous "portraits" of George Washington painted by Gilbert Stuart; there is no question that he is shown as a man who has risen above the pettiness of politics. The fact that Washington only sat briefly for any of Stuart's paintings is rarely mentioned, and indeed the "portraits" are for the most part pure conjectures and inventions. Nonetheless, for two centuries the conventional wisdom has it that, if Washington ever came back and did not look like Stuart portrayed him, he would be condemned as an imposter and charlatan. The most famous of Stuart's portrayals can be viewed online at www.nga.gov/exhibitions/ 2005/stuart/philadelphia.shtm. For other iconography in the same vein, readers should look at John Trumbull's *Signing of the Declaration of Independence*, 1817, currently in the Art Gallery at Yale University; and Howard Chandler Christie, *Signing of the Constitution*, 1940, currently hanging in the east stairway, House wing of the United States Capitol. Both paintings are entirely products of the artists' imaginations and are not historically accurate, and yet have achieved the status of historical correctness.[14]

Americans' jaundiced, negative view of politics and government continues to this day. The Pew Research Center for People and the Press recently concluded a longitudinal study of Americans' trust in government from 1953–2013. The trend line is almost consistently downhill.[15] Trust in government is of course an indirect measure of attitudes towards politics and politicians, but other work supports the claim that Americans don't much like politics.[16] It's not a long empirical or logical jump to observe that there is undoubtedly a spillover effect: just as Americans hold dim views of politics, so too do they hold dim views of campaigns.

But as one might expect, matters are more complicated than this. We know, for example, that Americans pay attention to campaigns, or at least the political advertisements which inundate them on television and by mail and by digital means; and we know that those ads make a difference, and can influence voter attitudes.[17] We also know that attitudes towards campaigns are deeply dependent on the extent of voter engagement or involvement in politics. Those who follow politics, and are committed to and active in it, view campaigns far more favorably, and even want more "substance," than those who take a stand-offish, detached, indifferent, essentially negative attitude towards politics.[18]

Even in the nineteenth century, well before the advent of electronic media and when the mass media were largely limited to urban areas, people followed political campaigns. We know that, when a campaign came to a small hamlet or town, it was cause for celebration, as it was a big event, a release from the chores and hardships of everyday life.

In a very real sense, it is probably correct to say that Americans have at best held an ambivalent attitude towards political campaigns: a necessary evil, but one that could provide diversion, entertainment, whiskey, and even cash for those who cared to join in. And for those who liked or were interested in and followed politics, they provided a source of energy and excitement, possibly even inspiration; indeed, of the many varieties of political junkies, one of the most common is the devotee of political campaigns.

But, as interesting as is the topic of Americans' views of campaigns, even more central is the question of whether the criticisms made of them have any validity. Obviously we cannot discuss each of the many criticisms that are often heard. But three are of such importance that they merit consideration:

Are American political campaigns too long? Do they cost too much? And do they emphasize platitudes, clichés, and bloviation at the expense of substance?

A word of caution before the discussion: attitudes towards campaigns can be highly subjective, personal, even idiosyncratic. What strikes one person as empty-headed might strike another as appealing. Too many negative attack ads might seem to someone else as a hard-fought, aggressive campaign. Partisanship of course influences how one views campaigns, perhaps especially depending on how the favored candidate is doing, but the matter goes beyond party identification or loyalty; one hears the same complaints about non-partisan campaigns as well. The point is, one always has to take complaints about campaigns with a grain of salt; there is no fully objective way to measure or test their validity.

## Are Campaigns Too Long?

The question is so vague as to be meaningless. What does one mean by "campaign?" Or "long?" An active campaign, involving advertising, events, forums and debates, meet-and-greets, rallies, television appearances, photo-ops, and so forth might only last a few weeks or months for local races, but for statewide and of course presidential contests they will be much, much longer. But the "active phase" of a campaign is only the tip of the iceberg. Even campaigns for local offices require months and months of organization, fund-raising, support building and endorsements, strategizing, locking-in and expanding the base, etc., etc., etc. The campaign that is thrown together over a couple of weeks prior to the qualifying date is not likely to succeed. Even modest contests for city council or county commission require a good deal of behind-the-scenes preparation before the "active" campaign unfolds.

In the case of major statewide (for governor or senator, for example) and presidential contests, the preliminary work can take years. In a large, complex state like California or New York or Florida a great deal of spadework has to be undertaken before a credible statewide race can be mounted. Even in more modestly sized states there is still a tremendous amount of organizing required, which might take a year or more. And for the presidency, given that both the presidential nomination process involving primaries and caucuses and the general election all go forward on a state-by-state basis, the amount of on-the-ground preparation, as well as the overall direction, organization, and operation of the campaign, is staggering. It is no exaggeration to say that the skills required to mount and run a large state campaign, or especially a presidential race, are comparable to those needed for running large corporations, even governing nations.

Some Democratic nations limit the length of active campaigns. In Great Britain they are a month to six weeks; in Australia, about six weeks; in France, active presidential campaigns last only for two weeks before the first ballot, and for a week if a second ballot is needed, while for the General Assembly campaigns are limited to 20 days before the first ballot; in Israel, the campaign lasts 101 days before the date fixed by the Knesset, the Israeli parliament.[19] France, Ireland, Belgium, and Turkey do not allow paid political advertising on television, and in some cases radio, during campaigns, although print advertising is permitted.[20] Of course these rules and regulations only limit the time and scope of active campaigns; just as in the United States, a great deal of political organizing and campaigning goes on behind the scenes before the active phase starts, in order that once it begins, no time is wasted.

Should the United States also adopt time limitations on active campaigns? Congress could certainly enact such laws, but they would apply only to federal contests (President and Vice President, Senate, U.S. House of Representatives). Individual states, and possibly local governments, can also create such laws that would apply only within their jurisdictions if they so chose; the result of course might well be a hodgepodge and crazy patchwork of rules and regulations. Nonetheless, it must be said that serious proposals are on the table to limit the length of campaigns in the United States, even as they never seem to be enacted.[21]

Still, it has to be recognized that there are many people, including politically engaged people, for whom campaigns are too long and too distasteful; how many people feel this way is not known, as measuring such attitudes would be both difficult and expensive, but given how often critical voices are heard, the number is surely non-trivial.

But before either Congress or states begin to contemplate seriously limiting the duration and scope of active campaigns, weight must be given to the view that the eminent political scientist Stephen Hess put forward some years ago.[22] Hess argued that it would be a mistake to limit the length of presidential campaigns, at least, because their length, complexity, requirement of stamina and clear-headedness, ability to respond to crises and unexpected turns of events, and so forth actually mirror the presidency. Thus, by observing how the candidates comport themselves during the potentially years-long campaign, voters can get a sense of how they might behave, act, and respond to the pressures of the presidential office itself. The campaign of course is a marathon; but so is the presidency.[23] Thus, in Hess's view the presidential campaign is a sort of trial by fire, and by observing it voters can test the mettle of the candidates. Although Hess does not do so, the same argument he makes defending the length of presidential campaigns applies to those at the state and local level as well.

## Campaigns Cost Too Much

A second commonly voiced complaint about political campaigns is that they cost too much. The implication is that spending money on campaigns is wasteful, and perhaps the funds should either be saved or spent on something more worthwhile. The complaint is an old one—Andrew Jackson's successful presidential campaign in 1828 is thought to be the first million-dollar one, a sum that at the time seemed staggering.

It is indeed true that political campaigns have become very expensive. The Center for Responsive Politics is one of the major organizations that systematically tracks money spent on campaigns. It reported that, in 2000, a presidential election year, a total of just over $3 B was spent on national political races: $1.7 B for Congressional races, and $1.4 B for the presidential contest. In 2012, those numbers rose to nearly $7 B for the national races: $3.7 B for Congressional races and $2.6 B for the presidential race, an increase of 104 percent over the 12-year period.[24] In 2014, an "off-presidential" election year, campaigns cost about $3.8 B, up slightly from 2010 ($3.6 B), another "off" year.[25] Space does not permit a detailed examination of the costs of state and local races, but even a cursory glance reveals that they have become overwhelming: In 2010 Michael Bloomberg spent $108,371,685.01 to win a third term as Mayor of New York City; Rick Scott spent $85 M to become Governor of Florida; in 2012 Elizabeth Warren spent upwards of $42 M in her successful Senatorial Campaign in Massachusetts.[26] Even in small communities the amount of money spent for local commission and council races can raise eyebrows: in a spring, 2014 non-partisan City Commission race in Gainesville, Florida, a city of 126,000, one candidate spent over $43,000—and lost! Her winning opponent spent "only" $31,000.[27] Clearly, running a political campaign has become a very, very expensive proposition, and anyone thinking of running for office must seriously address the questions of how much money will be needed, where will it come from, and does he/she want to do the things that must be done in order to raise it? It is also one of the reasons that increasingly political candidates, especially in major contests, tend to be wealthy and can use their personal assets to partially bankroll their campaigns.

Again, it needs to be pointed out that what one person thinks is wasteful might be someone else's good investment. There is no objective way to determine if spending money on campaigns is foolish and wasteful, or something that advances the interests of the nation, or a state, or a candidate, or groups and individuals supporting the candidate. If, for example, one feels that the results of campaigns matter, and their outcome is important, or at least are non-trivial, because Candidate A and not Candidate B is elected, or this constitutional amendment passes and that one does not, then spending money on campaigns is worthwhile. If one feels the opposite, that it does not matter who is elected or what ballot initiatives succeed or fail, then campaign donations and expenditures might indeed look worthless, even recognizing that the money spent provides jobs and income for the many, many people who make the campaigns go forward.

But there is another way to examine the question of whether campaigns are too expensive: too expensive compared to what? Consider the following:

- In 2011, the top 7 corporations in terms of advertising budgets (Proctor and Gamble, L'Oréal, General Motors, Chrysler, Verizon, Time-Warner, and Pfizer) spent a combined total of $11.4 B.[28]
- In 2013, Americans spent $56 B on pet food, supplies, and care.
- In any given year, Americans spend about $33 B on cosmetics and beauty care.
- In 2011, Americans spent the following amounts on:
  - beer: $96 B
  - romance novels: $10 B
  - engagement and wedding rings: $11 B
  - gambling: $35 B
  - chocolate: $16 B
  - bottled water: $11 B
  - fast food: $117 B
  - credit card late fees: -$18 B
  - lawn care: $40 B.
- And finally, in 2011 the tobacco industry spent $8.4 B on cigarette advertising in the United States. In that year Americans bought 293 billion cigarettes, approximately 14.7 billion packs. At an average cost of $5.51/pack (although the range across the 50 states was from $4.96 in Kentucky to $14.50 in New York), the total amount Americans spent on cigarettes alone was just under $81 B. But this figure is deceiving, because the cost of medical care for smokers and for lost productivity because of tobacco-related absences from jobs (including to second-hand smoke) between 2009 and 2012 was over $289 B.[29]

What are we to make of this? That Americans spend about 7 times as much on chocolate as to elect the President? Or that the total cost of electing all of our national political leaders was only slightly more than one-third of what Americans pay on delinquent credit card fees? Again, what one regards as money well spent or as money wasted is highly individual, very much in the eye of the beholder. But the data bear witness to the fact that, compared to the things that American consumers buy, spending for political campaigns is small potatoes.

In any case, as we briefly noted earlier and will investigate in detail later in the book, the amount of money involved in politics is not really the issue. Far more important are the sources of the funds, and especially—indeed crucially—whether those sources are publicly accountable and transparent, or not. To the extent that there are problems with accountability and transparency in money for political campaigns, so are the integrity and robustness of democratic elections compromised.

## American Political Campaigns Lack Substance, Gravitas

A third common complaint about American political campaigns is that they lack substance. They emphasize the trivial, the personal, the beside-the-point, the horserace. There is not enough discussion of "issues" and too much discussion of "character" and "qualifications"—especially when speaking of opponents—and not enough specifics about what the candidate(s) will do if elected to office. Or the campaigns just consist of empty rhetoric, meaningless phrases, vague promises, and blather. And they dwell heavily on the negative, emphasizing attacks and even character assassination, instead of outlining agendas and developing plans for "doing something" once elected. In brief, campaigns are not what our well-intentioned grade school teachers said they should be: a frank, candid, open presentation of policy alternatives so voters can make informed, careful choices about the candidates and cast ballots accordingly.

We can of course excuse our teachers for painting an unrealistic picture of our campaigns and elections, so we need not pursue that point. But there is something much more important at stake here, anyway. What is an "issue?" And why is a campaign that focuses on character and qualifi-cations less "weighty" or less informative than one which drones on about issuing bonds for bridge and highway construction and maintenance, or teachers' salaries, or even national security? Indeed, it is not unreasonable to assert that it is as essential for voters to make choices about candidates based on their character and experience, voters' belief that one (or another) of the candidates will do his or her utmost to uphold the public trust given by them to act in a public-spirited manner, to behave honestly and responsibly, and to make him or herself fully accountable to the public, as it is to decide based on the candidate's alleged position on this issue, or that one.

This is not to say that bonds for maintaining our infrastructure, or teachers' salaries (or public school expenditures generally) or national security are trivial; far from it, they are all public questions and matters—that is, issues—of great importance and weight. But why is it that we expect political campaigns to be the "right" forum for their consideration? Each of the three issues mentioned—and there are dozens more—are exceedingly complex, call for much more detailed and informed discussion than a political campaign could possibly offer or have time for, and require massive input from knowledgeable specialists who are not even in or a part of the campaign, in order to decide what is best to do.

And so, as a result, campaigns discuss "issues" in highly political and partisan terms, using catchy sound bites to attract votes or to lambast opponents, that is, if they do so at all. There is nothing functional, from a candidate's standpoint, about trying to "teach" voters about municipal bonds, or the various interests and pressures that go into a consideration of "national security." One thinks of the hapless Al Gore, who tried, seriously and even passionately, to inform voters, to talk knowledgeably with them about weighty matters. His strenuous efforts resulted in putting voters off, and in many instances putting them to sleep.[30] Policy wonkery and winning campaign strategy are not compatible and essentially exist in different political universes. Even our most successful policy wonk President, Bill Clinton, very much minimized substantive discussion of policy issues during his campaigns, in favor of presenting his personality and style to the public and only offered the most vague outlines of what he planned to do as President.[31] It worked, twice.

From the candidate's and campaign's standpoint, issues are, with some exceptions, a nightmare. The reason is that they tend to be divisive. For every vote a candidate attracts by outlining a detailed policy proposal, he/she is likely to put off others, possibly even lose votes. So candidates shy away from specifics, instead offering banalities, platitudes, and clichés. Or they talk about the failings and weaknesses and incompetence of their opponent(s). The result of course is that voters might scratch their heads wondering exactly what a candidate thinks about an issue, or what he/she proposes to do about it. But that's exactly what the candidate wants: it allows him/her maximum wiggling room and puts off as few potential supporters as possible.

The exception mentioned is when one or more issues can be used to back opponents into a corner. This is especially true of so-called "wedge" issues: those that are inherently divisive, in which the proponent of one side uses his or her views to seize the moral/religious/political high ground and leave opponents struggling to justify their views. Examples are legion: abortion rights; gay marriage; creationism in science classes; sex education; gun control; use of torture; equal pay for women; voter ID laws; no rights for illegal immigrants or their children; interventionist foreign policies; minimum wage laws, etc., etc., etc. Wedge issues can be effective political weapons because they force an either/or choice or dichotomy onto the voter: "You're either with me or against me!" "I am taking the moral high road; my opponent sold out!" "My opponent is soft on 2nd Amendment gun rights!" And of course it can readily be seen how manipulating wedge issues goes hand-in-glove with attack ads and negative campaigning. Whether or not this sort of absolutist divisiveness makes for good governance and sound policy making is another matter entirely; but it can make for winning campaign strategy, certainly in particular times, circumstances, and locations.

There is another consideration of issues that should be re-emphasized after mentioning it earlier in the chapter. Only the most politically involved, engaged, and committed voters really want to hear about "issues." As we will see in the next section of this chapter, many—perhaps most—voters have neither the time nor desire to focus on policy substance; so they use cues and shortcuts to make up their minds (including whether or not to vote), and they are as much, or more, likely to decide based on reasons which some people—especially those who take campaigns and politics seriously—might regard as trivial or incidental: partisanship; "likeability" and personality of the candidate; whether the candidate is African-American or Hispanic-American or gay or a woman or some combination of these (each of these characteristics can be positively or negatively determinative for individual voters); what the boss wants; where the paycheck comes from; what the minister says; what dad or mom or brother or sister prefer; what a friend or partner or spouse or golfing buddy thinks; what the people in the office discuss; what the shop steward says to do.[32]

For many of these voters, it's not that "issues" don't count or matter. It's rather that they only care to hear snippets and sound bites and 30-second ads about them because that's all they really care about or have time for; they are much more likely to cast a ballot for someone they like and trust— or against someone whom they find distasteful and unacceptable—than because he or she can lecture knowledgeably about utility rates or the defeasance of municipal bonds, the intricacies and complexities of home rule, the politics of state budget making or school-funding formulas, the pros and cons of a new, advanced weapons system, or some other impenetrable and incomprehensible "issue."

This is not to say campaigns always have to follow the "KISS" principle: Keep It Simple, Stupid. Many, perhaps most, voters expect more than this, and certainly none will respond positively if they suspect the candidate is being condescending to them, or treating them like dummies. On the other hand, quick, direct, readily comprehensible messages are far more appealing, and will attract far more voters, than long, drawn-out, ponderous, opaque explanations of, say, utility rates, or workmen's compensation rules, or agricultural subsidies.

Thus, based on this discussion, it's surprising that there is any discussion of "issues" at all in campaigns. One suspects that they are foisted off onto candidates by the media, who like to pretend that they are above the political fray and are interested in "substance," and by that portion of the voting population that wants to hear about weighty matters of public concern (or at least their concern/self interest), that is, "issues." But candidates for the most part would rather talk about something else, like the soundness of their credentials and experience, or the moral failings of an opponent, or how far out of touch and out of step with mainstream voters the opponent is.

## Creating a Political Persona

There is one final point to be made in conjunction with this discussion of campaigns and the public. Candidates increase their chance of success if

---

### How Our View of "Political Time" Has Changed

In the nineteenth century political events and speeches and rallies could be interminable. For the famous Lincoln–Douglas debates in 1858, for example, the first speaker would talk for an hour; his opponent then had 90 minutes for rebuttal, followed by 30 minutes for the first speaker. Perhaps people had more time on their hands then; perhaps that was what they wanted. But nowadays nobody would put up with political speeches of this length; there are even complaints that the so-called TV political debates, generally 90 minutes or so in length, are too long, and viewers mentally "tune out" after the first 15 or 20 minutes, even if they leave the TV on. Attention spans of modern-day Americans, of all ages, seem to be contracting; hence the need for snippets, sound bites, and 30-second spots.[33]

---

they effectively present themselves as appealing, credible, trustworthy men and women to voters in particular, and the public generally. We call this creating a "political persona." It's not so much a superficial statement of what they are like, but fundamentally what kind of individuals they are: likeable; trustworthy, strong and decisive, honest and virtuous. Or, friendly and approachable and engaging, the sort of person one would like to spend time with, or bend an elbow with at a bar. Or serious, thoughtful, emotionally withdrawn, disengaged. The political persona must be well drawn, believable, appealing, and consistent if a candidate wants to attract voters. In recent years Al Gore, John Kerry, and Mitt Romney all saw the results of not presenting an attractive persona clearly defined to the public: each lost. They never were able to convincingly show the public what kind of individuals they were. This was not the only reason for their defeats, of course, but when one thinks of opposite examples—Ronald Reagan, Bill Clinton, and George W. Bush come to mind—one sees the advantage of letting the voting public know clearly and forcefully who one "is." Some might object that Barack Obama was not very good at presenting an appealing, well-defined political persona to the public, and one is inclined to agree. But his major opponents—Hillary Clinton, John McCain, and Mitt Romney—were worse at it. And each lost. The same could be said of George H. W. Bush, who campaigned against the doomed, unknown Michael Dukakis; Bush Senior had a very poorly defined political persona, but Dukakis had none at all.

Thus, the conclusion seems inescapable: in modern American political campaigns, it is probably more important that voters gain a clear picture of who are the candidates, and whether they embody qualities in their political persona that they find attractive and appealing, than that they spend time discussing their views on "issues." Because of this essential task of the campaign, and of the candidates, it cannot be said that they lack "weight" or "gravitas" or are trivial. Other aspects of the campaign might be—attack ads, character assassination, silly campaign antics—but not when the candidates are revealing to voters who, and what kind of people, they are. It is a central, essential, and very difficult, task.

## Three Axioms of Modern Political Campaigns

Every year, or at least every two, even-numbered years, there are thousands of political campaigns in this country. They range in scope from races for council or commission in tiny hamlets to state legislatures, Congress and, every four years, the Big Enchilada, the contest for the presidency. Each of these campaigns is different, based in specific times, circumstances, and locations. And yet they share certain commonalties, in terms of the hurdles they face, and how they must be overcome. We can call these "axioms of campaigns," and while there are many, here we can focus on the three most important.[34]

### *Finding a Way To Win*

The first of these axioms is that campaigns are designed to win; there is no silver medal or second-place trophy when it comes to political campaigning. The goal of even the most hopeless candidate/campaign is not to lose, even when it is clear that defeat is staring them in the face, or, if not that, then to avoid as much as possible an acute embarrassment.

But a winning campaign must do more, much more, than just try not to lose; in this sense campaigns are different from the cautious, defensive, even timid, strategies used by some coaches of sports teams in order to get through a game successfully. And it is exactly at this point that some political campaigns begin to veer in ethically dubious directions and engage in ethically challenged practices. Dirty tricks, lies, deceptions, sleight-of-hand, bombast—virtually nothing is out of bounds for the campaign that is anxious, even desperate, to win. Campaigns will do essentially anything—*anything!*—to gain a winning edge, even if the managers and candidates are not sure that they can get away with it. The Watergate break-in during the 1972 presidential campaign might be the most infamous example of "do-anything-to-win" dirty tricks in the last 100 years; but it must be remembered that the perpetrators almost did get away with the job, or at least they thought they could, and cover it up if discovered.[35]

---

### Dirty Tricks in Campaigns Happen at All Levels

Dirty Tricks *à la* Watergate are by no means limited to presidential campaigns. They can infect even modest local ones. In Miami-Dade County, Florida, in the late 1980s a nonpartisan County Judge race was coming to an end. One of the candidates, a young woman, looked like a sure loser. Her campaign manager, a well-known political operative of dubious reputation, on the Friday night before the Tuesday election plastered major roadways and bridges in the area with billboards and posters accusing his own client of major ethical violations and then loudly complained to the media that her opponent was playing dirty tricks. Of course it was too late for the opponent, who had no part in any of this, to do anything except fulminate in anger and rage that it was not him, but his opponent's own campaign, that had put up the signs. But no one believed his side of the story: what campaign would do such a thing to its own candidate? The young woman won when the election ended on Tuesday night.

---

But what happens if they don't get away with it? What happens if complaints are filed or, if truly prohibited activities are alleged, legal action is started? The answer is a resounding, "Not Much!" Generally speaking, the resolution of complaints occurs after the conclusion of the campaign, too late to matter. If fines are involved, they can be paid after the fact with no change to the election's outcome. If the issue involves serious legal questions, they too can stretch out until after the election results are in, and very, very few judges are willing to throw out the results no matter how nefarious the deeds alleged.[36] The Watergate episode is of course the great exception.

High-minded readers who find this offensive or unacceptable need to remind themselves that the ethical, legal, and behavioral standards for campaigns are different from those of many—perhaps most—other parts of public (and private) life. Truth-in-advertising rules and laws, for example, do not apply (with rare exceptions) to political campaigns. State and local elections officials, the media, even judges, seem willing to "cut the campaign some slack" when it comes to determining the boundaries of appropriate/inappropriate campaign behavior; of course, the amount of slack cut is often a function of whether the behavior in question is perpetrated by favored candidates, or opponents. But, more generally, a sense of "Well, that's politics, what do you expect?" accompanied by a shrug or a rolling of eyes seems to pervade the determination of just how far campaigns can go, and whether or not they should be held accountable. The result, of course, is that there is very little accountability, and campaigns will do what they can to win, all under the long-recognized-and-time-honored dictum of Boss Plunkitt: "I seen my opportunities, and I took 'em!"[37]

### Is Anybody Out There Listening?

The second axiom is that campaigns have to ask, "Is Anyone Paying Attention?" In this country politics is too often viewed as an unpleasant inevitability, like death and taxes. Campaigns have to draw Americans' attention to them, because for many, politics resides outside of what they generally think is important, or are worried about: jobs, money, bills, mortgage, family, illness, marriage, divorce, school, children, elderly parents, home and hearth, nosy or noisy neighbors, an impossible boss, the weather, What's for dinner?, Who will win the World Series?[38]

But it is not just that politics occupies a lowly position on the American totem pole. There is additionally the bombardment—24/7/365—of commercials, announcements, information, digital and electronic noise, sound and visual pollution, which every American faces constantly. Not only can one not take it all in, the real issue is that one must create elaborate, complicated perceptual screens to keep most of it out. Failure to do so means that a person could literally drown in the auditory and visual cacophony competing for even a nanosecond of his/her time, or just go crazy.

The consequence for political campaigns is obvious: how to break through? How does the campaign discover ways to make sure its message is heard and not blocked out like most of the other racket obstinately, aggressively, even rudely, vying for a place in the viewer's/listener's consciousness? Even the politically pre-disposed, the regular voters, the junkies—people who can be depended on to show up at the polls, perhaps even volunteer or make a donation—have to be informed, persuaded, reinforced. Taking any of these for granted almost always spells defeat for a campaign.

---

### The Speaker Gets His Comeuppance

There is a famous anecdote, perhaps apocryphal, about the late "Tip" O'Neill, long-time member of the U.S. House of Representatives from Massachusetts and its Speaker in 1977–1987. After chalking up another re-election victory, he met his neighbor one morning on the front walk, and asked her if she had voted for him. "No." was the reply. O'Neill, astounded, asked, "Why not?" "Because you didn't ask me," was the reply.

Campaigns therefore have to find a way to grab a voter's attention. Colorful antics, outrageous claims, outright lies, deception, and especially a big heap of negativity might just do the trick; bland, wholesome, and positive won't. So what if the message is not true, or is in bad taste, or defames an opponent? So what if it does the candidate no credit? If it helps the campaign sell its message, it will be used. Indeed, the more egregiously outrageous the message, the more likely it is to break through the voters' perceptual screens. Is it any wonder, then, that the modern political campaign relies so heavily on distortion, outlandish language and claims, fabrications, half-truths, lies, and twisted contexts to make sure it is heard? Indeed, does it have a choice?

### Campaigns and Popular Culture

The third axiom of political campaigns is that they must recognize that they are part and parcel of American popular culture. As such, they are as much in the entertainment business as Hollywood, Big Time Sports, Television, Music, Fashion, and other phenomena that both shape and reflect American taste. Because campaigns are not in the education or civic engagement business but are rather in the business of winning elections, they must bring to bear the same techniques of marketing and advertising as the businesses of selling movies, rock stars, cars, beer, TV shows, pet food, and other commodities to the public.

---

### Popular Culture and Political Campaigns

Popular culture of course does not simply entertain; it can help Americans understand the world around them, in this case, political campaigns. For example, a recent Hollywood movie, *The Campaign*, and TV series (*The Good Wife*) portray just how down and dirty modern political campaigns can get. Both of these examples of popular culture entertain; but they also inform, as viewers get very dramatic and powerful, and all too accurate, portrayals of how actual political campaigns go forward in this country, why they take the forms they do, and what—sometimes pernicious, ugly, and nasty—characteristics they have.[39]

---

Thus campaigns must recognize how important it is to entertain the voting public. Boring them, as Jimmy Carter and Al Gore found, to their dismay, does not bring victory: How could either of these intelligent, earnest, sincere, well-meaning but dreary candidates possibly compete successfully with the irrepressibly sunny and optimistic Ronald Reagan, or the folksy cowboy George W. Bush?

Entertaining the voting public includes negativity built on deceptions, lies, viciousness, and meanness of spirit. Indeed, it may well be that, at the present time, massaging some decidedly unpleasant characteristics of our popular culture—rudeness, greed, violence, self-centeredness, sanctimonious religiosity, xenophobia, racism, misogyny, for example—may be highly appealing, as evidenced by these and similar themes showing up in many popular contemporary movies and TV shows. They may be the best ways to get voters to pay attention.

In fact, when one thinks of some of the major features of modern television shows and movies, not to speak of the more lurid parts of the Internet, explicitness and what a generation ago could not be publicly shown is now the norm, not the exception. Now there is no distinction between public and private, now there are no secrets or privacy,[40] now there is no tale too shocking or revealing that it will not rapidly find a wide audience. Movies, television programs, and the Internet cater to the voyeuristic, sensationalistic appetites of a public that dotes on the openly public behavior of celebrities, sports stars, politicians, musical entertainers, and talent-challenged self-promoters who seem to offer nothing else but an ability to reveal the most intimate details of themselves.

For campaigns, then, the sky is the limit, and anything goes. If popular culture and public taste now readily accommodate a population wanting and demanding full revelations of private lives, so campaigns are not only free to go along: they must. Otherwise, the public will pay little or no attention. And even if the candidate has much to offer in the way of ideas or the promise of useful public service, he or she will not win the hearts and minds of a voting public ready and willing to abandon him or her in favor of a new and sensational titillation from a source able to provide it.

## Notes

1   Such comments continue to be found, especially but not exclusively among conservatives. See, for example, Edward Glaesser, "Campaigning is Over, Time to Govern," e21, Economic Policies for the 21st Century at the Manhattan Institute, November 6, 2013, viewed online at www.economics21.org/commentary/campaigning-over-time-govern; and Jim Nolan and Olympia Meola, "'Campaign's Over, Time to Govern' for McAuliffe," *Richmond Times-Dispatch*, November 12, 2013, viewed online at www.timesdispatch.com/news/state-regional/virginia-politics/campaign-s-over-it-s-time-to-govern-for-mcauliffe/article_2fdf0afc-4131-5865-b566-94d1ca0a1ca5.html; both viewed May 16, 2014.

2   See, of many possible examples, Gregg Easterbrook, "The Perpetual Campaign," *The Atlantic Monthly*, January, 1983, viewed online at www.theatlantic.com/past/docs/issues/83jan/easterbrook.htm, June 16, 2014; Joe Klein, "The Perils of the Permanent Campaign," *Time*, October 30, 2005,

viewed online at http://content.time.com/time/magazine/article/0,9171, 1124332,00.html; Thomas E. Mann, "From Campaigning to Governing: Politics and Policymaking in the New Obama Administration," *Brookings*, Research, April 21, 2009, viewed online at www.brookings.edu/research/ speeches/2009/04/21-governance-mann; "Governing in a Campaign Year: What's Next for Policy in 2013," *The Conversation*, February 4, 2013, viewed online at http://theconversation.com/governing-in-a-campaign-year-what-next-for-policy-in-2013-11898; Diane Roberts, "America Is Stuck in Perpetual Campaign Mode. It Stinks," *guardian*, November 14, 2013, viewed online at www.theguardian.com/commentisfree/2013/nov/14/obama-fundraising-2014-citizens-united; all viewed May 16, 2014; see also, Pippa Norris, *A Virtuous Circle* (New York: Cambridge University Press, 2000).

3  See Lyn Ragsdale, "Disconnected Politics: Public Opinion and Presidents," n.d., viewed online at http://elections.gmu.edu/Classes/GOVT311/ Ragsdale.pdf; viewed May 16, 2014.

4  George C. Edwards, III, "The Permanent Campaign: Why Does the President Go Public," *Public Opinion Pros*, 2005–2007, viewed online at www.publicopinionpros.norc.org/inprint/2005/june/edwards.asp, May 16, 2014. The piece is actually an excerpt from Edwards's book, *On Deaf Ears: The Limits of the Bully Pulpit* (New Haven, CT: Yale University Press, 2005).

5  See, for example, Kenneth T. Walsh, "Obama, Democrats Locked in Perpetual Campaign," *Us News*, July 15, 2010, viewed online at www.usnews.com/ news/articles/2010/07/15/obama-democrats-locked-in-a-perpetual-campaign; Noah Rothman, "Obama's Perpetual Campaign: When Will the Nation Tire of Not Having an Executive in the White House?' *Mediaite*, November 28, 2012, viewed online at www.mediaite.com/tv/ obamas-perpetual-campaign-when-will-the-nation-tire-of-not-having-an-executive-in-the-white-house; and Jeff Mason, "Obama San Francisco Fundraiser Addresses GOP Relationship," Reuters and Huffingtonpost.com, April 4, 2013, viewed online at www.huffin-gtonpost.com/2013/04/04/obama-san-francisco-fundraiser_n_3011459.htm; all viewed May 16, 2014.

6  The breakdown of the distinction between campaigning and governing is a theme in many of the writings of the prestigious journalist Elizabeth Drew; see *Washington Journal: The Events of 1973–1974* (New York: Random House, 1974); *Portrait Of An Election: The 1980 Presidential Campaign* (New York: Simon and Schuster, 1981); and *The Corruption Of American Politics* (New York: Kensington Publishing, 1999).

7  Sources: William March, "Florida Governor's Race Will Top $150 Costliest in US," *Tampa Tribune*, viewed online at http://tbo.com/news/politics/fla-governors-race-will-top-150-million-costliest-in-us-20141101; "Wisconsin's Governor's Race Cost Nearly $82 Million," *Wisconsin Democracy Campaign*, March 9, 2015, viewed online at www.wisdc.org/pr021715.php; Steve Esack and Laura Olson, "Pennsylvania Governor's Race Cost at $54 Million and Counting," *The Morning Call*, October 24, 2014, viewed online at www.mcall.com/news/nationworld/pennsylvania/mc-pa-governor-race-fundraising-20141024-story.html; and Christopher Keating, "Governor's Race Cost More Than $30 Million," *Hartford Courant*, November 7, 2014, viewed online at www.mcall.com/news/nationworld/pennsylvania/mc-pa-governor-race-fundraising-20141024-story.html; all sites viewed June 27, 2015.

8  A very effective and persuasive, albeit older, examination of the traditional, now largely obsolete, style in American politics can be found in Charles E.

Lindblom, *The Policymaking Process*, 3rd edn. (Upper Saddle River, N.J: Prentice-Hall, 1992).

9 Any number of journalistic accounts of some U.S. Senators, Congressmen, even governors substantiate this point. See, for example, the series in Huffingtonpost.com on Senator Ted Cruz of Texas,n.d., www.huffingtonpost.com/tag/ted-cruz-texas; Jason Zengerle, "Did Somebody Say Fringe?," GQ Online, www.gq.com/news-politics/politics/201010/rand-paul-gq-aqua-buddha-jason-zengerle, October, 2010 (on Rand Paul); the *New York Times* series on Congressman Alan Grayson of Florida, n.d., http://topics.nytimes.com/top/reference/timestopics/people/g/alan_grayson/index.html; the Huffingtonpost.com series on Governor Nikki Haley of South Carolina, n.d., http://topics.nytimes.com/top/reference/timestopics/people/g/alan_grayson/index.html; all viewed July 19, 2014. Other examples of candidates and office holders who illustrate the increasing tension between political style and institutional norms could be cited, including 2010 U.S. Senate candidates Christina O'Donnell (Delaware), Sharron Angle (Nevada), and Carly Fiorina (California), and 2012 U.S. Senate candidate Linda McMahon (Connecticut).

10 See Robert Reich, "Are You Robert Reich? You're a Commie Dirtbag," Salon.com, September 26, 2013, viewed online at www.salon.com/2013/09/26/are_you_robert_reich_youre_a_commie_dirtbag_partner, September 27, 2013. See also Robert J. Samuelson, "Ideology Is What Has Won in the Shutdown Debate," *Washington Post*, October 6, 2013, viewed online at www.washingtonpost.com/opinions/robert-samuelson-the-shutdown-is-a-triumph-of-ideology/2013/10/06/1bc17054-2d4c-11e3-97a3-ff2758228523_story.html, May 15, 2014. See also Jack Torry, "Broken Congress: Scorching Rhetoric Dominates Today's Sentate," *Pittsburgh Post-Gazette*, June 5, 2014, viewed online at www.post-gazette.com/business/powersource/latest-oil-and-gas/2014/06/05/Broken-Congress-Scorching-rhetoric-dominates-today-s-Senate/stories/201406050338 and Jessica Wehrman, "Politics over Policy in House," *Dayton Daily News*, June 6, 2014, viewed online at www.arcamax.com/politics/politicalnews/s-1534607, both viewed June 9, 2014. See also Thomas Frank, *What's the Matter with Kansas?* (New York: Holt Paperbacks, 2005).

11 *Citizens United vs. Federal Election Commission*, 558 U.S. 310 (2010).

12 *SpeechNow.org vs. FEC*, no. 08-5223 (2010).

13 *McCutcheon vs. FEC*, 572 US ____ (2014)

14 Trumbull's painting can be viewed online at www.google.com/imgres?imgurl=http://upload.wikimedia.org/wikipedia/commons/thumb/1/15/Declaration_independence.jpg/600px-Declaration_independence.jpg&imgrefurl=http://en.wikipedia.org/wiki/Trumbull's_Declaration_of_Independence&h=183&w=276&tbnid=PHLmMXThp2QIxM:&zoom=1&tbnh=160&tbnw=241&usg=__B1ksADWkFC9X4EjkIoHhCKIDJ4s=&docid=K0XoKRYGZ_SznM&itg=1&sa=X&ei=fvqFU9amIM70oATijoLYCg&ved=0CMQBEPwdMAo; Christie's at http://edsitement.neh.gov/constitution-day/visualizing-founders.

15 Pew Research Center for People and the Press, "Public Trust in Government 1953–2013," October 18, 2013, viewed online at www.people-press.org/2013/10/18/trust-in-government-interactive, May 17, 2014. See also Gallup, "Trust in Government 1993-2010,"n.d., viewed online at www.gallup.com/poll/5392/trust-government.aspx, May 17, 2014.

16 See, for example, Thomas Patterson, "Why Do So Many Americans Hate Politics," *History News Network*, August 9, 2005, viewed online at http://hnn.us/article/1127; Ryan D. Enos and Anthony Fowler, "Do Americans

Care About Politics?" *Yougov*, December 10, 2010, viewed online at http://today.yougov.com/news/2010/12/10/do-americans-care-about-politics; Ezra Klein, "Americans Don't Like Politics—And That Matters," *Washington Post*, February 25, 2011, viewed online at http://voices.washingtonpost.com/ezra-klein/2011/02/americans_dont_like_politics_-.html; all viewed May 17, 2014.

17   The literature on these propositions is immense, occupying long shelves in libraries. Two readily available sources comprehensible to the general public are R. Michael Alvarez, "Campaign Ads: Do Voters Pay Attention and Do They Matter," *Psychology Today*, March 29, 2011, viewed online at www.psychologytoday.com/blog/the-psychology-behind-political-debate/201103/campaign-ads-do-voters-pay-attention-and-do-they-; and Sadie Dingfelder, "The Science of Political Advertising," *American Psychological Association*, April, 2012, viewed online at www.apa.org/monitor/2012/04/advertising.aspx; both viewed May 17, 2014.

18   See Keena Lipsitz, Christine Trost, Matthew Grossmann, and John Sides, "What Voters Want from Political Campaign Information," *Political Communication* 22: 337–354 (Routledge, Taylor and Francis Group, 2005), viewed online at http://home.gwu.edu/~jsides/polcomm.pdf, May 17, 2014.

19   See The Law Library of Congress, "Campaign Finance: Comparative Summary," May, 2009; viewed online at www.loc.gov/law/help/campaign-finance/comparative-summary.php#duration, May 19, 2014.

20   Centre for Law and Democracy, *Regulation Of Paid Political Advertising: A Survey*, March, 2012; viewed online at www.law-democracy.org/wp-content/uploads/2012/03/Elections-and-Broadcasting-Final.pdf, May 19, 2014.

21   See, for example, Keli Goff, "What England Can Teach Us About Getting Elections Right," Huffingtonpost.com, January 4, 2011, viewed online at www.huffingtonpost.com/keli-goff/what-england-can-teach-us_b_804112.html, May 19, 2014.

22   Stephen Hess, *The Presidential Campaign* (Washington, D.C: Brookings, 1988).

23   Jules Witcover's fascinating book on Jimmy Carter's pursuit of the presidency is, in fact, entitled *Marathon: The Pursuit Of The Presidency 1972–1976* (New York: Vintage, 1977).

24   Center for Responsive Politics, "The Money Behind the Election," OpenSecrets.org, n.d., viewed online at www.opensecrets.org/ bigpicture, May 20, 2014. These data do not include money spent on state and local races. The National Institute on Money in State Politics tracks money spent there, through its website www.followthemoney.org and its more recent iteration, www.betafollowthemoney.org.

25   Center for Responsive Politics, OpenSecrets.org, October 29, 2014; viewed online at www.opensecrets.org/news/2014/10/overall-spending-inches-up-in-2014-megadonors-equip-outside-groups-to-capture-a-bigger-share-of-the-pie, June 27, 2015.

26   Frank Lombardi, "Bloomberg's Campaign Tab," *New York Daily News*, January 15, 2010, viewed online at www.nydailynews.com/news/bloomberg-campaign-tab-108-371-685-01-relected-term-nyc-mayor-priceless-article-1.460319; Scott Powers, "It's Official: Rick Scott Is the All-time Big Spender," *Orlando Sentinel*, February 2, 2011, viewed online at http://articles.orlandosentinel.com/2011-02-02/news/os-gov-race-finances-20110201_1_rick-scott-big-spender-democrat-alex-sink; and "Open Secrets,

Congressional Elections: Massachusetts Senate Race: 2012 Cycle," n.d., viewed online at www.opensecrets.org/races/summary.php?id=MAS1&cycle= 2012; all viewed May 20, 2014.

27 Alachua County Supervisor of Elections, Campaign Reports, viewed online at www.voterfocus.com/ws/WScand/candidate_pr.php?c=alachua&el=29, May 20, 2014. The race required a run-off; the candidate spending the most money received 9,943 votes for both elections; her per-vote cost was $4.43; the winning candidate received 10,187 votes; her per-vote cost was $3.04.

28 Figures from 2011–2013 because they serve as benchmarks for the presidential campaign of 2012.

29 Janet Fowler, "7 Companies with Big Advertising Budgets, *Investopedia*, June 18, 2012, viewed online at www.investopedia.com/financial-edge/0612/7-companies-with-big-advertising-budgets.aspx; CBS News, "Americans Spent a Record $56 B on Pets Last Year," March 13, 2014, viewed online at www.cbsnews.com/news/americans-spent-a-record-56-billion-on-pets-last-year; "How Much Do Americans Spend on Cosmetics?," Ask.com., n.d., viewed online at www.ask.com/question/how-much-do-americans-spend-on-cosmetics; Lucas Reilly, "By the Numbers: How Americans Spend Their Money," MENTAL FLOSS, July 17, 2012, viewed online at http://mentalfloss.com/article/31222/numbers-how-americans-spend-their-money; Centers for Disease Control and Prevention, "Economic Facts About Tobacco Production and Use," n.d., viewed online at www.cdc.gov/tobacco/data_statistics/fact_sheets/economics/econ_facts; and Sarah Jampel, "The Price of Everything: What a Pack of Cigarettes Costs Now, State by State," *The Awl*, July 12, 2013, viewed online at www.theawl.com/2013/07/what-a-pack-of-cigarettes-costs-now-state-by-state; all viewed May 20, 2014. See also Chris Cillizza, "The 2014 Election Cost $3.7 Billion. We Spend Twice That Much on Halloween," *Washington Post*, November 6, 2014, viewed online at www.washingtonpost.com/blogs/the-fix/wp/2014/11/06/the-2014-election-cost-3-7-billion-we-spend-twice-that-much-on-halloween, June 27, 2015.

30 Two-time presidential candidate Adlai Stevenson was quoted as saying, "I have tried to talk about the issues in this campaign {...}. But, strangely enough, my friends, this road has been a lonely road because I never meet anybody coming the other way." Stevenson lost twice against Dwight D. Eisenhower. From *Speeches of Adlai Stevenson, 1952*, quoted in https://en.wikiquote.org/wiki/Adlai_Stevenson; viewed online June 27, 2015.

31 Perhaps the best illustration of this point comes from a work of fiction, but one based on Bill Clinton, presidential candidate. See Anonymous (Joe Klein), *Primary Colors*, 10th anniversary edn. (New York: Random House, 2006).

32 Footnote 4 of the Preface provides an overview of important scholarly literatures on how, or whether, people decide to vote. For the non-specialist, a very helpful overview can be found in Bryon Allen and Chris Wilson, Wilson Research Strategies, "Heuristics: Shortcuts Voters Use to Decide Between Candidates," *Campaigns And Elections*, April 26, 2010, viewed online at www.campaignsandelections.com/print/175742/heuristics-shortcuts-voters-use-to-decide-between-candidates.thtml, May 22, 2014.

33 On the Lincoln–Douglas debates, see National Park Service, "The Lincoln–Douglas Debates of 1858," n.d., viewed online at www.nps.gov/liho/historyculture/debates.htm. Criticism of presidential debates is widespread; a useful source is Open Debates, "What is the CPD?," n.d., viewed online at www.opendebates.org/theissue/whatisthecdp.html; on the problem of short attention spans for modern consumers, presumably consumers of political

information as well, see the helpful post by Rob Weatherhead, "Say It Quick, Say It Well—The Attention Span of a Modern Internet Consumer," *Guardian*, February 28, 2014, viewed online at www.theguardian.com/media-network/media-network-blog/2012/mar/19/attention-span-internet-consumer; on the effects of TV debates, see for example John Sides, "Do Presidential Debates Really Matter," *Washington Monthly*, September/October 2012, viewed online at www.washingtonmonthly.com/magazine/septemberoctober_2012/ten_miles_square/do_presidential_debates_really039413.php?page=all; viewed May 23, 2014.

34 These are also discussed in the author's previous version of this book, *The Modern Political Campaign* (Armonk, N.Y: M. E. Sharpe, 1997). That presentation is still timely and relevant today.

35 The most famous account of Watergate is of course *All The President's Men*, by Carl Bernstein and Bob Woodward (New York: Simon and Schuster, reissue edition June 3, 2014), see also J. Anthony Lukas and Joan Hoff, *Nightmare: The Underside of the Nixon Years* (Athens: Ohio University Press, 1999).

36 In 1998 a Miami judge threw out the results of a mayoral election in the City of Miami because of fraudulent use of absentee ballots. This was a highly unusual and controversial step for a judge to take. See Mireya Navarro, "Fraud Ruling Invalidates Miami Mayoral Election," *Miami Herald*, March 5, 1998, viewed online at www.nytimes.com/1998/03/05/us/fraud-ruling-invalidates-miami-mayoral-election.html, September 4, 2013.

37 A comment made by one of Tammany Hall's most famous characters, George Washington Plunkitt.

38 Evidence for this statement abounds. To cite but two examples from many, one thinks of the individuals with whom Barbara Ehrenreich worked and about whom she wrote in her book *Nickel and Dimed* (New York: Picador, 2001 and 2011), or whom Robert Kuttner cited for his book *The Squandering of America* (New York: Vintage, 2008), all of whom stated, so the authors tell us, that politics meant nothing to them and had nothing whatsoever to do with their lives.

39 "The Campaign" can be found at www.imdb.com/title/tt1790886; readers are especially urged to look at A. O. Scott's review of the film, *New York Times*, August 9, 2012, viewed online at http://movies.nytimes.com/2012/08/10/movies/the-campaign-starring-will-ferrell-and-zach-galifianakis.html?pagewanted=all; season 2 of *The Good Wife* features an especially nasty political campaign; it can be viewed at www.imdb.com/title/tt1442462/episodes?season=2; both viewed September 20, 2013.

40 This is not a unique observation. See, for example, *TED Radio Hour*, "The End of Privacy," NPR, January 31, 2014, viewed online at www.npr.org/programs/ted-radio-hour/265352348/the-end-of-privacy; "The End of Privacy," Huffingtonpost.com, April, 2014, viewed online at www.huffingtonpost.com/news/the-end-of-privacy; "The Death of Privacy: *guardian*, August 3, 2014, viewed online at www.theguardian.com/world/2014/aug/03/internet-death-privacy-google-facebook-alex-preston; and "The End of Privacy," Special issue, *Science Magazine*, January 30. 2015, viewed online at www.sciencemag.org/site/special/privacy/index.xhtml; all viewed June 28, 2015.

# 2  American Political Campaigns in Historical Perspective

History by itself tells us very little, if anything. It's what one puts into its telling and writing, and into its reading or hearing, that can be instructive. A history, for example, is never complete, because no historian, no matter how skilled, can fully create a past reality. He or she must always be selective in choosing what to write or say or, more importantly, what to leave out. And, as the eminent British historian Simon Schama has so convincingly shown, in searching for the meanings and lessons of history, too often we focus on the wrong things, or draw the wrong conclusion, or just see in a historical account what we want to.[1] Thus one needs to proceed with more than an abundance of caution in trying to ferret out the "lessons" of history.

On the other hand, examining past events and occasions through the lens and perspective of years gone by can be illuminating. Why? Because, in the case of political campaigns, for example, we learn that what happened long ago parallels much of what happens now. One does not have to be a historical determinist to realize that, with American political campaigns, the more things change over time (sophistication of technology, extent and speed of access to voters, political agendas and styles of conveying them, limits of "acceptability," strengthened or atrophied partisanship and ideologies, how the media covers them, how they are paid for, etc.), the more they look like things that happened before. The vicious struggle to win between Federalists and Jeffersonian Republicans in 1800 is remarkably similar to the ugliness of the presidential elections of 2008 and 2012 and, most likely, 2016. And the extortionist tactics of Mark Hanna in 1896 were reborn, in very similar styles and tones, in 1988, when Lee Atwater created the modern negative campaign, and were continued in presidential as well as state and local campaigns ever since.

By placing the modern political campaign in its historical context, we will then be able to see what, in its most recent manifestations, is both similar to and different from the past. Even if in reading about recent campaigns one has the sneaking suspicion that one has seen all of this before, there are significant changes, add-ons and extensions and new developments from what happened earlier, and the way they happened.

## How Bad Were They?

Pretty bad, depending on one's point of view of course, and what one expects a political campaign to be. A Norman Rockwellian image of a campaign moment, if one exists, would not be accurate. Enlightened political debate, rhetoric that stuck to the facts and rationally drew conclusions for the benefit of voters, and policy proposals that reflected popular will as well as goals for the public good exist only in civics texts and the exhortations of our grade school teachers who gamely and sincerely sought to teach us the rules and customs of Democracy, but certainly not its carbuncles, wiles, and dark spaces.

Gentlemanliness, good sportsmanship, decency, respect, and measured speech—these were not characteristic of American political campaigns in years gone by. Quite the opposite, in fact, to such an extent that in an earlier version of this book it could rightly be said, "Mudslinging: As American As Apple Pie."[2] Indeed, even as campaigns in former times could be ugly, so could they be fascinating, intriguing, exciting, engaging, even riveting, in the same sense that one watches in horror as a car crash unfolds, unable to take one's eyes away.

America's first real presidential election (because George Washington was not on the ballot) came in 1800, with Thomas Jefferson and John Adams slugging each other in a notoriously vicious campaign. In those days presidential candidates relied on surrogates and did little campaigning on their own; that did not begin in even the most modest ways until the late 1830s and 1840s, although it was the twentieth century before serious traveling, whistle-stopping, and major speeches by candidates began in earnest. During our early years it was regarded as "unseemly" to campaign for the august office of President; candidates for other offices were free to do so, however, and did.

Both Jefferson and Adams relied on friends and supporters and newspapers to campaign for them; in those days, and indeed throughout the nineteenth century newspapers were far more openly partisan than they are today. Newspapers entered the 1800 fray with vigor, openly pushing their favored candidates. Also, the distinction between what we now call "news stories" and "editorials" was decidedly muddied:

> Murder, robbery, rape, adultery and incest will all be openly taught and practiced, the air will be rent with the cries of the distressed, the soil will be soaked with blood, and the nation black with crimes.

So said the Federalist-supporting *Connecticut Courant* about the likely consequences of a Jefferson victory.[3] Newspapers favoring Jefferson shot back at Adams with equal venom and vituperation.

But this was just the tip of the iceberg. Jefferson was called an infidel, an atheist, a debaucher of young women and sire of mulatto children, and, perhaps worst of all in an age of verbal excess, a Jacobin:

> Can serious and reflecting men look about them, and doubt that if Jefferson is elected, and the Jacobins get into authority, that those morals which protect our lives from the knife of the assassin—which guard the chastity of our wives and daughters from seduction and violence—defend our property from plunder and devastation, and shield our religion from contempt and profanation, will not be trampled on and exploded?
>
> (Scher 1997)

The Jeffersonians fought back with everything they had. Adams, they shouted, was "a fool, hypocrite, criminal and tyrant" … his presidency was one "continued tempest of malignant passions." It was claimed that his goal was to establish a presidential dynasty for his family, and it was even alleged that he sent a member of the distinguished Pinckney family to England to fetch a mistress for him; Adams, devoted to his wife Abigail, apparently laughed at that one, but there was little else to find amusing during the campaign.

The presidential campaign of 1800 is worth noting because it illuminates how early in our history verbal histrionics and sharply negative language were part and parcel of our political campaigns. It also demonstrates that our Founding Fathers, our national quasi-deities and secular saints, were, in spite of their silks and velvet culottes and powdered wigs, not above mudslinging and character assassination when it came to campaigning for office.

And so it continued throughout the nineteenth century. Examples are legion. In 1828 the incumbent John Quincy Adams exchanged vitriolic unpleasantries with the man whom he had defeated 4 years earlier, the irascible military hero from Tennessee, Andrew Jackson. Jackson, the Quincy Adams forces declared, was ignorant, reckless, inexperienced, a blasphemer, bastard, and adulterer (allegedly because he had married before his new wife was divorced) and, worst of all, a murderer: not because he had massacred untold numbers of Seminoles, but because he had murdered some of his own men in cold blood. Some of Quincy Adams's handbills, circulated with drawings of what were supposedly their coffins, still survive.

But, try as the Quincy Adams campaign did to make Jackson lose his temper publicly, they failed. Instead, the Jacksonians hit back hard. Quincy Adams, they claimed, was a monarchist, a "squanderer of the taxpayers' dollars on silken fripperies, a Sabbath breaker [for riding on Sunday] and pimp"; this latter because allegedly Quincy Adams had procured American girls for Czar Alexander I while serving as minister to the Russian Court.

Jackson of course won, because he rode a tide of increasing democratic populism cresting across the nation at that time. But he was aided by a huge campaign treasury; allegedly the campaign of 1828 was the first million-dollar one in American history and the first in which money—heavily favoring Jackson—made the difference in the outcome.

The presidential campaign of 1840 was the direct precursor of the one in 1968; both featured a wholly "invented," or "remade," candidate; put differently, both campaigns were based on neatly constructed fables: William Henry Harrison in the case of the former, and Richard Milhous Nixon in the latter. Both were made out to be individuals they decidedly were not.

Harrison was actually born into comfortable circumstances in Virginia and had a modest if unremarkable military record. Nonetheless, the kingmakers of the day made him into a child born in a rough frontier log cabin, who rose to become a military hero fighting Indians. The whole conceit was a fraud, a Potemkin village, but the public didn't care. They loved the toy log cabins that the campaign passed out as souvenirs and the hard cider it provided those coming to rallies as enticements; and even more they loved the huge balls of tin, paper, and other materials rolled from village to village to "get the ball rolling" for Harrison. His opponent, in contrast, was the elegant incumbent Martin Van Buren, supposedly a dandy who liked fine clothes, sat on velvet chairs in the White House, and drank French wines from silver goblets.

Harrison's campaign successfully did its utmost to paint the contrast between the candidates in the starkest possible terms. In the face of the pseudo-populist, rough-and-ready Harrison campaign, which lost no opportunity to remake Harrison into a red-blooded American war hero, Van Buren never had a chance. His supporters' efforts to show the obvious fakery of the Harrison campaign fell on deaf ears, nor could they find a way to overcome the popularity and appeal of trinkets and parades and music and large rallies featuring hard cider—all the trappings of a circus, and the first time in American history that such gimmicks were used in a presidential campaign. It was a masterpiece of deception, an archetypal use of smoke-and-mirrors, bait-and-switch political tactics designed to propel a phony to victory. It worked, brilliantly.

In the 1860s even northern newspapers blasted Lincoln as a "drunk," a "baboon," "shattered, dazed, and utterly foolish," and the "craftiest and most dishonest politician that ever disgraced office in America."[4] A famous, vicious Currier and Ives cartoon of Lincoln in the 1860 presidential campaign called "The Rail Splitter" would, by today's standards, be considered tasteless and racist, but even a cursory examination of campaign cartoons published in newspapers and magazines at the time reveals that, compared to others, it is not unique in descending to a low level in terms of its offensiveness and nastiness.

---

**The New Nixon**

Richard Milhous Nixon had a reputation as something of a political thug ever since his emergence onto the national political stage as an anti-Communist crusader during the McCarthy era. His years in the Eisenhower administration, even his appearance during the presidential campaign of 1960 (dark circles under his eyes, heavy beard, jowly), and his sour-grapes remarks after losing the California gubernatorial campaign in 1962 did nothing to soften his image. By 1968, however, his handlers had completely remade him, and the public was told of the "New Nixon," who, however, turned out to be very much like the old one.[5]

---

Indeed, Lincoln's opponents—inside and outside of campaigns—seemed never to miss a chance to verbally or pictorially assault and mock him viciously, intemperately; it was probably Lincoln's self-deprecating sense of humor which helped him shrug off the hurtful invective hurled at him.

But, for sheer vituperation and ugliness, the presidential campaigns of 1884 (Grover Cleveland vs. James G. Blaine) and 1896 (William McKinley vs. William Jennings Bryan) can hardly be surpassed. In the former race, newspapers and other political opponents repeatedly attacked Blaine's character and ethics, often using vicious cartoons.[6] Indeed, much of his entire political career seemed to consist of ethically challenged behaviors and deeds, all of which were repeatedly dredged up. Blaine himself always seemed to have the slightly sour aura of the sleazy miscreant about him. He was a favorite target of the famous political cartoonist Thomas Nast, known for the shrewdness, sharpness, and sometimes bitterness of his portrayals, and it is highly likely that Nast's attacks did as much to defeat Blaine as did Cleveland and the Democrats.

In 1896 William McKinley did little actual campaigning, but he did not have to. His campaign was run by Mark Hanna, a brilliant and conniving Ohio politician; Hanna was to McKinley what Lee Atwater was to George H.W. Bush and Karl Rove to George W. Bush in modern times. He played Wall Street and the media like a virtuoso, raising fears of the Populist Bryan and his "free silver" economic policies, but that was the least of it. Cartoons and newspaper stories and campaign broadsides vilified Bryan repeatedly and even compared him to anarchists and President James Garfield's assassin Charles Guiteau.[7] To raise money, Hanna engaged in outright extortion, going to Wall Street and other corporate and financial headquarters, demanding that they contribute lavishly to McKinley's campaign or he would publicly assail them as likely Bryan supporters.

Indeed, there is evidence that Hanna set a minimum "floor" or quota for each corporation to contribute, or it risked public embarrassment.

It was probably not the first time in American presidential campaigns that blackmail was used to force contributions; but Hanna raised the tactic to an art form, one that was widely copied in any number of twentieth-century campaigns. Commentators and pundits of the day noted that they could not recall the level of vicious calumny, financed by Big Money and orchestrated by Hanna, heaped on Bryan, at least not in a very long time.

---

### Political Blackmail

During the 1972 presidential campaign it was widely rumored, if not always substantiated by facts, that the Committee to Re-Elect the President (CREEP, as its astonishing moniker was known) used threats of Internal Revenue Service investigations to force political cooperation and quiescence and, most likely, campaign "contributions." And of course political blackmail was the stock-in-trade of Lee Atwater, campaign manager and political adviser to George H.W. Bush in 1988.[8]

---

## What Can We Learn?

As it happens, we can draw some conclusions from the spectacles and circuses of nineteenth-century political campaigns, which illuminate those of the twentieth and twenty-first centuries. Readers can decide for themselves if they represent the "lessons" of history; less grandly but probably more helpfully, they help us connect with our own political traditions because, while the names and places and specific contexts change, the way in which our campaigns are conducted show remarkable continuity.

## Negativity Reigns

If there is one overriding constant in our tradition of campaigns, it is that negativity reigns. It is essentially always there; the only variation is the quantity and quality and style of negativity, not its presence.

But what is a negative campaign? How do we know? Scholars, journalists, pundits, and candidates might all disagree on a definition, because one person's negative campaign is another's hard-hitting, go-for-the-jugular style. Negative campaigns are not simply comparative; showing or highlighting the record of one candidate in relation to others is not in itself necessarily negative, because the public record (and, perhaps sometimes, the private record) of candidates is fair game in a campaign.

Nor is painting an opponent in the most unfavorable light possible necessarily negative—as long as it's true.

Indeed, this brings us to the very essence of negative campaigns. There are at least two important criteria to consider. First is veracity and accuracy. If allegations of acts/behaviors/statements by an opponent are true—according to the accepted standards of publicly verifiable evidence—then they are not negative. The target of the attack may not like them, nor his supporters either, and they of course are free to question the interpretation and "slant" that opponents put on them. But, even as they decry them as "personal assaults" or "character assassination" or "dirty tricks," as long as the public evidence supports the allegations and charges, then it is hard to argue that they are negative. But of course if the allegations are false and cannot be substantiated—then the attack is purely a negative one, part of a strategy of deception and lies, of smokescreen and bait-and-switch politics, designed to fool voters and win support. It is exactly the same technique as the magician in the circus uses: distract the audience, divert its attention elsewhere, to keep it from finding out the truth.

Second, one has to ask, What is the purpose of the attack? Is it to illuminate a shady portion of an opponent's past, or is it just character assassination? Is the charge or language relevant to the office (or issue) being sought or pushed, or is it just a slanderous attack, a side-show, smoke and mirrors, or something ultimately based on bigotry designed to appeal to narrow-mindedness and prejudice? For example, when Lee Atwater in one of his early efforts fostered a whispering (and, eventually, overt) campaign that the opponent was Jewish, that was negative. Being Jewish was not relevant to the political office being sought, as religious tests for office were abandoned early in the nineteenth century. Atwater's tactic was just a way to massage the basic bigotry of the rednecks whose votes Atwater needed for his candidate to win. The same would have been true if he had been Catholic, or Muslim, or gay, or (possibly) a woman, or something else unacceptable to local cultural norms at that time.

Thus it is entirely relevant, when assessing whether or not a campaign is negative, to ask about the purpose of the attacks. Are they designed to build support for one candidate at the expense of another? Is their purpose to compare the qualifications and record and ability of the candidates for the office being sought? Or is the purpose, as many will suspect while a vicious negative campaign is underway, to deflect public attention away from defects in the candidacy of the campaign conducting it? And further, if the purpose is to destroy, to humiliate, to demean, to link the candidate with the dark prejudices and hatreds inherent in the culture at any given time and place so that they become the sole currency of the campaign—then the attacks are negative.[9] And of course if the purpose is deliberately to hurt—the candidate, a family member, his/her associates and friends—then the attacks reach the seventh circle of negativity.

It must be noted that often these kinds of tactics work.

But not always.

Sometimes the mud thrown by each side has a way of balancing out. One can perhaps see this in the election of 1800, when it would be difficult to say whether the supporters of Adams or Jefferson were more vitriolic and nasty; even in that era of verbal excess, there was plenty hurled by each side and, in the end, they may have cancelled each other out.

And sometimes the candidate hit the hardest by negative campaigns wins anyway. In 1828 Jackson was probably hit harder than Quincy Adams. Even then, allegations of murder were serious business, in spite of the fact that Jackson was never investigated or indicted for murder, much less convicted. Indeed, reports of his possible bigamy may well have resonated with voters at that time more than the (remote) possibility that he was a murderer; and of course no one seemed to care that he had butchered the Seminoles. But Jackson won handily, in spite of the calumny heaped on him.

The same was true of Abe Lincoln in 1860 and 1864. The assaults against him were vicious in the worst way and were all part of a major effort at character assassination totally devoid of anything that was relevant to serving as President, but rather were designed to de-legitimize him and make him seem unfit for the office. They failed, as they did in 1884 when a startling revelation appeared that Grover Cleveland, the Democratic candidate, had fathered a child out of wedlock. At first the allegation seemed to torpedo Cleveland's candidacy, but then Cleveland stepped forward and said that it could be true (actual paternity was never established) and he had taken steps to provide for the child. How much responsibility Cleveland bore was not clear but he took on its mantle, and, while undoubtedly the issue and charge against him were distasteful to many, the attack was not seen as negative. Indeed, Cleveland's willingness to step forward and accept both blame and responsibility seemed to defuse the whole matter, and the attention of voters returned to the campaign and the eminently disreputable Blaine.

Blaine himself was inundated by personal attacks and robust charges against his public and private ethics. While it was never clear how much was actually true, Blaine was the sort of shady, dubious character—in modern campaign language, we would say he had "high negatives"—for whom they might as well have been true, and they stuck to him as if his clothes were made of Velcro.

The 1884 presidential campaign occupies a sort of "never-never" land in the realm of negativity. A lot of the rhetoric and written materials were sour, condemnatory, outraged. Bitterness and nastiness were abundant. But, while so much of it had the air of negativism about it, because so many of the charges and counter-charges were true, or at least could not be disproved, it would be hard to characterize the total campaign as nothing but negative. Foul, putrid, in bad taste, demeaning to everybody (including the voters), the worst kind of low comedy, absolutely. But negative? Cleveland managed to overcome the hurtfulness hurled at him by candidly addressing charges against him. Blaine made them worse by prevaricating, hiding, acting coyly, dissembling.

But maybe none of this mattered anyway, because remarkably, on a single day close to the election (Wednesday, October 29), Republicans managed to make two staggering blunders that cost them the White House prize. Both mistakes resulted from bad judgment, bad timing, and stupidity, rather than from negative Democratic attacks. In the morning of that day, the eminent Protestant clergyman, the Rev. Samuel Burchard, uttered his infamous, ugly, bigoted diatribe against the Democratic party of New York, dominated by the Irish, whose ancestors he claimed were "Rum, Romanism, and Rebellion." Within hours the phrase circulated widely in Irish wards and precincts of the city, mobilizing them to vote for Cleveland; their votes previously had been up for grabs, but the insults from Burchard pushed them to Cleveland.

In the evening of the same day, Blaine attended a lavish dinner at Delmonico's, the swankiest restaurant in New York and possibly in the entire United States at the time.[10] Present also were commercial, financial, and industrial moguls and fat cats such as Jay Gould, John Jacob Astor, Levi Morton, and Cyrus Field, all universally detested by Democrats. This widely publicized incident—again, true—poured gasoline onto the conflagration already consuming Blaine. Negative? The Reverend's remarks certainly were, but it was an odd example in that a supporter's negative attack against the Irish hurt his own candidate; Blaine's presence at the dinner given by the wealthiest Titans of finance and industry was a tactical blunder of epic proportions, perhaps matched subsequently only by the leaked tape of Mitt Romney during the 2012 campaign as he addressed a crowd of very wealthy donors and berated the lower 47 percent of the population whom he characterized as "takers."[11]

And then of course there were the numerous campaigns where negativity carried the day. The personal assaults on Van Buren in 1840 were prodigious, largely unfounded and absurdly overstated, but persuasive at the time. But they pale in comparison to 1896, in which Mark Hanna completely destroyed Bryan's character, with no other purpose than to do so. As bad as campaigns were in 1988 (George H.W. Bush against Michael Dukakis, orchestrated by Lee Atwater) and in 2008 and 2012 against Barack Obama (with Karl Rove a major background player), it is unlikely that, for sheer hatefulness, any American presidential campaign comes close to 1896. Hanna's tactics were of course successful; perhaps the most unfortunate part of the vilifications heaped on Bryan, who later became one of America's most distinguished statesmen, was that they were all so unnecessary, because America was not ready for midwestern populism, and Bryan would undoubtedly have lost anyway.

What seemed to make the difference in the effectiveness of negative campaigns? This is a question that continues to puzzle students of American politics, but at least three major indicators leap from our overview of nineteenth-century campaigns.

First, candidates who had a public image problem seemed especially susceptible to negative assaults. As noted above, nowadays we call them candidates with high negatives—meaning that there is much about them of which the voting public is suspicious. They project an aura of phoniness and insincerity or worse. They just don't seem very "likeable" or "trustworthy." They could not pass the 2000/2004 George Bush test: voters, recognizing his limitations, nonetheless were clear that they would rather have a beer with him than either the cerebral Al Gore or the remote patrician, John Kerry.

And so it was in the nineteenth century: neither of the Adamses could connect with the public on a personal, human level, and neither could Van Buren. Blaine looked and acted like a crook, and the cartoons of Nast and others showed him no mercy; it is worth a moment of speculation to imagine how the Disney Studios or, in a different vein, the French creators of "Ernest and Celestine," would have portrayed Blaine as the bad guy.[12] Bryan never really got out of the starting gate; Hanna had him pegged publicly as a naïve and unqualified immature, baby-like candidate who would ruin the country. On the other side, Jefferson seemed far more likeable and human than Adams. Both Jackson and Harrison were "men of the people," even if the latter had to be faked as one. Cleveland looked honest and competent, if boring; the scoundrel, even villainous, Blaine could not compete with a Boy Scout. And McKinley appeared states-manlike and above it all or, in the inimitable phrase of a contemporary political observer, he was someone "who walked among men like a bronze statue determinedly looking for a pedestal."[13] How could such a candidate possibly lose an election?

The second major determinant of the effectiveness of negative campaigns appears to be contextual and situational. What is the local political culture, style, and tradition? Does it relish, welcome, like, accept, tolerate, or reject negative campaigning? How much do local mores and customs at any given moment in time and space—in other words, what has worked or not worked in the past to elect or defeat a candidate— influence voters' attitudes towards their candidates? For example, Lee Atwater could negatively exploit a candidate's Jewish religion in rural, Bible belt, fundamentalist South Carolina; in much of Brooklyn, then and now, being Jewish would likely be to the advantage of a candidate.

And so it was. Quincy Adams and Van Buren had the misfortune of having reputations as patricians and (at least in Van Buren's case) something of an aesthete at a time when America was rapidly democra-tizing, and "red blooded" men of the soil were seen as more acceptable;

John Kerry of course ran into the same problem in 2004, when his patrician airs and Francophilia made him seem distant and remote and slightly condescending, compared to the Texas cowboy George W. Bush. Undoubtedly the same set of attitudes helped Lincoln against both Douglas and McClellan: he was plain and unpretentious; they had "airs" about them. Blaine appeared too much the embodiment of the widespread political corruption of the day, and Bryan was made to seem like a loony, ready and willing to overturn dominant values of American capitalism during the Gilded Age.[14]

Finally, how well does the victim of a negative campaign respond? Can he do so effectively and convincingly? Neither of the Adams candidates seemed to know what to say in response to attacks on them. Neither did Van Buren. For that matter, Blaine seemed to make things worse every time he opened his mouth, or his campaign surrogates opened theirs. And Bryan's campaign never had any traction; Hanna had him on the ropes before the campaign really started, and he was beaten from the outset. There are many parallels in later campaigns: probably the two most prominent were Dukakis in 1988 and Kerry in 2004; both seemed stunned by the negative assaults against them and never responded in a strong or credible manner.

Thus, in determining whether or not negative campaigns worked, or might work, in any given election, one has to ponder whether or not the attack will successfully "stick" to a candidate or fall harmlessly off. Similarly, does it "fit" within the political style and boundaries of acceptability in a given area, recognizing that these can and do change over time? And how did the target of negativity handle it? Was he paralyzed into inaction or did he come out forcefully and convincingly swinging back, defending himself?

## Shady Dealings and Dirty Tricks

Shady dealings and dirty tricks are part of the campaign circus, occupying prominent and long-standing pride of place in a variety of arenas. And they are also a major portion of the negative campaigning repertoire, but are so important that they deserve a separate mention here.

What is perhaps most worth noting is how early on shady dealings and dirty tricks became a part of presidential (and presumably other) campaigns, and how pervasive they have been. They can of course take a variety of forms, but for our purposes we can lump them into two categories.

The first we can call lies and fabrications. These are nothing other than efforts to invent new realities and to deny what rational people can see right in front of them. Many modern observers might argue that the campaigns of 2004 and 2012, especially, saw Republican candidates living in alternative universes, constructing realities that seemed divorced from the lives that most people experience.[15] But this kind of thing has been going on for a long time. In 1800 and 1828 opponents of the Adamses tried to paint them as wannabe monarchs, which was just silly but did achieve some traction. More serious were charges in 1800 that Jefferson had died during the campaign (actually a slave of that name had died, not the candidate); that Adams sent a political ally abroad in search of a mistress and that in the 1828 campaign Quincy Adams was portrayed as a procurer for the Russian Czar; or that in 1828 Jackson had murdered his own men; and in 1896 Bryan was a dangerous radical intent on destroying American capitalism.

Readers might object that all of these examples were just campaign nonsense and should have been ignored and given no credit; but that is exactly the point. In those times communication was difficult and slow, and alternative sources of information few and far between. Newspapers were far more openly partisan than today, and the slogans "Fair and Balanced" and "We Report, You Decide" had not yet been invented. So lies, invective, innuendoes, fabrications, and just stuff made up had substantial circulation and credibility if it was skillfully done, with little to refute it. By the time the "truth" (whatever that meant) became known, the damage had been done.

The other kind of dirty tricks can be called strong-arm tactics. These too are of ancient (by American standards) vintage. They did not begin with Watergate in 1972 or Willie Horton in 1988. From the moment the Whigs created a phony candidate in the form of William Henry Harrison in 1840, and ran a campaign based on gimmicks and souvenirs, it became common to undermine whatever tactics the opponent was using by crashing rallies, destroying posters and handbills, disrupting parades. But this was small, petty stuff compared to 1896, when Hanna never blinked an eye or thought twice about using extortion and goon-style tactics to extract money for McKinley from corporations, banks, industrial giants, and wealthy individuals.

Indeed, one can justly say that it would be rare to find a campaign at any level in America that did not involve some kind of shady dealings, dirty tricks, or something close to them. They may well be the lifeblood of campaign politics.

## Issues

"Issues? Why, son, they don't have a damn thing to do with it."[16] This famous remark by a North Florida county judge in 1949 is not exactly true of early presidential campaigns, but it is not far off the mark either. Issues were present, often important ones if we define "issues" as key or critical public questions of the day. But they did not always come out

## House of Cards

Readers are especially invited to view the Netflix series, *House of Cards*, based on the English TV series of the same name, to substantiate the point that dirty tricks may be integral to our campaign politics. While not dealing specifically with presidential campaigns, it portrays in realistic fashion the kind of shady dealings that go on in Congressional politics, including campaigns. See http://movies.netflix.com/WiMovie/House_of_Cards/70178217? locale=en-US for details. Episode 3, for example, deals extensively with a fictional, cynical, but realistic Congressional campaign in South Carolina featuring religious hypocrisy and political blackmail. It was all based on a house of cards, virtually none of it was true, but nonetheless it was effective. It—indeed the entire series—is a superb portrayal of dirty tricks politics, including betrayal and backstabbing, and is entirely credible.

during campaigns, nor were they always directly, let alone seriously, addressed. More often, they were covered up by diversionary, bait-and-switch tactics like mudslinging and character assassination.

In 1800, for example, the nation was deeply immersed in a struggle to determine its rightful place on the world stage, especially its relations with England and Napoleon's France. There was divisiveness over the *Alien and Sedition Acts*, which called into question just how far First Amendment freedoms of speech and press extended. And questions of federal versus states' rights continued to dog the new country.

None of this mattered. As an earlier version of this book noted, "It was all submerged under an avalanche of scurrilous attacks, character assassination, charges and countercharges, allegations of corruption, and worse."[17] While the issue of "The Bank" was clearly important in 1828, it was not the focus of the campaign; character assassination of both Quincy Adams and Jackson held center stage. Slavery was widely discussed in 1860, and the future of the nation in 1864, but they appeared mainly as vehicles for attacks on Lincoln, not as critical moral and political questions for the nation. In 1896 the future of the American economy was very much in the balance, as the debate between gold and silver (hard money versus easy credit) raged. So too were farm prices, interest rates, and monopoly and trust regulations on the table. But little about them was heard, because of the inundation of *ad hominem* attacks on Bryan.

Why? Why did issues play such minor, even invisible, roles in early presidential campaigns? Did not school teachers, pundits, and do-gooders back then stress their importance to democratic governance even as they do today? The answer, then as now, is that issues are more likely to lose votes than win them. For every assenting nod in a crowd at a rally as a candidate reveals an issue stance, there will be as many if not more shakes of the head and frowns, perhaps catcalls. Wedge issues, in particular, are designed to be divisive; while helpful in sorting out those who are in the candidate's circle from those who are opposed, wedge issues are better at preaching to the choir, or rallying and mobilizing the troops, than attracting votes by changing opponents' minds.

Thus there is a tendency in general elections, including presidential ones, to address public questions in bland, vague, often meaningless terms, if at all. To do otherwise, in general, risks alienating voters and losing votes. So too, politicians generally, and candidates in particular, resist the kind of commitment or "pigeon holing" that issues can require. Better to stay loose, flexible, go with the prevailing political flow. Better still to criticize the opponent for being out of step, out of touch, with mainstream American values, or for shady dealings, or being untrustworthy, or not sufficiently Christian. There are far more votes to be gained by impugning an opponent's character than by elucidating a position on a national bank, or slavery, or tariffs, or tax reform, or the desirability of a full-blown Palestinian state.

## The Politics of Personality and Sloganeering

Given that issues were generally hidden under layers of campaign dirt, and even when they surfaced they hardly merited serious discussion but instead received short shrift, of what did campaign rhetoric consist? In other words, what did candidates talk about? What did their handbills, posters, and supporting newspapers print?

The answer is pretty straightforward: the emphasis was on personality and sloganeering.

"Personality" of course means many things, especially in a campaign context. But there are two aspects of personality that stood out in our older campaigns. The first dealt with character. While a maddeningly vague term, generally discussions of character (particularly by surrogates of the candidate) were designed to show voters that he could be trusted with whatever office was being sought, for example, the presidency. But, even more importantly, discussions of character were perfect vehicles for vitriolic attacks on opponents. We have already cited so many examples in this chapter that any more would be superfluous. But the message was really quite clear: our candidate can be trusted, the opponent is a bad guy, evil incarnate, the Great Satan, a drunk, a murderer, a fornicator, a traitor. And worse. In other words, his "character" did not measure up to the demands of the presidency, or any other office.

The other aspect of personality that often appeared was "qualifications." Like "personality," there has never been any agreement as to what "qualifications" meant. Fitness for office based on experience, presumably; but how does one gain the necessary experience for American public office before one actually holds it? The tautology is as true for a village council or commission seat as it is for the presidency. So, like "character," "qualifications" are in the eye of the beholder. One's favored candidate is by definition, *ipso facto*, "qualified," just as he/she has the necessary "character." The others don't, even though they may have impressive resumes.

Of course, discussion of "qualifications" in campaigns is often, probably always, a surrogate for deeper and darker concerns: race, gender, social class, religion, social connections, the "right" family history, the "right" schools and colleges, the "right" views on whatever are the public questions of the day, and the like. When voters or pundits or colleagues ask about a potential or actual candidate's "qualifications" or "fitness" for office, they could well be raising questions that have nothing to do with ability, but rather with pedigree. "Polite" discussion of "qualifications" would exclude overt remarks such as "He's a Jew," but by merely using the word "qualification" the speaker makes very clear what he or she means. Thus, like so much else in the circus world of campaign politics, "qualifications" is really a smokescreen, a diversion from the message that the speaker or writer actually wants to convey.

What is particularly interesting is that the issue of "qualifications" could arise even in the case of incumbents seeking re-election. Both John and John Quincy Adams had to endure endless nitpicking that they were not qualified to be President, even though both were sitting in the White House. So did Van Buren. The same allegations were made against George W. Bush in 2004 and Barack Obama in 2012; opponents attacked them mercilessly as unqualified for the office they already held. In both cases voters disagreed. It is of interest that in the nineteenth century the two Adamses and Van Buren lost re-election bids, although it is not at all clear that the allegations of being "unqualified" swayed voters. More important were the candidates' public images and public personae as distant, removed, disengaged, haughty, and pretentious, including an inability to connect with "everyday" people.

What we can say more definitively is that sloganeering was a common and powerful force in our early campaigns. Jackson's moniker, "Old Hickory," used even before 1828, might seem corny to modern voters but it was persuasive and confidence building to voters then, because it not only gave him a clear, rural, Western (in those days Tennessee was the West), popular, democratic, non-establishment identity, but also one of toughness and reliability and trustworthiness like the hickory stick souvenirs that his campaign passed out to supporters. "Tippeecanoe and

Tyler Too" in 1840 was part of the manufactured identity of Harrison; but, for voters, it conjured up what was supposed to be one of the candidate's major military victories over the Indians, thereby making him a robust, manly candidate far superior to the allegedly effete, passive Van Buren. The slogans made up about Blaine in 1884 (Blaine! Blaine!/The Continental Liar/From the State of Maine!) and Bryan in 1896 (he was repeatedly stung by variations on the theme of "Free Silver") stuck like glue to both candidates, much to their undoing. So too did the slogans "Rough Rider" and "Charge Up San Juan Hill" stick to Theodore Roosevelt as the century turned, but with much more favorable results.

Slogans of course are important for all sorts of reasons. They provide an identity and a ready tag for voters. They might not know anything about the candidate; they may not even know his name. But they know the slogan: "Old Hickory" was undoubtedly far more meaningful to average voters than a substantive elucidation of Jackson's platform or agenda; so were slogans like "New Deal," "Fair Deal," "New Frontier, "Great Society," and "It's Morning in America." Nicknames can play the same role as slogans, offering an identity, a "human" face behind which candidates can hide. "Ike," the nickname/slogan for Dwight D. Eisenhower, which was not an easy name to remember or pronounce, undoubtedly made him seem more avuncular than he would have without it; so too did the nicknames "Jack" Kennedy and "LBJ" convey more of a sense of familiarity, of "human-ness," than their full real names. But whether or not the jocular moniker "Shrub," conveyed on George W. Bush by the late, lamented journalist Molly Ivins,[18] cost Bush popular support is uncertain, but doubtful.

More importantly, slogans can obfuscate. "Old Hickory" hides the fact that, while Jackson may or may not have been a murderer, he did kill people in duels and he did massacre Indians, and, while he probably did not commit bigamy, his slogan obscures the fact that many people thought he did. A hickory tree is strong, and inspires respect; that was the point of linking Jackson to *Carya tomentosa*. The slogans of both the "New Frontier" and "Great Society," evocative of a great mission and a grand future, obscured the fact that they ignored or deliberately left out significant needy or disadvantaged portions of the population.

And of course slogans obviate the need for discussion of issues or policies. Why worry about U.S. expansion into the West; "Tippecanoe and Tyler Too" said all the voter needed to know: Harrison was a military hero, what better person to have in the White House? The "Great Society" had a persuasive and appealing ring to it, but did not address the questions of "great society" for whom and how it would be achieved. Slogans, then, become shields, instruments of protection behind which candidates and campaigns can hide. It's no wonder that the use of slogans in political campaigns continues to the present. Indeed it does, but we generally call them something else: "sound bites," perfect for press conferences, TV commercials, short blogs on the Internet, Tweets, and the like. They are devoid of content, but can be very meaningful and evocative of what the candidate "stands for" without saying anything substantive or making a commitment to a position or course of action.

---

### Political Slogans

In 2012 Mitt Romney's campaign used the slogan "Believe in America." The Obama campaign adopted "Forward." Most analysts thought the Obama slogan was more effective. It is of interest, however, that "Forward" was the title of Mussolini's house newspaper, *Avanti*! It was also similar to the slogan of one of Hitler's youth movements, "*Vorwärts*." It is not clear how many Americans knew this, or cared, or even if the Obama campaign was aware of the term's provenance. Some slogans are so vague as to be meaningless; one thinks of John McCain's "Country First" (2008) in this regard. Others quickly ring hollow: "Change you can believe in" (Obama, 2008) is an example.

---

## Money

Another feature of our early campaigns that is now central to modern ones—even for modest races in small communities—is money. Indeed, it is no exaggeration to say that money now counts more than voters in the outcome of elections because, without sufficient funds, a campaign won't garner any votes. Money might well be the Great Satan of modern political campaigning—in a later chapter we will see how new campaign finance practices have potentially compromised democratic elections—but it has certainly become the *sine qua non* of modern campaigns.

What is of interest is that pundits and observers of campaigns, even early in the nineteenth century, expressed concern over how much they cost. It is thought that Andrew Jackson's campaign in 1828 was the first to break the $1 M mark, a sum which bothered many observers. While, in 2014 dollars, this might not seem like an impressive amount for a presidential campaign[19]—it would be about $21 M[20]—one has to remember that in 1828 the electorate was still very small.

"National" campaigns barely reached the Mississippi river but really were focused farther east, and there was no need for extensive and expensive advertising, polling, and high priced consultants, none of which existed then.

---

### How Much is $1 M?

In 1828 $1 M was a non-trivial amount of money. The entire federal operating budget for fiscal year 1828 was about $18 M.[21] The Erie Canal, completed in 1825, cost a little over $7 M;[22] the first U.S. railroad founded to carry passengers and freight, the Baltimore and Ohio in 1827, was financed by an initial stock offering of $3 M.[23] In 1829 $1 M would buy more than 8,300 head of cattle (@ $12); in 1823 that amount of money would buy 500,000 acres ($2/acre) of land in parts of South Carolina: nearly 3 percent of the state's total land area.[24] In 1830 there was only about $93 M of money in total circulation in the United States.[25]

---

It is difficult to get a firm grip on the use of money in presidential, and other, political campaigns during the nineteenth century. For the most part, political parties ran them and they were not required to submit any kind of financial statements to either state or federal officials. Indeed, until the landmark U.S. Supreme Court decision of *Smith v. Allwright* (1944),[26] political parties were regarded as mainly private agencies, not subject to public scrutiny or supervision. In addition to the financing of campaigns by parties, candidates were allowed to "cut deals" with individual donors to raise funds for campaigns, sometimes to their detriment; both Lincoln and Teddy Roosevelt were accused of being a little too cozy with some of their major, wealthy financial backers and received criticism for it. But none of this required any official reporting.

Perhaps the lid started to blow off the boiling campaign finance pot in 1896, when Hanna extorted every cent he could from Big Money. He himself claimed to have raised $3 M, but others claimed it was more than $16 M. Hanna used to complain about industrialists, bankers, and other wealthy targets who tried to get off cheap when he came around demanding donations, calling them a "a lot of God-damned sheep."

Following Hanna's excesses and Teddy Roosevelt's relationship with bankers, Progressives did begin to make noises about campaign finance reform. The best known of these efforts culminated in the *Tillman Act* of 1907.[27] But neither it nor others associated with various reform efforts, including the *Federal Corrupt Practices Acts* of 1910, 1911, and 1925, proved effective instruments of campaign finance reform, largely because they were unenforceable. It would not be until another election that featured an excess of Big Money, largely from corporations, in 1972 that the first real efforts to create stringent federal campaign finance laws bore fruit.

## Public Dissatisfaction

The last characteristic of campaigns found early in our history to be noted is public dissatisfaction with them. Since the early 1800s vilification of political campaigns has been one of Americans' favorite pastimes, matched in recent years only by widespread criticism of the U.S. Congress, whose prestige and popularity have fallen, as the astute political observer and satirist Stephen Colbert succinctly noted, below that of colonoscopies.[28] It is doubtful that any other aspect of our politics has been more vilified than campaigns.

In Chapter 1 of this book we discussed public attitudes towards campaigns and, rather than repeat what was said, readers are invited to review that section. What is of interest is that criticism of the length and emptiness and triviality of presidential, and presumably other, campaigns has long been a part of our history. For example, in 1840 the *Philadelphia Ledger*, a Democratic foe of Whig William Henry Harrison, wrote:

> The log cabin campaign was a 'national drunken frolic' and a disgrace. The worst part of it was … that many ladies went to the open-air meetings, strained their voices shouting 'Huzza,' drank hard cider from gourd shells, and devoured baked beans with their fingers from barrels. 'Was this the proper sphere of women? … Was this appropriate to her elevating, refining influence? Did such things improve men? No. They merely degraded women, and made men still more degraded than they were before.[29]

Aside from the gender stereotyping in the quote, similar sentiments have been expressed numerous times over the decades to the present. Perhaps it is appropriate to end this chapter with quotations from six astute observers of American political campaigns. They summarize brilliantly what seems to be the prevailing view that Americans have had about them over the years:[30]

- "Political campaigns are designedly made into emotional orgies which endeavor to distract attention from the real issues involved, and they actually paralyze what slight powers of cerebration man can normally muster" (James Harvey Robinson, *The Human Comedy*, 1937).
- "We'd all like to vote for the best man, but he's never a candidate" (Kin Hubbard).
- "I offer my opponents a bargain: if they will stop telling lies about us, I will stop telling the truth about them (Adlai Stevenson, campaign speech, 1952).

- "Every two years the American politics industry fills the airwaves with the most virulent, scurrilous, wall-to-wall character assassination of nearly every political practitioner in the country—and then declares itself puzzled that America has lost trust in its politicians" (Charles Krauthammer).
- "The [candidates] were talking themselves red, white and blue in the face" (Clare Boothe Luce).
- "When one may pay out over two million dollars to presidential and Congressional campaigns, the U.S. government is virtually up for sale" (John Gardner).

## Notes

1 See, for example, his "Prologue: Iowa Waltz," in *The American Future: A History* (New York: Harper Collins, 2009).
2 Richard K. Scher, *The Modern Political Campaign* (Armonk, N.Y.: M. E. Sharpe, 1997) p. 27.
3 Scher (1997), p. 31.
4 Quoted in Douglas Walton, *Ad Hominem Arguments* (Tuscaloosa: University of Alabama Press, 1998), p. xii.
5 See, for example, Lewis Chester, Geoffrey Hodgson, and Bruce Page, *An American Melodrama: The Presidential Campaign of 1968* (New York: Viking, 1969) and Gary Wills, *Nixon Agonistes* (Boston, M.A: Houghton Mifflin, 1970, 1979).
6 See James G. Blaine cartoons, cartoonstock.com, also viewed online at http://cartoons.osu.edu/nast/harpers.htm, viewed online May 15, 2012; a number of the historical sources listed above also include illuminating cartoons of Blaine, almost always making him look sneaky, elusive, a skulker, and worse.
7 See, for example, *Harper's Weekly*, October 24, 1896; viewed online at http://projects.vassar.edu/1896/1024hw.html, May 15, 2012.
8 See *Boogie Man: The Lee Atwater Story*, a documentary by Stefan Forbes (2008). A description can be found at www.imdb.com/title/tt1262863.
9 Some of the attacks on Michael Dukakis in 1988 and John Kerry in 2004 by independent groups descended to this level. See *The Living Room Candidate*, 1988, 2004, viewed online at www.livingroomcandidate.org/commercials/1988 and www.livingroomcandidate.org/commercials/2004, June 9, 2014.
10 See Judith Choate, James Canora, and Steve Pool, *Dining At Delmonico's: The Story Of America's Oldest Restaurant* (New York: Stuart, Tabori and Chang, 2008); William Grimes, *Appetite City: A Culinary History of New York* (New York: North Point Press, 2010).
11 The tape can be viewed at www.youtube.com/watch?v=M2gvY2wqI7M, September 18, 2012.
12 See the official site, Walt Disney Studios, waltdisneystudios.com; and the official site, "Ernest and Celestine," www.ernestandcelestine.com.
13 The remark apparently was made by the distinguished American journalist, editor, and leader of the Progressive movement, William Allen White; his characterization is quoted in PBS, "The American Experience: President McKinley and American Expansion," viewed online at www.pbs.org/wgbh/amex/1900/peopleevents/pande20.html, February 4, 2013.

14  Mark Twain coined the phrase in 1873; it became even more appropriate as the nineteenth century moved towards the twentieth.
15  See for example Ron Suskind, "Faith, Certainty, and the Presidency of George W. Bush," *New York Times Magazine*, October 17, 2004, viewed online at www.nytimes.com/2004/10/17/magazine/17BUSH.html?_r=0, June 9, 2014.
16  Quoted originally in V. O. Key, *Southern Politics* (New York: Vintage, 1949), p. 94. The line has been quoted in so many other places and contexts that one might suspect it was apocryphal.
17  Scher (1997), p. 30.
18  She often used the term. See Molly Ivins, *Shrub: The Short but Happy Political Life of George W. Bush* (New York: Vintage, 2000). Ivins underestimated Bush's political longevity, but she never failed to poke holes in him, until her dying moments.
19  Michael Bloomberg spent about $108 M on his third re-election campaign in New York City (see Huffingingtonpost.com, January 15, 2010, viewed online at www.huffingtonpost.com/2010/01/15/bloomberg-campaign-spendi_n_425240.html, February 8, 2010. Huffingtonpost.com also reports that Governor Rick Scott of Florida planned to spend upwards of $100 for his 2014 re-election campaign; see www.huffingtonpost.com/2013/02/06/rick-scott-reelection_n_2630020.html?utm_hp_ref=politics, viewed online February 8, 2013.
20  Using the Federal Reserve Consumer Price Index data on comparing dollar values over time; the arithmetic is 2012 Price = 1828 Price x (2012 CPI/1828 CPI), where the 1828 price is $1 M, 2012 CPI 687.5, and 1828 CPI 33. See www.minneapolisfed.org/community_education/teacher/calc/hist1800.cfm?, viewed online February 8, 2013.
21  See U.S. Government Spending, 1828; viewed online at www.usgovernmentspending.com/year_spending_1828USmf_13ms1s, February 8, 2013.
22  See  http://news.google.com/newspapers?nid=1499&dat=19821106&id=S3UfAAAAIBAJ&sjid=3SkEAAAAIBAJ&pg=4325,4205486, viewed online February 8, 2013.              .
23  This was the figure given by Dave Shackelford, Chief Curator of the Baltimore and Ohio Museum, Baltimore, M.D., in a personal email, Monday, February 11, 2013. Shackelford lists several works corroborating this figure in his communication. Other sources give a figure of $4M; see www.ushistory.org/us/25b.asp, viewed online February 8, 2013.
24  See  http://247wallst.com/2010/09/16/the-history-of-what-things-cost-in-america-1776-to-today/2, viewed online February 8, 2013.
25  See http://research.stlouisfed.org/wp/2003/2003-006.pdf, p. 46l viewed online February 8, 2013.
26  *Smith vs. Allwright*, 321US 649 (1944).
27  See, for example, "Turn of the Century Timeline," viewed online at www.polisci.ccsu.edu/trieb/turn.htm, February 9, 2013 and Larry J. Sabato and Howard R. Ernst, *Encyclopedia Of American Political Parties And Elections*, updated (Info Base Learning, Facts on File e-book, 2006), p. 146; viewed online at http://books.google.com/books?id=d-379E2mFmYC&pg=PA146&lpg=PA146&dq=tillman+bill+1907&source=bl&ots=IBw8m_qAfx&sig=uUf1mUlc9URehDjGlR8-WYAZb6o&hl=en&sa=X&ei=mnMWUauYMea42QWYmICoBw&ved=0CFAQ6AEwBQ#v=onepage&q=tillman%20bill%201907&f=false, February 9, 2013.
28  See  Huffingtonpost.com,  February  8,  2013,  viewed  online  at www.huffingtonpost.com/2013/02/08/stephen-colbert-house-democrats_n_

2646759.html, February 9, 2013.

29　Quoted in Scher, p. 39.

30　All the quotes can be found in Welcome to the Quote Garden, "Quotations about Politics," 2014, viewed online at www.quotegarden.com/politics.html, June 10, 2014.

# 3 Candidates and Campaigns

People who study social and political phenomena, whether professional scholars or beginning students, are inclined (indeed the professionals are so trained) to think in macro-level terms. There are legitimate reasons for this, mostly involving efforts to be as "scientific" as possible (which generally require substantial data sets) and to draw conclusions and create generalizations, even build theory, about the phenomena under investigation.

The weakness in this approach is that it is easy to lose sight of individuals, of people, of human beings. Campaigns, for example, involve intensely human, individual-level activity. Unless the campaign is about an issue, a referendum, or amendment, the focus is on a single individual, the candidate, and his/her very human opponent(s). It is certainly possible to study campaigns at the macro level, and in this book we do a good deal of that. But every campaign is unique, no two are ever the same (even the campaigns of candidates running, successfully, for re-election time after time), every candidate has his or her very personal quirks and qualities, likes and dislikes, ways of campaigning, responses to the inevitable bumps and setbacks that the campaign trail always offer up. Anyone interested in political campaigns, whether a scholar, student, journalist, or interested bystander, would do well never to forget just how "human" candidates really are and how individualistic, even idiosyncratic, each campaign is.

So in this chapter we try to take a step away from the macro-level analysis of campaigns to focus on the individual candidate. The key point for readers to remember is that candidates are very much flesh and blood, and their personality and style very much color what their campaign is like. The crucial questions that we will ask are: Why would anyone ever run for office?; What are the pros and cons of doing so?; How does campaigning affect them as people, their families, their business and professional associates?; and What happens if they lose or, even more importantly, what happens if they win?

Thus our major purpose now is to show the very human side of political campaigns. Towards the end, in discussing the emergence of a new kind of candidate, we will return to a more macro-level analysis. But, even then, it is important that the reader keep in mind that campaigning is a very, very human, individual, activity.

## Running for Office

Why would anyone run for public office? To succeed into elective office one has to endure a campaign: expensive, disruptive of personal and professional life, noisy and disconcerting, usually negative and potentially down and dirty, always humbling and often humiliating even in victory and almost assuredly in defeat, and rarely a credit to the abilities and reputation of the candidate(s). In the event of victory, what has the winner gained? Not a high salary or access to (legal) sources of money, nor elevated social status, unless he or she is elected President, or Senator, or perhaps Governor; however, he or she does get demands on his/her time and energy 24/7/365 while having to smile into a camera even when seething or crying inwardly, almost constant criticism (including from inevitably disappointed supporters) for what was done or said, or not said and not done, and (among many other things) the elimination of even the semblance, the mere shadow, of a private life. The list makes losing seem almost more desirable.

Why do it? Perhaps the famous Civil War General William Tecumseh Sherman had it right when he was quoted in 1884 while the Republican Party tossed his name about as its possible presidential nominee: "If nominated I will not run; if elected I will not serve."[1] Evidently Sherman saw what was coming and headed the other way as fast as he could.

But many do not. Every year, or at least every other year, thousands of men and women, of all shapes and sizes and political stripes, throw their hats into various rings and run for elective offices, ranging from a seat on the town council of a tiny crossroads hamlet in the middle of nowhere to the most exalted office of all, the presidency of the United States. The reasons they do so, and choose to endure the discomforts, surprises, vagaries, and likely disappointments[2] of a campaign are as varied and idiosyncratic as those who decide to file papers and plunk down the required fees, for reasons of their own or for reasons of which they may not even be conscious.

In this chapter we cannot, obviously, survey all of the reasons why people make a decision to run and proceed to declare their candidacy for elective office.

But we can look at the hurdles that candidates—potential and real— must overcome to mount a campaign. We can also look at some of the major payoffs or benefits from running for office, benefits which clearly outweigh the costs of running, even if from a statistical standpoint any given candidate is more likely to lose than win. We will then look at two important features of modern candidates: one is the criticism that they don't measure up to those of mythical days of yore, when candidates were larger-than-life giants; and the other is that the way many contemporary candidates emerge has produced a new type of office seeker who may not always be healthy for American democratic elections.

## The Costs of Running for Office[3]

As with so much that can be said about political campaigns, the costs of running can be idiosyncratic: what might be so much of a burden/cost for one potential candidate that it compels him or her not to run might well be shrugged off by another as incidental or irrelevant. Nonetheless, the potential costs featured in the following brief discussion represent those that every prospective candidate needs to consider; how prohibitive or incidental they are is generally highly personal. Moreover, the calculation/determination of costs can change during a campaign: what seemed minor at the outset might suddenly loom so large that it causes the candidate to withdraw. And one or more costs that at the outset might have seemed overwhelming could, over time, appear much less heavy had the candidate stuck with it.

---

### Deciding Not To Run

The author recalls a Florida candidate, scion of a very prominent political family, who neglected to reveal an episode with marijuana in a distant state some 25 years earlier, because he thought it was of no consequence. When the opponent got wind of it and very loudly broadcast it, suddenly it appeared definitively consequential, and he was forced to drop out. In two other instances the author had spoken with potential candidates exploring possible runs; one had been treated, successfully, for a severe mental illness, and the other had endured a very public messy divorce. In the end both felt that these facts would wreck their candidacies, and decided not to run, even though some of their supporters pointed out that with fully candid disclosures these matters could have been overcome, since as times change the public's acceptance of human frailty, when accompanied by frankness and honesty, has broadened.

---

### Time

Without doubt the most serious cost to anyone campaigning is time. Unlike virtually any other resource, it can never be recouped. Today's innocent remark can be seen tomorrow as a blunder and the next day as a nightmare and the beginning of the end. Apologies and retractions can flow like a torrent but, in the end, whatever was said cannot be retracted because the moment it happened can never be reeled back, nor the episode undone. In political campaigns, time never stands still and certainly never goes backward; it only goes inexorably forward, and the closer election day looms, the faster it seems to run. Physics teachers trying to explain theories of relativity to students should have them join a political campaign; the lesson will quickly be learned.

The time cost of campaigns can be seen in any number of ways, but for our purposes here three will suffice.

First, time spent campaigning cannot be spent doing something else: walking the dog, enjoying a glass of wine, going to work, closing a business deal. Thus, if one contemplates a run for office, one has to ask, What will I give up as I spend my time campaigning? Serious campaigns are all-consuming, requiring the full attention of the candidate (and often those closest to him); not to devote full time to the campaign invites failure and defeat. So what kinds of activities is the potential candidate willing to give up, and force those nearest to him give up as well?; Is it worth it?; Is that seat on the town council so important that family time can be sacrificed, the Saturday golf game with friends abandoned, languid Sunday afternoons lamented as a thing of the past?

Second, in the hurly-burly of a campaign there are frequent dilemmas for the candidate's use of time. Should he go to this event at this time, or another one? Should she send a surrogate instead and, if so, whom? Should she spend the time dialing for dollars or visit the nursing home or community center?

---

### Dialing for Dollars

Even in this day of digital communication, calling supporters and potential supporters for money is still called "dialing for dollars," a throwback to antediluvian rotary telephones.

---

At any given moment, the campaign may well require the attention of the candidate (and staff) for a number of competing activities; but choices have to be made as to how the time will be spent, because the same time cannot be used for more than one purpose. How to know which is the right expenditure of time? What if none of the available choices seems palatable, or especially functional? In the heat of the campaign, one still feels obliged to do SOMETHING, go SOMEWHERE! A victory on election night will probably be interpreted as vindication that the right choice of time use was made; a defeat will just as likely be viewed as a misuse of time. In the end, the candidate and his/her campaign has to forge ahead and use time in what appears to be the most beneficial way. But, no one will ever really know if that was indeed the case.

Finally, campaigns now are endless, and the time they take seems to flow forever. There are two parts to this point.

First, the planning of a political campaign can go on for extended periods; as a general rule, the "higher" the office, the longer it takes.[4] But even a campaign for a local office, if it has a genuine chance of success, cannot be thrown together in a slap-dash manner. Aside from the money that the campaign will cost, and the very difficult question of how to get the money if it is not candidate-financed (which includes the question of whether the candidate is willing to do/say or not do/not say what is necessary to get the money), there are issues that take months, even years, to resolve: candidate credentials; candidate visibility; candidate reputation; candidate name-recognition; candidate credibility; massaging the media; determining and creating a winning coalition; identifying and locking down the candidate's "base"; securing the necessary funds. These are just some of the very complex and difficult matters that require careful attention if the candidate is going to make a serious run for office. Indeed, even for a campaign for a minor local office, candidates would be well advised to think in terms of a year or preferably more, in order to be well prepared, well positioned, and well financed for a credible race. Deciding on the afternoon of the last day of qualifying that one wants to run for office is sure to result in a campaign that goes nowhere.

But there is more. Let us remind ourselves of the discussion in Chapter 1: the distinction between governance, whether in Washington, D.C. or in a miniscule crossroads village, and campaigning has broken down. Successful candidates who become office holders can never really stop campaigning, because it is necessary in modern times to campaign continuously to have a chance at accomplishing one's political goals; the era of quiet negotiating and painstaking, point-by-point discussion and consensus building (or at least compromising) to accomplish a purpose or reach a goal seems like a relic of a quaint distant past. Political goals by office holders are now reached by shouting into microphones on radio or television, or making ever bolder claims in blogs, emails, and tweets. So, even as the successful candidate enjoys his victory toast on election night, the realization that he or she has to start campaigning again in the morning—or at least the moment he takes the oath of office—might well spoil the taste of the sweet victory nectar. The lesson is abundantly clear: campaigning is a time-eating activity of major proportions, and there is never—NEVER—a moment to lose.

## Opportunity Costs

The opportunity costs of campaigning follow from the previous discussion. They accrue because campaigning eats up so much of the candidate's time that he/she cannot do something else.

For example, if one is campaigning, one is not working at one's job—selling insurance, representing clients in legal cases, building houses, laying bricks, manufacturing and shipping widgets from here to there, writing novels or poems, teaching algebra to eighth graders. It is of course possible to calculate how much income one loses by dialing for dollars or glad handing at the weekly Rotary Club instead of attending to one's occupation. For economically vulnerable potential candidates, these opportunity costs can rise to such levels as to render taking time out to run for office impossible, especially if there is a family to support and a mortgage to pay. Is it any wonder that so many office seekers and holders are wealthy people? Given how we conduct campaigns—full time, over a considerable period even for local offices—candidates have to raise the money or pay out of their own pockets, since as a practical matter public financing of campaigns in this country does not really exist. Thus, given the cost of modern campaigns, we have effectively eliminated all but the top 20 percent of the population, and for major offices all but the top 1 percent, from running.[5]

But opportunity costs are not always numerical, or financial. Time used for campaigning means not going to the school play, or soccer game, or sometimes rushing in at the last moment to avoid totally disappointing one's child; eating cold pizza at a campaign event instead of dining with one's spouse or partner or parent or friend or child, even if the pizza at home or in a restaurant is just as rubbery and tasteless as at the campaign venue; standing in the hot sun or driving rain while pretending to enjoy oneself instead of surfing the Net or happily reading a book or going for a walk or downing a cold one while watching TV: the list is endless. The point is, the opportunity costs of campaigning can be staggering, sufficiently so that they discourage otherwise able people from even considering a run for office. Too often, those opportunity costs are not sufficiently thought through ahead of time, and the candidate finds out in the course of the campaign just how high they are, for himself, his loved ones, his business associates, his friends.

## Outlay of Personal Resources

The political campaign does not exist that requires no outlay of personal resources, especially money. They accrue from the very outset of the campaign. If the candidate is a first-timer, he or she cannot raise funds until a campaign account is opened; most banks require at least a minimum initial deposit ($5? $100? $500?) to open one. The funds are almost always from the candidate, unless he/she is an incumbent, in which case the campaign account already exists, and leftover funds from previous campaigns are already deposited in it. There are other start-up costs as well: unless one has secured a donated space, a headquarters needs to be arranged and paid for; even if it is in the candidate's house, that means the dining room or spare bedroom or study must be transformed for the duration of the campaign. Computers, smart phones, cards and stationery, flyers and banners, buttons and stickers, and all of the other flotsam and jetsam that campaigns require—the money for these has to come from someplace, and unless money starts pouring into the campaign account from the moment it is opened, at least many of these initial expenses will be the candidate's.

True, most of these are reimbursable; the candidate, in general, can use campaign donations to replenish his own bank account, if desired. But is that the best use of money donated to the campaign? Is that what most donors really want—for the candidate to pay himself back at the donors' expense? Indeed, the candidate has to decide, long before he or she opens an account, how much of his or her own personal funds he or she is willing to use.

Of course, if the candidate is a billionaire like Michael Bloomberg, former Mayor of New York City, or even just a modest multi-millionaire like Rick Scott, Governor of Florida, these start-up costs are incidental, and indeed both of these wealthy candidates spent vast personal sums on their campaigns.[6] Spending personal wealth on one's political campaigns has become much more than a cottage industry. The Center for Responsive Politics, through its Open Secrets Blog, reported that in 2012 candidates for a variety of offices spent over $130 M in personal funds.[7] But of course this raises very fundamental questions about the health of our democracy: Does one have to be wealthy in order to run for office? What about otherwise able people who have limited or no personal resources to commit to their campaigns—are they disqualified, or just doomed from the outset because they cannot compete with wealthy opponents?

And there are other personal costs to the candidate in carrying out his or her campaign. Presidential and U.S. Senate candidates (except in the smallest of states) usually fly from one campaign venue to another. But Congressmen, state legislators, and local candidates generally have to use a personal car; if the campaign account is flush, perhaps renting a car is possible, but many candidates choose not to use scarce resources on a rental, preferring to pay for media and advertising, or polling, or consultants instead. Candidates might even need new clothes, since these are part of the all-important image and political persona that the candidates want to create and project. And campaign volunteers and workers need to be fed and refreshed; campaign funds can be used for this, but many donors would react negatively to find that their money was used to buy pizza and peanuts and bottles of water instead of campaign ads or opposition research. Much better if the candidate uses his or her own money for campaign snacks and refreshments, in the event that he cannot secure in-kind donations of food and drink.

---

### How the Candidate Should Dress

Some years ago a candidate for the Florida state legislature decided to make the official announcement of his candidacy around the swimming pool in his back yard, instead of arranging another, more public venue. It was a hot day, but the candidate chose to stand in the sun while delivering his statement. He was a short young man with sandy hair and a sallow complexion. He wore a tan suit, pale cream-colored shirt, and light-toned tie of uncertain color. From across the pool, where most of his supporters stood in the shade staring into the glare of the blazing late afternoon sun, he could barely be seen. The next day his wife and campaign staff took him to a men's store, to buy some dark suits and jackets, in hopes that in the often blinding Florida sunshine the candidate might actually be visible.

---

### Stress and Strain on Family Life

Without doubt, the stress and strain that the demands of a campaign place on the candidate's family represent the greatest non-financial cost that he or she must face. Of course if the candidate is single, and without any kind of companion, then these costs do not accrue. Even if he or she owns a dog or cat, however, the campaign will take its toll in terms of abrupt changes in the pet's routine and schedule because of comings and goings at all hours of day and night, strangers marching in and out of the residence, and so forth.

But if there is a family, and especially if there are children, the stresses and strains can be staggering. In the author's experience, no marriage or partnership is unchanged by a campaign (this point is effectively, and at times brilliantly, portrayed in the television series *The Good Wife*[8]). Sometimes it is strengthened, but too often it is weakened to the point that a break-up is inevitable if not immediate. There is no such thing as a relationship-neutral campaign, because of the tensions and pressures inevitably felt. This remains true even when the campaign is seemingly over for the day (or night), and the door is closed and the house quiet; in fact, the campaign never gives the candidate and his/her family a moment's respite or peace.

## Campaign Stresses and Strains

The discussion has emphasized psychological and emotional stresses and strains on the family unit. But there are often physical effects as well. Candidates, and their spouses or partners, generally gain or lose weight during the campaign; rare are the exceptions. Pre-existing physical conditions, such as high blood pressure or a tendency toward migraine headaches, can be exacerbated by campaign pressures. And physical problems can occur on the campaign trail as well. Perhaps the best known came in 1960, when Richard Nixon banged his knee getting into a car after a campaign stop in Greensboro, North Carolina. The abrasion became infected, and he landed in Walter Reed Hospital in Washington, D.C., just before the first Presidential Debate since 1858. As he arrived at the TV studio in Chicago to take part, Nixon AGAIN hit the knee, and according to on-site reports his face turned chalk-white. He refused to accept make-up and during the debate clearly showed his pain and discomfort. How much the injury contributed to his ultimate defeat is a matter of conjecture, but clearly it did not help him.[9]

With children, matters get more complicated. Can or will they play a role in the campaign? Perhaps, if they are old enough, but do they want to? What if they are not old enough, and suddenly one of the parents or major adult care-givers in their lives is absent, out campaigning, when children are in need of their presence? How do the children deal with the absence of a parent or step-parent from the science fair, or school supper, or ball game, or band concert, or just bed-time, because the campaign required that the grown-up be elsewhere? How do the children deal with the inevitable "playground" comments that they will hear from their peers about their parent or step-parent who is the candidate? Resentments, anger, disappointments, feelings of abandonment—all of these and more are inevitable when children get sucked into the campaign, as they will be, whether by choice or by the whirlpool effect that campaigns have on the candidate's family. And what happens to spouses and partners and children if the candidate loses? Or wins? From their standpoint, it's hard to know which might have the more substantial, even devastating, impact.

Some readers might object that only the most callous individual would ignore these matters beforehand. Surely months, perhaps years, of family preparation are needed and will take place before the official announcement of a candidacy is made! Surely the conscientious spouse, partner, and parent will have made all the necessary preparations and arrangements ahead of time! Sadly, not always. The collateral damage on family members, and number of casualties resulting from the stresses and strains of a campaign on the family, especially if there are children, all too often resemble those of a bad car accident, devastating illness, or train wreck.

## Stresses and Strains on Friends and Business Associates

Everything in the previous section also applies to the candidate's friends and business associates during the campaign. While the candidate might assume that his golfing buddies and poker circle "of course" support him, it is not a given, and indeed they may not. The same is true with his or her law partners or members of his or her insurance or real estate agency: it is no more certain that all of them are supporters than it would be if they were members of the candidate's church or synagogue or Kiwanis club. Presumably the candidate has worked out arrangements with business associates because inevitably someone(s) will have to take up the slack while the candidate is out campaigning. But that does not mean that resentments and discontents and ill-feelings will not arise.

And the same is true of friendships. Some may not care that the candidate is no longer available for Tuesday night poker or Saturday golf; others will be annoyed or hurt, and regard the absent candidate as ignoring both his buddies and the obligations that friendships entail. And this does not even begin to speak to the question of differences of views and opinions on issues of the day, or partisanship. One can be very happy in a golf foursome of individuals with very different political views; but the moment one becomes a candidate, divisive lines are drawn, often with a damaging impact on the personal dynamics of the foursome. Inevitably, the friendships will be changed, even if they survive a winning, or losing, campaign. The same is true with business associates; relations among partners or colleagues will never be the same again once the hat gets tossed into the ring.

## Serendipity, and the Slings and Arrows of Outrageous Fortune

As the iconic bumper sticker says, "Things Happen." And political campaigns are no exception. Things happen along the way, sometimes propelling the campaign forward, sometimes becoming a train wreck, derailing it completely. When they are of the latter sort, the cost to campaign and candidate can be devastating.

To paraphrase former Secretary of Defense Donald Rumsfeld, a campaign faces a variety of unknowns, both known and unknown.[10] A carefully crafted campaign plan tries to anticipate possible difficulties along the way and how they should be dealt with—these would be the potential "known unknowns." Architects of the campaign plan (including the candidate) might have a sense that a difficulty might arise if something becomes public knowledge and morphs into a political albatross. The sudden revelation, discussed in the previous chapter, that 1884 presidential candidate Grover Cleveland might have fathered a child out of wedlock may possibly be the archetype of a "known unknown" in a political campaign. But of course Cleveland was prepared for it and immediately knew what to do.

But it's the "unknown unknowns" that cause the greatest trouble. The "discovery" of the excesses of the Reverend Jeremiah Wright during Barack Obama's first presidential campaign (2008) caused no end of public relations disasters, as his critics and political opponents (and they were by no means only Republicans) pounded him mercilessly with a "guilt by association" media campaign. That Mr. Obama responded, finally, with not only one of his finest speeches, indeed one of the greatest statements on issues of race in contemporary America, in no way hides the fact that the whole episode was a classic example of an "unknown unknown" almost wrecking his campaign.[11] No one really saw it coming, the campaign appeared totally blindsided, initially it was unclear what, if anything, should be done or said in response, and it was not until the wheels threatened to come off the campaign cart that Mr. Obama moved to speak about it.

Another "unknown unknown" with an even more devastating impact occurred during the Mitt Romney presidential campaign in 2012. It became known as the "17%" incident, in which a secretly recorded video was leaked of the candidate speaking to wealthy supporters where he made disparaging remarks about the "47%" of Americans who "took" from government and gave nothing back in the form of federal income taxes.[12] In spite of all the political gymnastics that it could muster, the campaign never recovered from this egregious blunder; it will assuredly be remembered in the future as a classic example of "unknown unknowns" happening during a campaign and hampering it seriously.

But not all of the known and unknown unknowns that occur during a campaign are of the "slings and arrows of outrageous fortune" variety. Often they are just things "that happen" out of the blue. Serendipitously, they can benefit the candidate and campaign: a powerful opponent is forced to drop out; the candidate receives an unexpected but welcome endorsement; fund raising meets or exceeds expectations. In the campaign just mentioned, Mr. Obama was lucky that the Reverend Wright episode occurred in the early spring of the primary season, before he was even the nominee; by the time he officially became the Democratic presidential candidate, the whole business was but a footnote, and Republican efforts to drag it again out of the closet failed. And when Republican candidate John McCain unexpectedly suspended his teetering campaign in late September, 2008, allegedly to return to Washington, D.C. to "fix" the growing financial crisis, he not only confused his supporters but provided a huge public relations opportunity for the Obama campaign, one that they quickly turned to their advantage.[13]

But the costs of "things happening" during the campaign extend beyond serendipity, or the way in which odd things can suddenly occur. Some costs may be systemic, that is, they may be "known unknowns," in that their appearance can be anticipated, but their true cost cannot. The impact of sharply negative campaigns on a candidate, and especially on his family and closest friends, cannot always be fathomed, especially not before the fact. The psychic damage that negativity can produce may fester for months or years before its real cost is realized; the same can be said of public humiliations that even victorious candidates have been known to suffer, although the ignominy of a devastating defeat is assuredly the most profound humiliation a candidate can endure, and its psychic costs undoubtedly the greatest.[14]

## The Positives of Running for Office

Readers at this point might well be asking, Are there any positives to running for office? Any kind of rewards? The answer is, yes indeed! Our discussion will emphasize personal, largely psychic rewards that campaigning can bring to the candidate. But it must also be noted that a spin-off of campaigning can have financial benefits. Because of the publicity and even modest media coverage that local campaigns generate, the candidate who is a lawyer might attract more clients; the insurance or real estate agent may find new customers as he or she moves through various campaign venues. There have also been cases—usually isolated and local—of candidates paying themselves salaries from campaign donations, which is legal in many areas, but we leave them aside as aberrations that defy any but the most kooky notions of campaign ethics.

## The Pursuit of Power

Many—perhaps most—individuals run for public office to achieve political power. The point seems so obvious as to require little or no comment. The very nature of holding public office implies that inherent in the position are tasks, responsibilities, authority—that is, power, the capacity to get things done, all cloaked with Constitutional and legal legitimacy.

The more interesting issues are not that they seek power, but why, and for what purpose? We will address these questions as this section of the chapter unfolds. For now we need to note that candidates may have seriously wrong illusions about how much power they will actually have and be able to use if they succeed to office, and what they can accomplish. How many candidates have made promises they cannot possibly keep once they win their election? Are they liars? Possibly some are; more likely the vast number really have only the dimmest notion of what it is possible to achieve once in office. There are no—absolutely no—public offices or positions in this country which provide the incumbent with absolute power. From the President on down, officials are constrained by the Constitution, laws, court decisions, precedents, customs and mores, public opinion, political culture, and of course other office holders, thus limiting what they can actually do.

We need only add that candidates, whether they are aware of the constraints that they will face or not, pursue power will all the fervor of a chase for the Holy Grail. If they were not interested in the exercise of power—whether real or illusory—most would have absolutely no reason to run for office. How candidates justify or rationalize or cloak the pursuit of power—to themselves certainly, sometimes to their families, supporters, and the public at large—constitutes part our discussion for the remainder of this section.

## Civic Duty

Cynics might scoff at the idea that candidates run out of a sense of civic duty, but the truth is that some actually do. There are candidates who take seriously the Rockwellian idea[15] of civic involvement, that it is the responsibility of the citizen to offer him- or herself for public service. To the cynic, the whole notion may seem absurdly romantic and reek of third-grade civics lessons.

But the idea of stepping forward to run for office out of a sense of duty cannot be dismissed so easily, even if it also masks the pursuit of power. Deeply imbedded in American political culture is the belief that with citizenship comes responsibility, and part of that responsibility is to serve. In this current era of antipathy towards government, and suspicion of if not outright hostility towards public officials, the idea that public service is a worthy activity may have gone into eclipse. But not so long ago it was very popular, especially but not only among the young: the success of the Peace Corps, Volunteers in Service to America (VISTA), Teach for America, and other such programs is testament to how powerful has been the sense of public service in the past. And even if one wants to argue that much of the "civic duty" rhetoric that some candidates espouse is just opportunism and ambition, one does have to recognize that a major credo of the American political heritage is the idea that civic duty, and serving the public, are critical components of our version of democratic governance. Running for public office is but one of many ways to offer service, and those who offer themselves assuredly deserve our respect, regardless of what are their politics.

## Giving Back to the Community

Related to the ideas of public service and civic duty is the notion of "giving back something to the community." For some candidates this can be a powerful motivation, because they deeply believe that just as their community (or state, or nation) provided them with an opportunity to succeed, so too do they have an obligation to return some of that "success" (however measured or defined) so that others may also have the same opportunity. This kind of motivation represents a very specific dimension of public service, one focused on their own roots and not simply a reflection of a more generic desire "to serve."

Again, cynics can have a field day with candidate expressions of "giving something back," but as before they may not have the final word. Particularly when candidates overcame financial or other hardships in order to "succeed," one has to recognize that, at least in some cases, their desire to give back may well be genuine. A case in point could well be Florida's junior Senator, Marco Rubio. Whatever one may think of his politics and possible presidential aspirations, and even if there is evidence that he embellished his life story,[16] Rubio has made very clear how profoundly he feels his deep roots in Miami's Cuban community and how not only does he wish to carry its torch but to pave the way for others to follow. It is his way of "giving back" to his community. And there are others like him.

## A Desire To Do Good

The author, who has met perhaps hundreds of candidates and potential candidates over the years, has sometimes been asked (usually by students) if they have any commonalities, recognizing that they come in all shapes and sizes. The answer is that there are at least two.

The first is a desire to do good. There has probably never been a candidate who wanted to hold public office to do bad things. In fact, it is always the opposite. Voters, among other people, may of course have very different views from the candidate about what constitutes "doing good." But that is an integral part of the political game: people have widely, sometimes wildly, differing views on what should and should not be done, and which course of action (if any) does the most good. And even if the candidate's view of "doing good" is to take revenge on another official, or even private citizen, or to right some real or imagined "wrong" perpetrated in the past, the candidate and his/her supporters will dress up what he/she is doing by arguing that a "wrong" is being "righted," hence, they are doing good.

The point here is neither to disparage nor applaud the dynamics of how "doing good" is to be determined. Rather, it is to recognize that candidates, probably universally, step forward because they have definite views of what kind of good they want to do and why their version of "good" is the right one. Doing good, in other words, appears to be a fundamental component of becoming a candidate; without it, one wonders why anybody would bother.

## Ego Gratification

The second commonalty that candidates share, in the author's experience, are outsize egos. Not only that, but it is his long-standing impression that candidates have a need, or desire, or both, to foist those egos onto the public. The campaign becomes a way of making this happen, while at the same time massaging and gratifying those egos. The author, who is not a psychologist, also recognizes that this characterization of candidates may not sit well with all of his readers. And he certainly does not wish to suggest that having outsize egos means that candidates are all awful, boorish, or insensitive clods. Far from it, in fact. No one would ever get elected if this were the case. Many candidates know how to use their egos to attract people, voters in particular, and ingratiate themselves in order to create a winning coalition; once in office, that same capability can be very helpful in carrying out his or her agenda and in "doing good."

But the truth is, candidates generally have high opinions of themselves, strongly and positively felt, and they usually want to let the public know how good and capable and committed and trustworthy they really are. Some may say this is nothing more than a well-developed sense of self confidence. No argument there; self-confidence is a *sine qua non* for a successful candidate and office holder. So the question of candidate ego and ego gratification, and projecting self-confidence, really becomes a matter of creating a viable political persona, of defining him- or herself in a way that voters find appealing. The campaign is thus an exercise, for the candidate, of self-realization and -actualization, of deciding what and who one really is, and how one wants to convey that identity to the public.[17]

Not all candidates are successful in this regard. We saw in Chapter 1 that both Al Gore and Mitt Romney had problems defining themselves to the public, and so did Barack Obama. But some candidates are very good at letting the public know exactly who they are. Was there ever any doubt, as far as public persona is concerned, about who Teddy Roosevelt was, or F.D.R., or Harry S Truman, or J.F.K., or Ronald Reagan, or Bill Clinton? Governor Chris Christie of New Jersey is an excellent current example of a former candidate, now office holder, who channeled his obviously huge ego and almost overwhelming physical presence into a larger than life political persona; even after the potentially damaging fallout that he suffered from "Bridgegate," he literally dominates the political landscape merely by showing up.[18]

Thus the campaign is a mechanism for the candidate to express who he or she is to the public. And the campaign allows the candidate to relish and massage his or her ego, further energizing and motivating them (even in the difficult moments that all campaigns encounter). Can anyone doubt that F.D.R or Ronald Reagan or Bill Clinton found both joy and immense ego gratification in the way they conveyed their sense of self, their egos, their self-confidence, to the public? Indeed it is not too much to say that in the case of these three individuals—and there are others—their campaigns and subsequent administrations became inseparable from their very identities, as campaigning/governing/egos merged into one.

It is also true that candidates' egos, while often outsized, can be extremely fragile. One rarely sees this in public; Ed Muskie's breakdown in front of everybody, derailing his presidential campaign in 1972, was very unusual.[19] One is more likely to find the fragility of a candidate's ego in a quiet conversation late at night, after campaigning for the day is over, and the hurts and disappointments and frustrations that are an inevitable part of any campaign surface; or in a sudden lashing out at campaign workers and advisers, when someone—inadvertently or not—said something which stung the frazzled, very vulnerable and sensitive ego of the candidate.

Some readers might observe that the previous paragraphs read more like a cost to the candidate than a satisfaction, and perhaps should have been in the previous section. The observation would be correct. But one also has to remember that candidates, probably because of their outsize egos, are driven individuals, anxious to be in the public eye, determined to become a part of the publics' (especially voters') consciousness. They are willing to expose themselves to the slings and arrows of a campaign and to open their psychological vulnerabilities to the possibility of injury, even as most manage to hide how much they are hurting inside. Indeed, a thick skin—or even just the public appearance of one—is probably the most important asset a candidate can have. It not only protects the candidate, it can hide just how bruised and battered his or her ego might be.

The ego satisfactions of campaigning can be substantial. For those who seek or need public recognition and affirmation, there is nothing like it. Candidates are thrust, or thrust themselves, into the spotlight at every turn; during campaign season, candidates, even losing candidates, can (although not always) achieve near celebrity if not rock-star status. The media hang on every word that the candidate utters, if only so that they can hang him with those words, or hand them to his opponent to use as rope. For the candidate who needs public recognition, even a hanging party provides gratification, because he or she is the center of attention, at least until the trap door opens and the campaign collapses. For the candidate who is desperate to be in the public eye, even critical attention can be satisfying; better the media, the opponents, the public say terrible things about him or her, than nothing at all.

And for the candidate who draws psychic or physical strength from associating with the rich and/or powerful, a campaign is perfect. Raising money, unless one deliberately runs as the shoestring candidate, requires that he or she approach individuals who have wealth and are willing to spend it on political candidates. Nowadays, thanks to the U.S. Supreme Court and its decisions in *Citizens United vs. FEC* and *McCutcheon vs. FEC*, among others, candidates can also approach temples of capitalism to try to suck money from the citadels of our economy. What candidate in search of campaign funds would not derive satisfaction, and perhaps even feel that he belongs there, by sitting in a well-appointed corporate boardroom, or the private office of a mogul of Big Money?[20]

Similarly, candidates want to surround themselves with "successful" people, especially well-known ones. Celebrities, professional athletes, rock stars—it really doesn't matter because the candidate (and often public official) wants to be in the company of such individuals, hoping their aura and reputation and panache will rub off and enhance his or her campaign or stature. And what candidate would not feel a huge leap of psychic satisfaction, and gain political prestige, from an invitation to ride on Air Force One or have a drink and conversation in a prominent Governor's or Senator's private office?

---

### Richard M. Nixon, Football Coach

Richard Nixon, assuredly one of the most psychologically insecure of our Presidents, loved to invite sports celebrities to the White House, or visit them in their practice fields. It has often been rumored that he even suggested plays to his long-time friend George Allen, coach of the Washington Redskins, when he attended practice sessions, although it is difficult either to substantiate or invalidate the stories.[21]

---

And then, at least in terms of the psychic satisfactions and gratifications of running for office, there is the thrill of the chase, the emotional high that comes with competing. Candidates, as noted before, tend to be driven individuals. Many, assuredly most, are highly competitive. The chance to "strut one's stuff," to show off, to demonstrate that one is more popular— or at least can get more votes—than the other candidates, to bask in the limelight of publicity (even if it is unfavorable and negative): it is often hard to estimate how much these factors energize and motivate the candidate, because they are generally privately held, and perhaps may not be fully known even to the candidate. But it would be wrong to assume that many if not the majority of candidates are not at least secretly propelled in their campaigns by a competitive spirit, one which drives them forward to show that they can do better than the others. Indeed, it would make an interesting psychological study to see how many candidates have secret fantasy lives as race car drivers, or world class athletes, or concert violinists, or indefatigable lovers, any one of which would reveal just how deeply felt and powerful is their desire to show off as well as the strength of their competitive spirit.

Finally, we need to point out the ultimate psychic satisfaction, the greatest ego gratification of all: the possibility of electoral success and victory on election night. Very, very few (if any) are the candidates who enter the campaign circus thinking they will lose. Even the most unlikely, self-deluded, hopeless candidate feels, at least at the beginning, that he or she can and will win. The cold, dark, harshness of a collapsing campaign, or one that never got off the ground, may not manifest itself in the candidate's conscious mind for some time, but even if it does, a serious candidate would never admit publicly to self-doubts or the possibility of defeat; the image of Harry S Truman, soldiering on in 1948 in spite of all the pundits' trumpeting of his imminent rejection and demise, is a powerful motivator for a candidate whose campaign is caught in a downward death spiral.

But for those whose campaigns are viable and competitive, and who sense that they just might win (even if they ultimately do not), keeping their eyes on the prize of victory is not just a powerful motivator, it is immensely gratifying and a complete vindication of their decision to run. Indeed, if it were not, why would anyone put themselves, their families, their friends, and their associates through the meat grinder that is the modern political campaign?

### Where Are the Giants of Old?[22]

Buffoons. Morons. Clowns. Liars. Incompetent. Unqualified. Out of Touch. Self-Serving. Disgraceful. Insulting to the Public. Unworthy. We Deserve Better Than This.

These are some of the more polite words and phrases often heard to describe the list of candidates presenting themselves for public office. It is of interest that the terms exist with no reference to or implication of partisanship; they and others like them can be heard about candidates from both major parties, minor parties, and no parties. They are used at all levels of electoral activity, from the presidency down to the wannabes for the town council. "None of the above" is a choice many voters say they would like to have, but don't. Indeed, what would happen if they did, and "none of the above" received the most votes in an election?

What's the matter? Why do so many voters feel that the candidates from whom they must choose are unworthy of them and search for the "least awful," the "best of a bad lot," and hold their noses while they vote, unless of course they are so appalled and turned off that they don't bother to vote at all? Might not voter turnout be higher, and might not people take a more positive view of their elected officials, if they felt that their candidates were "better?"

Leaving aside the question of what "better" candidates might look like, we should observe at the outset that complaints about the quality of candidates is nothing new in the United States. Once the demi-god George Washington retired, the floodgates of criticism opened. Our political pantheon of "best" Presidents—Adams, Jefferson, Jackson, Lincoln, the Roosevelts, Wilson, Truman, Eisenhower, Kennedy, Reagan, Clinton— were all reviled during their campaigns as malicious incompetents and worse. Candidates of lesser stature, those who never made it into the Presidential Hall of Fame, or who served at lower levels of government, were treated even more harshly.

It may well be that Americans expect too much of their candidates, wanting them to be supermen and superwomen, and are disappointed when they turn out to be mere mortals with feet of clay. Ingrained in American political culture is the view that politics is some kind of giant morality play, and of course then we should expect our candidates, even for local offices, to embody the virtues that we associate with greatness: strength of character, vision, charisma, the capacity to rise above petty politics, an ability to create consensus, the moral suasion to see and do what is right, the power to defeat the forces of evil that would do us harm, the skill to get the job done and at the same time make it look easy, while maintaining calm, equilibrium, and a sense of identity with everyday people. It hardly needs to be observed that such a person has never existed and never will; but Americans keep hoping that he or she will show up in the list of candidates at the next election.

Other nations are different. The French, for example, start with realistic expectations of who their candidates are and what they can reasonably be expected to accomplish if elected. They are neither surprised nor disappointed to discover that their candidates and office holders often do not rise to the level of the bar that they have set so low. And given the revolving door that is Italian politics, is it any wonder that so many shrug their shoulders at the prospect of a new election, a new government? So what? Are these *buffone* any different from or better than the last bunch?[23]

The consequence of Americans' unrealistic pursuit of supercandidates is not just that we are disappointed to find that they are mere mortals. It is that we find ourselves pining for a past that never existed; 20:20 hindsight comes with highly prismatic glasses. The irony of course is that the glorious past, or at least the good old days, or even more minimally, "Back in my day, we actually had a choice of decent candidates!," never existed. It's all selective remembrance and a constructed history that is pleasing to think about, but wholly false. The candidates of former days for whom we are nostalgic were often viewed as vermin at the time, and certainly not of the quality that we the people deserve and would want to vote for.

But what does the evidence show? Are candidates today "worse" than in previous times? There is no doubt that they are different, because the tasks of campaigning are different. Campaign rhetoric, for example, is completely different now than formerly; we have traded the soaring language of Kennedy and Reagan for the 20-second sound bite; campaign ads seek less to introduce candidates and inform voters than to criticize opponents, usually as nastily as possible. Even the modes and schedules of campaigning have changed: it all happens at jet speed, roaring from one state to another in a single day, the candidates making brief appearances and delivering canned speeches at carefully staged events before disappearing into their metallic magic carpet and zooming off to the next venue; and from there, the digital campaign takes over, as tweets and text messages and emails and Facebook postings hurtle at light speed across the blogosphere, rallying supporters and trashing opponents.

But different demands on the candidates and different styles of campaigning do not necessarily mean worse candidates than before. At least two types of data can be gathered to show that in fact modern candidates may offer more to voters than in earlier times.

First are resumés and credentials. It is a reasonable argument that in today's political world, with very little privacy and an array of digital search engines able to pry into every corner of a candidate's background, candidates need to be completely above board about their resumés. Does this mean that a shyster like James G. Blaine (who bent over backwards double and triple to conceal his record) could not announce for presidency and make a serious run? Of course not. But he, or she, would be quickly found out. It's inevitable, as Gary Hart and Elliot Spitzer and Anthony Weiner and many other candidates, wannabes, and office holders have learned, that trying to deceive the media, or the public, won't work. Even at the local level, to be taken seriously, a candidate must present an honest resumé.

## The Costs of Fabricating a Resumé

The author recalls a prominent candidate for Sheriff in his home county, a public official who claimed to have played football at Alabama for legendary Coach Bear Bryant. When it was discovered that he did not even attend Alabama, much less play on the football team for Bryant or anyone else, he was laughed out of the race. Tragically, another candidate of his acquaintance, an able young woman, lied about her higher education credentials; she subsequently committed suicide when she was found out.

Just as crucial as honesty is the substance of candidate credentials and resumés. It is a reasonable argument that, even in small communities, to be taken seriously a candidate has to be viewed as one well versed in its ways and mores, who has volunteered and worked through community-based organizations to enhance its quality of life. So, too, must the candidate publicly demonstrate a commitment for the office, and jurisdiction, to which he wishes election. To announce for town council or city commission without having served on any city boards, or having spent years in volunteer work through such community-based organizations as United Way or Rotary or a host of others, is to ensure defeat. Why? Because he or she will not be considered a serious candidate, at best a Johnny- (or Susy-) come-lately and at worst an opportunist; the most likely result is that he or she will be unable to raise the funds needed to mount a serious campaign. Money seeks out winners in campaigns, or those who look like winners. "Follow the money" to see who are the powerful candidates is not an idle expression; while not infallible, it is probably still the best guide to who will win. It is certainly the best guide to which candidate(s) are taken seriously.

Candidates who are viewed as flakes, unqualified, inexperienced, pushy, self-serving, not ready, or not committed will inevitably file weak campaign finance reports, and their candidacies will founder. Aside from the money, if they are viewed as not well grounded in city or county or state affairs, voters will inevitably ask what they are doing in the electoral arena and shun them. Strong resumés and credentials therefore are essential elements of becoming a serious candidate. It is highly likely that today's litany of candidates, at all levels, have much stronger dossiers to present to voters, and the public generally, than at any time in the past.

A second set of data showing the improved quality of candidates over previous decades is inferential. If we look at the kind of people who occupy public offices, we can make inferences about who were the candidates for them; it is important to keep in mind that there is only one winner for each of the offices, but potentially two or more candidates for each.[24] Therefore, examining the demography of the winners reveals a good deal of who were the candidates.

Even if we only have space to examine legislative bodies, the discussion is revealing. A generation or so ago legislative bodies in the United States were still largely enclaves of white males. This is no longer the case, as the following tables point out. Table 3.1 shows that as late as 1990 there were only two women Senators, but by 2013 there were 20, the most ever. There were no African- American Senators in 1990 and still none in 2013, but by 2013 there were three Hispanic Senators, after none in 1990.[25]

Table 3.2 shows that in the 1990 U.S. House of Representatives there were 29 women, and by 2013 there were 78 women, the most ever.[26] In 1990 there were 25 African-Americans in the House, and by 2013, 43; in 1990 there were only ten Hispanics in the House, but 28 in 2013.[27]

*Table 3.1* Number and Percentage of Women, African-Americans, and Hispanics, 1990 and 2013, U.S. Senate

|  | Women | | African-Americans | | Hispanics | |
|---|---|---|---|---|---|---|
|  | No. | Percentage | No. | Percentage | No. | Percentage |
| 1990 | 2 | 2% | 0 | 0% | 0 | 0% |
| 2013 | 20 | 20% | 0 | 0% | 3 | 3% |

*Table 3.2* Number and Percentage of Women, African-Americans, and Hispanics, 1990 and 2013, U.S. House of Representatives

|  | Women | | African-Americans | | Hispanics | |
|---|---|---|---|---|---|---|
|  | No. | Percentage | No. | Percentage | No. | Percentage |
| 1990 | 29 | 7% | 25 | 6% | 10 | 2% |
| 2013 | 78 | 18% | 43 | 10% | 28 | 7% |

Similar increases can be seen at the state legislative level (Table 3.3). In the early 1990s, state legislators were about 18 percent women, 6 percent African-American, and 2 percent Hispanic.[28] As of 2013, women constituted about 24 percent of the total number; 10 percent were African American, and 4 percent Hispanics or Latinos.

Thus the conclusion is clear. Legislative bodies in America, at least at the national and state levels, now increasingly look like America as a whole: far more diverse than previously. They are not simply made up of white males any longer. And we can assuredly infer from these data that the list of candidates for offices is far more diverse than in previous decades. For those who believe that representative institutions are strengthened as they are composed of a broad array of Americans, so also can we say that the list of candidates for those offices is stronger than previously. The doors to public office are open wider for more kinds of people than at any previous time in our history; it is likely that, as more candidates from different demographic cohorts and segments present themselves as

*Table 3.3* Percentage of Women, African-Americans, and Hispanics, early 1990s and 2013, U.S. State Legislatures

|  | Women | African-Americans | Hispanics |
|---|---|---|---|
| Early 1990s | 18% | 6% | 2% |
| 2013 | 24% | 10% | 4% |

candidates, so will more enter public office. It would be hard to argue convincingly that this is not a healthy and welcome development in American politics.[29]

---

**State Legislators—As a Group, Well Educated**

The percentage of state legislators with college degrees has increased over the past decades. The top five states—California, Virginia, Nebraska, New York, and Texas—average 88 percent of their members as having at least a Bachelor's degree. The lowest five—Arkansas, New Mexico, Delaware, Maine, and New Hampshire—only average 58 percent college graduates. Overall, about 75 percent of state legislators have a Bachelor's degree or higher. Each of these figures is substantially higher than the population as a whole. About 30% of Americans hold a Bachelor's degree.[30]

---

Too much should not be made of these numbers, non-trivial as they are. Each of the groups mentioned is still under-represented in the population.[31] But arguing that groups should be represented according to their share of the population is sophistry. In the first place, the American system of representation in legislative (or executive/administrative/judicial) offices is not based on proportionality; it is common in other nations, but not here. More importantly, nowhere in the United States or any state Constitution is there a statement that says groups, especially minority groups, are either entitled or limited to their proportion in the population in legislative bodies. Thus, the goal should be to promote diversity, and create more opportunities for different kinds of people to become candidates for public office, not to limit them to their percentage in the population.[32]

## The New Candidate is the Big Money Candidate

In the old days, good or bad depending on one's point of view, political parties chose candidates. Part of the lore and mythology of American politics are the "smoke-filled rooms" at conventions and other sites, in which party bosses negotiated, horse-traded, and strong-armed one another to secure the nomination, and hence the candidacy, of their choices for particular office. The stories tend to focus on the presidency, but in fact the power plays and deals as to who would be the nominees took place over Senate, U.S. House, Governors, and the full range of "down-ticket" offices, including local ones, especially in our older, larger cities that had partisan elections and strong local party organizations.

The point to be made about all this is neither to extoll nor criticize what happened, but merely to note that it worked. When parties chose candidates who were accepted by rank-and-file members, they could mount viable, if not always winning, campaigns. When they could not reach agreement, and/or could not find a suitable candidate (or at least one around whom a consensus could be forged, or faked), the results could be disastrous. The classic example remains 1896, when Democratic leaders, holed up in their smoke-filled rooms at the Convention, could not agree on their presidential nominee. Then William Jennings Bryan, the nominee of the Populists, mounted the podium and gave his famous "Cross of Gold" speech and electrified those in the convention hall. Party leaders realized that they had little choice but to select him. The results, as they say, are history, because the "pros" knew they had the wrong candidate against William McKinley.

By the late 1960s and 1970s, and perhaps even earlier, parties had weakened considerably and lost much of their power in national, state, and local politics. With that decline came an atrophy of parties' ability to dictate nominees for office; it was replaced by a system of state-by-state party primaries. As a result, as the political scientists Barbara and Stephen Salmore have famously noted, a new kind of candidate began to emerge on the electoral scene.[33] These individuals were largely self-selected, because no longer could parties insist that candidates work their way up the ranks before the hands of leaders were laid on them as the Chosen Ones. With weakened parties, pretty much anybody could jump in and declare a candidacy. No longer was the preferred candidate of the party heavyweights the odds-on favorite for the nomination; the telegenic, well-financed individual who could create an electoral organization, whether for town council or the presidency, could now swipe the nomination right out from under the nose of whatever semblance of party organization remained. And they ran what came to be known as "candidate-centered" campaigns, in which they created their own organizations to run in the primary and general elections; they might include remnants or segments of the parties, but they might not, either.

The nomination process became highly fragmented, and the possibility of becoming a candidate one that was highly individualistic, even idiosyncratic, and entrepreneurial. The new candidate owed very little, if anything, to the party, even if he or she ran with the party label. They became largely independent actors in the political arena; their likelihood of electoral success was a function of their ability to create a viable campaign organization, hire quality consultants, find a good advertising firm, smile and not make a fool of themselves on camera, and mobilize voters to show up on election day; and all of this was dependent on a high-octane finance committee to raise funds to pay for it, not party coffers.[34]

## "Candidate-Centered" Candidates

At the presidential level, John F. Kennedy may well have been the first in modern times to run a candidate-centered campaign successfully, defeating party favorites Hubert Humphrey and Adlai Stevenson in primaries to secure the Democratic nomination in 1960. On the Republican side, Richard M. Nixon came back from the political dead in 1968, running a campaign outside of the party to secure the nomination. By 1972, Nixon's people shunned the Grand Old Party (GOP, i.e. the National Republican Party) almost completely, setting up an independent, candidate-centered re-election campaign organization called the Committee to Re-Elect the President, or CREEP as it presciently later became known.

Writing in the early 1990s, the astute, well-respected political analyst Alan Ehrenhalt took a look at what was happening and shook his head ruefully. In a thoughtful, reflective book called *The United States of Ambition*,[35] he noted that the pursuit of office had become so open that virtually anyone could, and did, jump into the ring. While he certainly did not espouse exclusionary politics, he did regret what was happening. Personal ambition replaced commitment to politics or public service as a motivator for seeking office. More importantly, the open door policy of candidacy meant individuals with no political experience of any kind could, with enough personality, money, and ambition, succeed to office.

At least in the old days, Ehrenhalt felt, parties served as a training ground, a socializing institution in which those potentially interested in running for office had to prove to party leaders that they were worthy and ready. In a sense, parties winnowed who actually understood not just the rules of politics, but its norms and mores. The flakes and nuts could be diverted, or if necessary prevented from running. Those succeeding to the ballot, if not to actual office, would not simply be presentable, they would undertake to further the institutional and political interests of the party, reach out to most if not all of its wings, caucuses, and factions, hopefully forge a consensus, and, at a minimum, represent the mainstream of the party.

But no longer. Anybody could run. And not only would they turn their backs on the party, Ehrenhalt feared, they would be unqualified to serve in public office should they win, because they had neither the background, training, outlook, nor discipline to understand what serving in public office really involved.

Ehrenhalt's argument is not simply the musing of a cranky conservative. It is far more serious than that. And, given the way in which some recently elected members of national, state, and local governments have contributed to gridlock, partisan stalemate, and the triumph of ideological purity over policymaking, one has to ask if Ehrenhalt does not in fact have a valid point.

Let us, however, make three observations.

The first is that the old party system, the one that Ehrenhalt admires, is dead and gone and is not coming back. Moreover, one wonders if in fact his view of the old system isn't through rose-colored glasses. The old, closed system was exactly that: old and closed. It kept women, African-Americans, Hispanics, Asians, the disabled, gays, and other marginalized groups out of the electoral arena from the 1860s to the late 1960s and beyond. Does anyone really want to go back to that?

Secondly, Ehrenhalt criticized what is often admired in other aspects of American life: an entrepreneurial spirit. It's true that blind ambition can lead people into perdition; but it is also true that individuals willing to take a chance, to start something unconventional and new, indeed, to dare to be different, have energized and fostered much in American life. Steve Jobs, the late head of Apple, is but one prominent example of entrepreneurs from the entire spectrum of American culture, including business and finance, entertainment, politics, sports, even academia, who have had a significant impact on how Americans live and what they think is important.

Third and most importantly, Ehrenhalt missed a crucial point, although he can hardly be blamed for not anticipating what the U. S. Supreme Court wrought 20 years after he wrote.[36] It is not so much the collapse of the ability of parties to control, even dictate, who would be the candidates that is problematic; it is that this very collapse allowed the entrance of private money, private Big Money, directly into campaign politics. To be sure, it has always been present, but it was largely channeled through parties. Parties are no longer gatekeepers of campaign finance; indeed, they have become supplicants in the pursuit of political money and for a time were limited in their ability to raise or spend money on or for candidates.[37]

The introduction of huge independent expenditures into campaigns has seriously eroded the traditional money gatekeeping role that parties have played, even if *McCutcheon* restores some of it. We will have much more to say about this point later, but we should end the chapter by noting that the New Candidate is the Big Money Candidate. She or he is the one with the most money, the one who is most beholden to big donors and special interests; those are the candidates who have a leg up (or more than one leg up) in determining the outcome of the election. Indeed, it is no exaggeration to say that Big Money has replaced parties as recruiters and supporters of candidates; Big Money controls more than candidate selection, it controls the very dynamic and outcomes of American electoral politics.[38]

## Big Money Candidates and Their Financiers

Are there Big Money candidates and office holders on the contemporary American political scene? Indeed there are. One could look at Senators Ted Cruz (R) and Elizabeth Warren (D) as examples of candidates who succeeded to office not through traditional recruitment paths but because of the power of Big Money behind them. Michael Bloomberg, Mayor of New York, and Rick Scott, Governor of Florida, are examples of Big Money candidates—both "outsiders" and political neophytes before announcing—who literally surged into office on the strength of Big Money—their own, and that of outside supporters. And there are others as well.

Both *The Atlantic* and *International Business News* during the spring, 2015, published lists of very wealthy donors and which candidate(s) they support. Perusing these articles leads to the conclusion that, certainly on the Republican side, each of the major contenders has one or more well-heeled, deep-pocketed "sugar daddies" or patrons or financiers behind them willing to spend whatever it takes to advance the candidacy of their Chosen One; and on the Democratic side Hillary Clinton appears to have locked up all of the Big Money.[39] More generally, the Center for Responsive Politics tracks the introduction of Big Money, including Dark Money (essentially unregulated, often anonymous donations) into the political arena on behalf of candidates and causes. On the right wing, the Koch Brothers have become the most famous of these donors; on the left, George Soros is perhaps most well known.[40]

In early August, 2015, the Koch Brothers hosted a weekend retreat for wealthy Republican donors at a swanky resort in Orange County, California and invited GOP candidates Jeb Bush, Ted Cruz, Carly Fiorina, Marco Rubio and Scott Walker to make their pitches for support from this elite group of the super-rich. It is the best possible example not only of the emergence of the Big Money Candidate, but of the centrality which wealthy *patróns* have to the viability and credibility of candidates.[41]

This last point is critical. The allegiance of the Money Candidate is mainly to private interests, in particular the money that was put forward for their campaigns. Some Money Candidates manage to retain a respect for the public interest, even if their view of it is not universally shared—Michael Bloomberg and Elizabeth Warren come to mind—but that would not be true of all Money Candidates.

Thus, in a sense, even as candidates for office nowadays are in some ways "better" than earlier ones, some—the Money Candidates—represent dangers to our democratic politics that are very real and very present. We shall return to this point later.

## Notes

1   New Perspectives on the West: "William Tecumseh Sherman," PBS, The West Film Project, 2001, viewed online at www.pbs.org/weta/thewest/people/s_z/sherman.htm, April 15, 2013. Instead of Sherman, the GOP nominated James G. Blaine of Maine.

2   Because in America elections are almost universally of the "winner-take-all," zero-sum variety in which there is no silver medal, no prize for second place, there are far more losers than winners, by a large margin.

3   In this section relevant literature will be cited as needed and required by the norms of good scholarship. But it should be noted that much of the material, and almost all of the anecdotes, come from the author's considerable experience running or consulting with political campaigns, over a more than 25-year period.

4   Readers are encouraged to review the discussion of the perpetual campaign in Chapter 1 of this book.

5   See "Trends in the Distribution of Household Income Between 1979 and 2007," Congressional Budget Office, October 25, 2011, viewed online at www.cbo.gov/publication/42729, May 15, 2013; Nathan Yau, "Wealth Distribution in America," *Infographics, Flowing Data*, April 16, 2013; viewed online at http://flowingdata.com/2013/04/16/wealth-distribution-in-america, May 15, 2013; and Richard Fryer and Paul Taylor, "A Rise in Wealth for the Wealthy; Declines for the Lower 93%," *Pew Research Social And Demographic Trends*, April 23, 2013; viewed online at www.pewsocialtrends.org/2013/04/23/a-rise-in-wealth-for-the-wealthydeclines-for-the-lower-93, May 15, 2013.

6   One New York newspaper reported that Bloomberg spent over $108 M on his third election campaign. See Frank Lombardi, "Bloomberg's Campaign Tab: $108,372,685.01," *New York Daily News*, January 15, 2010, viewed online at www.nydailynews.com/news/bloomberg-campaign-tab-108-371-685-01-relected-term-nyc-mayor-priceless-article-1.460319, April 26, 2013; Rick Scott spent over $70 M of his personal fortune on his successful bid for the Florida Governorship in 2010; see Steve Bosquet, "Gov. Scott Won't Dump His Personal Fortune Into Re-Election," *Tampa Bay Times*, April 24, 2012, viewed online at www.tampabay.com/news/politics/stateroundup/gov-rick-scott-wont-dump-his-fortune-into-re-election/1226653, April 26, 2013.

7   Dan Glaun, "Helping Themselves: 2012 Candidates Have Spent Over $130 Million Funding Their Own Campaigns," OpenSecrets.org, August 2, 2012, viewed online at www.opensecrets.org/news/2012/08/helping-themselves-2012-candidates.html, April 26, 2013.

8   *The Good Wife*, www.imdb.com/title/tt1442462; the series was originally produced by CBS and is available for viewing on Netflix.

9   See Brian Warner, "Nixon's Knee," *The Voter Update*, June 11, 2012, viewed online at http://thevoterupdate.com/articles/2012/6_11_12_nixons_knee.php, May 9, 2013.

10  John Ezard, "Rumsfeld's Unknown Unknowns Take Prize," *Guardian*, December 1, 2003, viewed online at www.guardian.co.uk/world/2003/dec/02/usa.johnezard, April 29, 2013.

11 The text of Mr. Obama's speech can be found in the Washington Wire blog of the *Wall Street Journal*, March 18, 2008, viewed online at http://blogs.wsj.com/washwire/2008/03/18/text-of-obamas-speech-a-more-perfect-union, April 29, 2013.

12 See Kasie Hunt, "Mitt Romney: '47%' Comments Were 'Just Completely Wrong,'" Huffingtonpost.com, October 5, 2012, viewed online at www.huffingtonpost.com/2012/10/04/mitt-romney-47-percent_n_1941423.html, April 29, 2013.

13 See Liz Halloran, "McCain Suspends Campaign, Shocks Republicans," *Us News* online, September 24, 2008, viewed online at www.usnews.com/news/campaign-2008/articles/2008/09/24/mccain-suspends-campaign-shocks-republicans, April 29, 2013.

14 While somewhat speculative, there is reason to think that Michael Dukakis, Democratic presidential nominee in 1988, never fully recovered from the devastating assault against him designed by Lee Atwater, who was Rasputin to George H. W. Bush. Evidence, or at least reasonable inferences, for this view can be drawn from the interviews with Dukakis in the documentary *Boogie Man: The Lee Atwater Story*, 2008. A full citation can be found in the previous chapter.

15 The allusion is to the famous painting of Norman Rockwell, one of the Four Freedoms series, in which a resolute young man, speaking at a New England town meeting, looks very much like he is either about to announce his candidacy for office or will find a delegation of his fellow townsmen on his doorstep the next morning urging him to do so. See www.kingsacademy.com/mhodges/11_Western-Art/27_Popular_Modern-Realism/Rockwell/Rockwell_1943_'Four-Freedoms'_Speech.jpg, viewed online May 8, 2013.

16 See, for example, Manuel Roig-Franzia, "Marco Rubio's Compelling Family Story Embellishes Facts, Documents Show," *Washington Post*, October 11, 2011, viewed online at www.washingtonpost.com/politics/marco-rubios-compelling-family-story-embellishes-facts-documents-show/2011/10/20/gIQA aVHD1L_story.html; and Arturo Lopez Levy, "Why Senator Rubio's Lies Matter," The Blog, Huffingtonpost.com, April 14, 2015, viewed online at www.huffingtonpost.com/arturo-lopez-levy/marco-rubio-cuba-family-story_b_7058486.html; both viewed July 4, 2015.

17 Readers are invited to review the discussion of creating a political persona in Chapter 1.

18 An excellent overview of Christie's political troubles caused by traffic jams created at the entrance to the George Washington Bridge can be found in Justin Worland, "Here's What You Need to Know About Chris Christie's Latest Bridge Scandal," Politics, 2016 Election, *Time*, June 20, 2014, viewed online at http://time.com/2918132/chris-christie-bridgegate, August 11, 2014; the piece contains links to earlier stories on the onset of Christie's bridge troubles. In late June, 2015, Mr. Christie announced his candidacy for the Republican presidential nomination. See Michael Barbaro, "Chris Christie Announces Run, Pledging 'Truth' About Nation's Woes," *New York Times*, June 30, 2015, viewed online at www.nytimes.com/2015/07/01/us/politics/chris-christie-presidential-campaign.html, July 3, 2015.

19 See "Remembering Ed Muskie," *Pbs Newshour*, March 26, 1996; viewed online at www.pbs.org/newshour/bb/remember/jan-june96/muskie_03-26.html, May 8, 2013.

20 See, for example, Julie Bykowicz, "Adelson Wooed by Republican presidential

Prospects at Vegas Meet," *Bloomberg*, March 30, 2014, viewed online at www.bloomberg.com/news/2014-03-29/republican-presidential-hopefuls-in-vegas-to-woo-donor-adelson.html, June 11, 2014. See also Ginger Gibson, "Election 2016: Candidates Court Mega-Donors," *International Business Times*, April 21, 2015, viewed online at www.ibtimes.com/election-2016-gop-candidates-court-mega-donors-1889562 and Russell Berman, "A Guide to the Billionaires Bankrolling the GOP Candidates," *The Atlantic*, April 24, 2015, www.theatlantic.com/politics/archive/2015/04/a-guide-to-the-billionaires-bankrolling-the-gop-candidates/391233; both viewed July 3, 2015.

21   See Brian Cronin, "Did Richard Nixon Call a Key Redskins Play," *ESPN Playbook*, ESPN.com, September 13, 2012, viewed online at http://espn.go.com/blog/playbook/fandom/post/_/id/9424/presidential-orders, May 8, 2013.

22   This and the following section are derived from an earlier version of this book, Richard K. Scher, *The Modern Political Campaign: Mudslinging, Bombast, And The Vitality Of American Politics* (Armonk, N.Y: M. E. Sharpe, 1997), Chapter 4.

23   On France, a long view of French attitudes towards politicians and government can be found in Theodore Zeldin, *The French* (London: The Harville Press, 1997); a more recent study by Pew confirms that the French have lost none of their skepticism and distrust towards their leaders or government. See "The New Sick Man of Europe: The European Union," *pew research global attitudes project*, May 13, 2013, viewed online at www.pewglobal.org/2013/05/13/the-new-sick-man-of-europe-the-european-union, May 15, 2013. Luigi Barzini's famous work *The Italians* (New York: Atheneum, 1964) is the classic account of Italian culture, and the Italian world view, including politics and government. More recent studies essentially reinforce Barzini's book. See, for example, Vito Laterza, "Italy's New Government and the Perpetuation of Minority Rule," *Al Jazeera*, May 3, 2013; viewed online at www.aljazeera.com/indepth/opinion/2013/05/201352638980219.html, May 15, 2013.

24   For the purpose of this discussion we leave aside races in which incumbents face no challengers.

25   Data on women in Congress for 1990 can be found in www.senate.gov/reference/resources/pdf/RL30261.pdf, viewed online May 13, 2013. Data on women in Congress, 2013, can be found in www.nytimes.com/2013/03/22/us/politics/women-make-new-gains-in-the-senate.html?pagewanted=all and womensissues.about.com/od/thepoliticalarena/a/Record-Number-Of-Women-In-Congress-In-2013-In-Both-House-Senate.htm; for 1990, www.senate.gov/reference/resources/pdf/RL30261.pdf, viewed online May 13, 2013.

26   See footnote 25 for references.

27   Data for African-Americans in Congress, 1990, can be found in www.senate.gov/reference/resources/pdf/RL30378.pdf; and for Hispanics, www.factmonster.com/spot/hhmcongress1.html#19, viewed online May 13, 2013. Data on African-Americans in Congress, 2013, can be found in www.infoplease.com/us/government/113-congress-african-americans.html; data for Hispanics are at www.huffingtonpost.com/2012/11/07/latino-congress-members_n_2090311.html, viewed online May 13, 2013.

28   Data on the demographics of women, African-Americans, and Hispanics in state legislatures were gleaned from www.csg.org/knowledgecenter/docs/WomeninStateGovernmentHistoricalOverviewandCurrentTrends-Carroll.pdf;

http://usatoday30.usatoday.com/news/nation/2009-03-05-blackleaders_
N.htm; http://latinola.com/story.php?story=9173, viewed online July 4, 2015.

29 In recent years, as Americans began to re-consider traditional policies on immigration, new voices of nativism and xenophobia have arisen. Many of these are atavistic outpourings of bigotry and prejudice. However, they have in some cases been given scholarly legitimacy; see for example Samuel P. Huntington, "The Hispanic Challenge," *Foreign Policy*, March 1, 2004, viewed online at www.foreignpolicy.com/articles/2004/03/01/the_hispanic_ challenge, May 13, 2013.

30 See "How Educated are State Legislators," *The Chronicle Of Higher Education*, June 12, 2011, viewed online at http://chronicle.com/article/ Degrees-of-Leadership-/127797, May 13, 2013; and Richard Peréz-Peña, "U.S. Bachelor Degree Rate Passes Milestone," *New York Times*, February 13, 2012, viewed online May 13, 2013.

31 See National Conference of State Legislatures, "Legislator Demographics: State by State," 2013, viewed online at www.ncsl.org/legislatures-elections/legisdata/legislator-demographic-map.aspx, May 13, 2013.

32 See Richard K. Scher, "Jim Crow Riding High: Trayvon Martin, Voting Rights and Equal Justice Under the Law," in *At Close Range: The Curious Case of Trayvon Martin: 2013 CSRRR Interdisciplinary Spring Symposium Proceedings* (Univ. of Florida Center for the Study of Race and Race Relations (ed.), 2013), available at http://scholarship.law.ufl.edu/csrrr_events/ 10thspringlecture/panels.

33 Barbara G. Salmore and Robert A. Salmore, *Candidates, Parties, and Campaigns: Electoral Politics In America* (Washington, D.C: CQ Press, 1989).

34 This statement is still true, although it is likely to be modified somewhat by the 2014 U.S. Supreme Court decision *McCutcheon vs. FEC*. The point will be discussed in a later chapter.

35 Alan Ehrenhalt, *The United States of Ambition: Politicians, Power, and the Pursuit of Office* (New York: Three Rivers Press, 1992).

36 The allusion is to *Citizens United vs. FEC* (2010), but the avalanche of Big Money in electoral politics, outside of party control, was notable as early as the late 1960s, and led to the Federal Election Campaign Acts of 1971 and 1974; more on those and *Citizens United* in a later chapter.

37 Jamelle Bouie, "What About the Parties?," *The American Prospect*, October 21, 2010, viewed online at http://prospect.org/article/what-about-parties-0, May 14, 2013. As we will see in a later chapter, the U. S. Supreme Court considerably loosened the restrictions on parties' ability to raise and direct funds in its 2014 decision *McCutcheon vs. FEC*. See also Adam Liptak, "Supreme Court Strikes Down Overall Political Donation Cap," *New York Times*, April 2, 2014, viewed online at www.nytimes.com/2014/04/03/us/ politics/supreme-court-ruling-on-campaign-contributions.html June 11, 2014.

38 See for example Simon Johnson, "The Quiet Coup," *The Atlantic*, May, 2009, viewed online at www.theatlantic.com/magazine/archive/2009/05/the-quiet-coup/307364, September 25, 2013; and Jacob S. Hacker and Paul Pierson, *Winner-Take-All Politics* (New York: Simon and Schuster, 2011); and Hedrick Smith, *Who Stole The American Dream?* (New York: Random House, 2013).

39 For references to these articles, see footnote 19 above. On Hillary Clinton, see Maggie Haberman and Nicholas Confessore, "'Super Pac' Raises $15.6 Million for Hillary Clinton Campaign," *New York Times*, July 2, 2015, viewed online at www.nytimes.com/politics/first-draft/2015/07/02/super-pac-raises-15-6-million-for-hillary-clinton-campaign, July 4, 2015.

40   See for example Dave Gilson, "Charts: How Much Have the Koch Brothers Spent on the 2012 Election,?" MotherJones.com, November 5, 2012, viewed online at www.motherjones.com/politics/2012/11/charts-map-koch-brothers-2012-spending, August 1, 2014. More detailed sources will be offered in Chapter 6.

41   Ben Jacobs, "Five Republican Candidates to Vie for Koch Brothers Backing at Donor Retreat," *Guardian*, August 1, 2015, viewed online at www.theguardian.com/us-news/2015/aug/01/republican-candidates-koch-brothers-backing-donor-retreat, August 1, 2015.

# 4 The Campaign Industry

In 1916 the Prohibition Party candidate for Governor of Florida was an itinerant Baptist minister from Alabama named Sidney J. Catts. He had moved to Florida to try to make a living selling insurance, but found himself attracted to politics. Although he failed to win the Democratic nomination for Governor, he did succeed in acquiring the mantle of the Prohibition Party. His campaign consisted of vicious anti-Catholic harangues and even worse hostility towards African-Americans.

Florida's population in 1916 was less than 1 million; it was the third least populated state east of the Mississippi River.[1] Except for Tampa and nascent Miami, most of the population lived along the Panhandle, between Jacksonville and Pensacola, some 350 miles apart, then two of the state's largest cities.

Catts' campaign consisted of two parts, both focused mainly in the Panhandle where anti-Catholicism and racism were rampant. He himself rode the few roads, almost none of them paved, in a model T Ford with loudspeakers attached to the roof. As he drove from hamlet to hamlet, he endlessly made the same populist demagogic speech and spouted his campaign slogan, "The working man has but three friends: Jesus Christ, Sears Roebuck, and Sidney J. Catts."[2]

The other prong of Catts's campaign consisted of a campaign aide, one Jerry Carter, dressed up as a Catholic priest, who traveled through the Panhandle repeatedly and robustly denouncing him. Catts also campaigned wearing a firearm on each hip, because he claimed Catholics had threatened him. Both tactics were obvious dirty tricks, but they worked, as they appealed to the strong anti-Papist sentiment in rural, poor, Bible-belt Florida at the time. Catts won the Governorship with 48 percent of the vote.[3]

The reason for beginning this chapter with this brief vignette is that it points out how small was the campaign organization and staff at that time. Catts and his campaign aide were really a two-man band, although they did use some advance men to go into isolated towns to let the residents know the campaign would soon arrive. But they indeed constituted the apparatus of almost the entire campaign.

In short, it was possible in those early days to mount and conduct even a state-wide campaign with just a few people. But this is really just the beginning of our focus in the chapter: the rise of the Campaign Industry. After all, Catts and Carter could not do everything by themselves. Granted, in those days a car driving into a small, isolated, rural town with loudspeakers blaring was something of an event sure to create interest and draw a crowd. But campaigns also needed the help of locals on the scene— if no one else, at least the County Sheriff (always a powerful political figure in the South) to spread the word and build support, others to tack up or pass out handbills, and still others to mobilize voters when election day rolled around.

## The Campaign Industry

It is possible to locate the very modest origins of what has become a mammoth Campaign Industry. Indeed, let us return for a moment to the historical evidence presented in Chapter 2, because it too suggests that campaign organization, even in the early days, was something with which a successful campaign had to be concerned.

In 1828, the Jackson campaign passed out hickory sticks as mementos at campaign events—someone had to arrange and pay for their manufacture, delivery, and distribution. Handbills were also important in that campaign, especially from the anti-Jackson campaign. How were they printed and distributed?

The quotation from the *Philadelphia Ledger* in 1840 cited earlier raises similar questions:

> The worst part of it was ... that many ladies went to the open-air meetings, strained their voices shouting 'Huzza,' drank hard cider from gourd shells, and devoured baked beans with their fingers from barrels.

Who organized the meetings noted in the quotation? Who went out and mobilized women—who could not vote but who could be involved in politics, including campaigns—to come to the meetings? Who paid for the hard cider? Who arranged for it to be available at the meetings? Who found the gourd shells, and had them *in situ* when the meetings took place? Who provided the barrels of baked beans? Who delivered them to the meetings? Who cleaned up the mess after the rallies?

In that same campaign, it will be recalled, supporters of William Henry Harrison made giant balls out of tin, paper and other flotsam and jetsam, pushing them from town to town to "get the ball rolling" for Harrison. Who arranged for the balls? Who coordinated their routes along the campaign trail? There were also buttons and miniature log cabins for

Harrison to be given out as well—who had them made and delivered to campaign venues? In 1896 Mark Hanna had small gold bugs made as reminders to voters that they should vote for the gold standard candidate William McKinley, not for the free silver candidate William Jennings Bryan. Again, to make this happen required a campaign staff, an organization.

Why is this discussion important? Because it points out that, from very early in our political history, as campaigns were increasingly designed to have broad popular appeal (the Jackson campaign of 1828 might have been the first in this regard), campaigns started to show signs of becoming a business. Expenses were involved, publicity had to be generated and distributed, advance men (and women?) had to be on site to plan campaign events and mobilize people—not only voters, because the size of the crowd was important in conveying a sense of the appeal, indeed the electoral inevitability, of the candidate—to show up. And even after the campaign event was over and the retinue had moved on to the next town, someone had to remain, or return, to keep up the level of enthusiasm, and mobilize voters to come to the polls on election day.

All of this required money, of course, but just as importantly it required planning and organization and coordination. Aside from the politicking, the business of campaigning required the same skills and knowledge that running any other kind of business did. Indeed, it seems fair to say that, by the middle of the nineteenth century, the business of campaigning was well on its way to becoming an industry, at first a cottage industry but by the end of the twentieth century, a major industry; by 2012, as we will see, the Campaign Industry, had it been a corporation, would have had a prominent position on the list of the *Fortune* 500.

## Professionalizing the Campaign Industry

Like many industries, political campaigning has a trade association, the American Association of Political Consultants (AAPC, website www.theaapc.org/default.asp?contentID=548). Anyone associated with campaigns, or even just interested innocent bystanders, can join. To quote from the Association's webpage,

> AAPC members consist of political consultants, media consultants, pollsters, campaign managers, corporate public affairs officers, professors, fund-raisers, lobbyists, congressional staffers and vendors. Membership is open to everyone associated with politics from the local level to the White House.
>
> AAPC members understand that, while we are often competitors on Election Day, we are all colleagues with similar

professional concerns that transcend "Republican," "Democrat" or "Independent" labels.

The Association is dedicated to improving the quality and professionalism of campaign consulting management, from whatever perspective or particular job members might have. It offers an array of services to members, including conferences and seminars held around the country, webinars, extensive networking, job and position notifications, and a code of ethics committing the organization and individual members to observe the highest standards of professionalism while going about the business of winning campaigns.

The Association is headquartered in McLean, Virginia, but has regional chapters across the United States.

In addition to a trade association, the campaign industry now produces an important journal called *Campaigns & Elections* in both hardcopy and online versions.[4] Part of its mission statement reads as follows:

> *Campaigns & Elections* is the preeminent "how-to" resource for politics, focused on the tools, tactics and techniques of the political consulting profession. Established in the spring of 1980 by Stanley Foster Reed, C&E was founded on the understanding that it's management that makes the difference, whether that's in business or on a political campaign.
>
> C&E's industry-leading training conferences bring together political strategists, candidates, elected officials, public affairs professionals, technologists, and campaign staffers to offer prime networking opportunities and the best campaign training in the business. C&E's core events include The Reed Awards Conference & Dinner, CampaignTech East, The Art of Political Campaigning, CampaignTech West, and The Campaigns & Marketing Summit.

The journal also sponsors seminars, roundtables, and meetings featuring the latest conceptual and technical developments in campaign consulting and management. In its articles, it works assiduously to bridge the gap between rigorous empirical research and on-the-street experience. *Campaigns & Elections* also provides an extensive list of campaign management and consulting firms and agencies; indeed it provides an index of more than 60 categories of companies involved in the campaign industry.

And a third piece of evidence on the increasing professionalization of the campaign industry is the growth of academic programs in campaign management or consulting. Either degree or certificate programs at the graduate (usually M.A.) level exist at George Washington University, American University, New York University, Fordham, and the University of Florida. There are also several online programs as well. These programs train advanced students in such matters as political communications, campaign strategy, lobbying, polling, and a host of other topics from which interested students can emphasize and specialize in their programs.

Some readers might wish to ask if the Campaign Industry really qualifies as an industry in the traditional sense? After all, the question might run, granted there is a huge amount of money involved, but is not the Campaign Industry primarily a seasonal one, not a permanent one? Is not the money really only focused on a relatively few months, every couple of years? Is not the Campaign Industry more like the hay fever season, or the Christmas season, or the basketball season, all of which have limited duration?

There is more than a grain of truth behind these questions. In a study published just after the midterm elections of 2014, the Pew Research Center found considerable fluctuation in campaign employment, depending on whether one looks at a presidential election year or a midterm year. For example, since 1978 there have been on average 1,810 political campaign organizations in presidential election years, and 1,743 in midterm years. In off-years, the odd-numbered years on the calendar, there are only a limited number of state and local elections; the number of campaign organizations in odd-numbered years falls to 1,575. Overall, however, since 1980 there has been a significant growth in the number of political campaign organizations, as counted by the U.S. Department of Labor Bureau of Labor Statistics: from 1,275 since the Reagan campaign of 1980 to 2,365 in 2012.[5]

Employment also fluctuates. Professional campaign work is a notoriously nomadic profession, and the variation in the number of filled positions is considerable. Pew reports that, going back to 2001, the average number of employed persons in October (just prior to elections) in presidential and midterm years was 19,754 and 14,607, respectively. But by December, when the elections were over, the numbers of those employed in campaign organizations rapidly dropped to 8,505 for presidential years, and 7,907 in midterm years. For non-election years, the average number of employed persons in campaign organizations is 6,839.[6]

Finally, Pew also notes that salaries in the Campaign Industry have risen considerably over the years. In 1978, the average campaign worker made $29,000. But in 2013, that number rose to $51,000, an increase of 76 percent.[7]

But there is another side to the issue of the seasonal aspect of campaign work, one we briefly examined in Chapter 1: campaigns go on all the time now. They may move from highly visible, highly public steamrollers that may seem to innocent bystanders like whirlwinds or hurricanes in their intensity as presidential and major statewide races move into high gear, to periods in which the public is really not aware of much, if anything, actually going on. But, in fact, as we pointed out earlier, even when campaigns are not very visible, there is still a good deal happening—fund raising, coalition building, organizing, planning, locking down endorsements, and the like. All of this requires money and personnel, and adds to the high costs that campaigning involves. Moreover, it is worth noting that the Federal Electoral Commission (FEC), when it issues its campaign finance reports, usually refers to campaigns in 2-year cycles (for example, 2011–2012, or 2013–2014). Thus it, too, is aware that campaigning is an ongoing matter over a 24-month cycle; it might vary in size and visibility, but it is rather more cyclical than sporadic or seasonal.

It may well be true that, for purely local races (city council, supervisor of elections, school board, and so forth), there are fairly long periods where campaigns appear to be dormant. But that is not always the case— races in large urban counties, for example, require attention to organizing and structuring a campaign over many months, and more, if it is to have a chance of success, especially if it is the campaign of a challenger against an incumbent, who probably already has the foundation of the next campaign in place.[8]

## The Size of the Campaign Industry

How large is the Campaign Industry? At the risk of overwhelming the reader, the best way to show its size is to show campaign expenditures. This is not to trivialize donations, but expenditures are a true measure of the resources that the campaigns accumulate and, more importantly, spend.

Let us first look at the presidential campaign cycle of 2012; it broke records for both contributions and expenditures. Later we will look at expenditures for both 2010 and 2014, both midterm, non-presidential election years.

In 2012, the Obama campaign spent just under $1.0 B and the Romney campaign $1.1 B, according to the authoritative Center for Responsive Politics.[9] These expenditures can be broken down as shown in Table 4.1.

But readers need to remember that there were many other elections, and expenditures, during 2012. About $3.6 B was spent on contests for the U.S. House of Representatives and U.S. Senate. And of course there were hundreds of races, not reported to the FEC but tracked by a number of groups at state and local levels. These can be difficult to assess, because states differ widely in reporting requirements. The National Institute on

*Table 4.1* Spending Related to the Presidential Race, 2011–2012

|  | For Obama | For Romney |
| --- | --- | --- |
| By candidate | $540.8 M | $336.1 M |
| National party spending | $292.3 M | $386.1 M |
| Outside spending | $131.3 M | $418.6 M |
| Total | $0.96 B | $1.14 B |

Money in State Politics (followthemoney.com)[10] estimated that, by June, 2012, races in 23 states had spent about $500 M, with four months to go of heavy campaigning[11] And the figure does not include purely local races, of which there were thousands.

What is the bottom line? How much money was spent on political campaigns in 2012? A conservative estimate provided by the well-regarded blog Politico.com suggests that $7 B would be an accurate figure, but only for the presidential campaigns.[12] Of this money, about $1.3 B came from outside sources, including SuperPacs, a new type of campaign-funding organization whose origin in 2010 and subsequent importance we will detail in Chapter 6. About one-quarter of the outside money (close to $300 M) was "dark," meaning its sources could not be traced, as donors' names did not have to be reported to the FEC.[13]

And what about state races? Followthemoney.com reported that, in the 2011–2012 election cycle, more than 16,500 state candidates and sundry political committees raised and spent more than $3.1 B, up from 2007–2008.[14]

In short, a reasonable but conservative estimate is that somewhere in the neighborhood of $10 B was spent on elections during the 2012 cycle.

---

## $10 B—Just the Tip of the Iceberg

Readers need to remember that the $10 B figure is *solely* for the 2011–2012 campaign cycle and is only expenditures. It does not include money from sources other than the American political campaigns. For example, it does not include campaigns in other countries in which American consulting firms may have participated (and were paid handsomely); we will briefly discuss these later in the chapter. Nor does it include retainers and other fees that large corporations (including non-profits), law firms, accounting firms, and other associations paid to political consulting firms on K Street in Washington, D.C., New York, Chicago, San Francisco, and other cities for "government relations," a euphemism for lobbying. As is well known, figures for lobbying can reach well into six figures even before much activity begins.

What about the election cycles of 2010 and 2014? So-called off-year elections generate far less interest, and far fewer dollars, than do those during presidential years. Nonetheless, the numbers are far from trivial. In 2010, between $3.5 B and $4 B was spent for primarily state and local races. This figure also includes the U.S. House of Representatives (435 members), whose members have to run every 2 years — although relatively few of these elections, given the 90+ percent success rate of re-election for incumbents,[15] are competitive—and about one-third of the U. S. Senate (which tends to be slightly more competitive).[16] In 2014, in spite of the lowest voter turnout in 72 years[17] and a seemingly somnolent electorate, campaign spending was up very slightly over 2010, to $3.8 B.[18]

## The Figures in Context

How many people can grasp what $1 B really represents? Or $10 B? The truth is that it is very hard to wrap one's head around sums of this magnitude. But placed in a familiar context, and compared to figures with which people are familiar, the numbers stand out in relief and achieve meaning.

For example, in 2012 the Sempra Energy Company of southern California had just over $10 B in gross revenues; it ranked 266 on the list of *Fortune* 500 companies that year.[19] BB&T, a large bank holding company headquartered in Winston-Salem, North Carolina, ranked 267, with gross revenues of just under $10 B.

In other words, had the 2012 Campaign Industry been a corporation, it would have ranked just past the half-way mark on the list of *Fortune* 500 largest corporations of that year.

---

### Besides the Expenditures in 2011–2012 for Political Campaigns in the United States, what else costs $10B? or $1B?

- A new Port Authority Terminal in New York City would cost $10 B.[20]
- Bloomberg estimated that the cost of re-building Nepal after the disastrous April, 2015, earthquake would exceed $10B.[21]
- Boston's later-abandoned bid to acquire the 2024 Olympics was estimated at $10 B.[22]
- Alaska's budget for 2016 will be $9.5 B.
- Montana's budget for 2015 was $10.9 B.[23]
- Budgets (2015) for some of the largest cities in the United States are in the same range:
  - Los Angeles, $8.5 B
  - Chicago, $8.9 B
  - San Francisco, $8.6 B.[24]

The Obama and Romney campaigns each spent about $1 B. What else can one buy for $1 billion and change?
- 3 Boeing 777 aircraft (@$320 M).[25]
- 2 Airbus A380-800 (@ $428 M).[26]
- 1 offshore oil rig costs about $600 M.[27]
- The most expensive cruise ship ever built, the Royal Caribbean "Oasis of the Seas," cost about $1.4 B (2009).[28]
- The world's tallest building, the 160-story Burj in Dubai, cost about $1.5 B to construct when it was finished in 2010.[29]
- Budgets of some major American cities (2015):
  - St Louis, $1.0 B[30]
  - Minneapolis, $1.2 B[31]
  - San Antonio, $1.0 B[32]
  - Phoenix, $1.1 B[33]
  - Detroit, $1.1 B.[34]

What are we to conclude from this examination of both the raw data on 2012 campaign expenditures and the data viewed in the context of other major private and public costs?

Most obviously, presidential campaigns, and indeed campaigns seen *in toto*, have become incredibly expensive. In 1960, Senator John F. Kennedy raised and spent about $9.8 million; Vice President Richard M. Nixon actually raised more money ($10.1 M) and lost.[35] In 1998, the total cost of all federal elections was about $1.6 B; as we saw, in 2012 it was about $7 B, an increase of about 338 percent.[36] And for 2016? There are estimates that Hillary Clinton alone will spend in the neighborhood of $2.5 B.[37] On the Republican side, Jeb Bush established early that his campaign was a money vacuum cleaner, raising about $103 M in just the first three months of 2015.[38] The Koch Brothers have already pledged close to $1 B in outside money.[39] Indeed, there is no reason to assume that in the next few presidential cycles there will be a decline in spending, barring serious changes in campaign finance laws at both federal and state levels.[40] Rather, the upward slant of the expenditure curve seems likely to continue unabated.

The costs of campaigning for public office, especially but not only for the presidency, are so staggering as to defy comprehension. *Fortune* magazine has further pointed out that startup costs alone for a credible presidential run are in the $10 M range, and these do not include the amounts that Republicans, at least in 2016, will have to spend in individual state primaries, which add millions in expenses per candidate, per state primary.[41]

Thus the conclusion is incontrovertible: not only is political campaigning now a major industry, it has joined the ranks of Big Business.

We leave for a later chapter a discussion of where the money comes from, and what are the consequences of candidates' having to raise these astronomical sums. For now we only need observe that the Campaign Industry in the United States is as mighty as some of the corporate giants of the nation, with all of the pros and cons that such status entails.

## The Campaign Industry as Big Business

What kind of a campaign can a candidate with more than $1 B in his/her war chest buy? The short answer is, a big one, with lots of bells and whistles. But there is much more to the question than might appear at first, for at least two reasons. First, if in fact campaigning has become an industry, Big Business, as this chapter contends, then examining how campaigns spend their money will tell us a great deal about what the industry is like. Second, looking at a particular campaign will demonstrate how it goes about the business of its campaigns as it allocates its resources to secure enough votes to emerge victorious at the end, because different campaigns will make those allocations differently.

A comparison of how the Obama and Romney campaigns spent their money during the 2012 presidential election will offer insight into both of these matters. Figures 4.1 and 4.2 provide the data:[42]

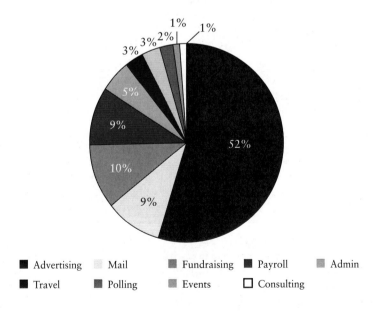

*Figure 4.1* Obama Campaign Expenditures as Percentage of Total

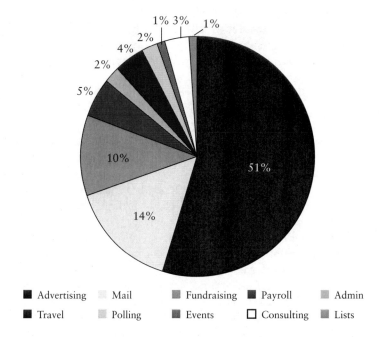

Figure 4.2 Romney Campaign Expenditures as Percentage of Total

What are we to conclude from these data?

First, Figures 4.1 and 4.2 show what kinds of activities these (and by extension, other) campaigns spend money on. There are ten categories of expenditures: Advertising, Direct Mail, Fundraising, Payroll, Administrative Costs, Travel, Polling, Events, Consulting, and Lists.

Of these, Advertising is by far the most important. The Obama campaign spent 52 percent of its total resources on advertising, and the Romney campaign, 51 percent. The overwhelming majority of these funds went to television advertisements, still the most effective way to reach voters. The Obama campaign outspent the Romney campaign more than 2:1 in buying online ads. Indeed, as early as June, 2012, Obama had spent over $16 M on online ads, compared to Romney's $7.8 M.[43]

Both campaigns spent heavily on direct mail, or, as it is more commonly known now, snail mail. The Republicans actually invented direct mail; as early as 1964, during the Goldwater campaign, they discovered how effective it could be for raising money, building support, and mobilizing voters.[44] Indeed, the Romney campaign spent 14 percent of its campaign money on direct mail, and the Obama campaign 9 percent. Given how committed the Obama Campaign was to digital forms of communication, including social media (a topic to which we will return in the next chapter), one might not have expected it to rely so heavily on snail mail, but on the other hand, some voters—probably especially older voters—are more comfortable with snail mail than with digital communications. And given a continuing digital divide in this country,[45] there is really no other way, except possibly by telephone, to reach them than by snail mail.

All told, the Obama campaign spent 61 percent of its operating budget on advertisements and mail; the Romney campaign, 65 percent.

The next largest budget item in the campaign was fundraising, about 10 percent of each's total. What this says is that campaigns have to spend money to get money, so in a sense they have to understand that fundraising efforts are part of the expenditure (investment?) that campaigns have to make in order to secure the resources needed for more immediate appeals to and communication with voters.

The same is true of administrative and payroll costs, that is, the costs of just running the campaign organization. We will have more to say about their significance later in the chapter. For now, we need to note that the Romney campaign spent only about 7 percent of its money on payroll and administration, while the Obama campaign spent at twice that rate, 14 percent. Whether this is a result of the Obama campaign paying higher salaries, having more foot-soldiers on the ground, not being efficient managers, or something else is not our concern here. What we can say is that the Obama campaign was willing to invest/spend a substantial amount on administration and payroll—that is, campaign infrastructure— as a way of making the campaign move forward.

It is in the last four major categories of campaign expenditures that we can see substantial differences, and not only in how the two campaigns went about their business of finding and securing voters, and what resources and assets of the Campaign Industry each chose to emphasize in order to do so. Readers will note that the Obama campaign spent more than twice as much as the Romney campaign on polling ($35 M to $14 M), more than three times as much on campaign events ($25 M to $7 M), and nearly twice as much on lists (including digital lists) as Romney ($17 M to $10 M). Only in hiring consultants did the Romney campaign outpace Obama's ($25 M to $13 M).

---

### Feeding the Campaign

All political campaigns, even the most modest, require long hours, expending lots of energy and effort, emotional fatigue, and patience on the part of participants. One of the ways campaigns help their personnel—volunteers and paid staff—cope with the highs and lows, fatigue and frustrations, is to feed them.

Even before either Mr. Obama or Mr. Romney had secured the presidential nomination of their respective parties, the *National Review*, no friend of the President, offered a slightly tongue-in-cheek assessment of how the Obama campaign spent money on food through mid-June, 2012:

- Catering—$96,389.41
- Big Delicious Planet Catering, Chicago—$13,128.72
- Subway (Columbus, Indiana) —$2,571.27
- Dunkin' Donuts—$552.67
- Einstein Bagels—$389.85
- Starbucks—$229.22
- Caribou Coffee—$183.15
- 7-Eleven—$239.38
- Domino's Pizza—$2,084.37
- Pizzano's Pizza—$1,774.78
- Papa John's Pizza—$1,167.45
- Pizza Hut—$834.03
- Little Caesar's Pizza—$362.00.

Finally, the *Review* notes an expenditure of $239.39 at a Krispy Kreme in Winston Salem, North Carolina, adding rather pointedly the question of whether Mrs. Obama, an outspoken and vigorous advocate of healthy eating, might have found out about the purchase, and, by implication, what she may have said about it.[46]

What are we to learn from examining these data on expenditures for each of the campaigns. A number of points emerge:

Advertising, especially TV advertising, is still king in campaigns, dwarfing all other expenditures. Even, as we will see in the next chapter, if much of TV advertising is wasteful, it is still the method through which most voters secure campaign/political information.[47] Moreover, there is a certain defensive stance in campaigns' investing heavily in TV ads; not to do so leaves the field wide open to opponents and so by necessity they have to have a TV presence. Indeed, the more important the office being sought and the closer election day nears, the larger that presence has to be.

It is of further interest that the Obama campaign opted to spend considerable sums on online ads. It seems highly likely that, in the future, digitally savvy campaigns will increase expenditures for online ads as a percentage of the advertising budget, as new techniques are developed for employing the Internet, in all of its manifestations, to reach likely voters.

Indeed, based on the last point and data from the expenditures shown, it can be said that the Obama campaign had a different view of the campaign business than did the Romney campaign. Bluntly, the difference can be described as future-directed in the case of Obama and tradition-bound in the case of Romney. The Obama campaign spent its money heavily on digital, high-tech, complex electronic wizardry to plan and carry out its mission: one sees this in the amount it spent on polling (which includes high-end, big data analysis, something we will discuss later in the book), online advertising, and lists, so that social media could be used to reach voters continuously, personally, and within nano-seconds.

The Romney campaign relied heavily on the traditional Republican use of direct mail and consultants—both of which are slow, and the latter in particular can be ponderous and cause confusion, even turmoil.[48] Indeed, a number of after-the-fact commentators noted that Romney probably relied too much on internal polls and/or did not commission enough polls (meaning, spend more money on them!), which led to mistakes in how campaign resources should have been allocated in the final, frantic days of the race.[49]

Finally, the Obama campaign vastly outspent the Romney campaign in putting on events, in which the candidate or his surrogate actually had personal contact (figuratively if not literally) with voters. Whether this means that the Obama campaign had a more retail view of what is important and effective within the confines of the Campaign Industry than the wholesale one of Romney is a subject for discussion. But what is clear is that local events, especially if they are designed as mass, come-one-come-all occasions, have powerful spillover effects, ripples that continue in the community where the campaign venue was located long after the candidate (or his surrogate) has departed to another venue. Thus the positive impact of a local campaign event on individual voters can be substantial.

In contrast, one thinks of the private event that Mr. Romney attended, at a ritzy country club in South Florida, where his unfortunate remarks about the 47 percent of "takers" were secretly recorded and then went viral over the Internet.[50] Events, like every other part of the campaign's business, have to be handled very carefully.

## The Business of Campaigns and the Business of the Campaign Industry

As we noted earlier in the book, no two campaigns are alike, even if they involve the same candidates running for the same office as previously. And they are structured differently—a gigantic organizational effort aimed at gaining the White House is quite different from one for town council in a small village. And yet, remarkably, all campaigns, of whatever size, share some commonalties. The reason is that they all share the same purpose and goal—securing more votes than the other candidate(s). In a real sense they are all engaged in the same business—finding ways of winning the election.

How is that business carried out? That is the business of the Campaign Industry. In the smallest campaigns it may well be that just a few people have to perform multiple functions to do that business, and few if any outsiders will be brought in to help. In the largest campaigns, hundreds of people have to be organized, and managed, in specific tasks; the organizational chart of a presidential campaign may very well look like that of a sizeable corporation.

Because candidates and their staffs of largely volunteers, or even paid generalists, did not have the skills or the time to carry out the complex business that the campaign demanded, specialized organizations—firms, agencies, companies, private consultants—developed to design and plan and even direct and manage them. And as political parties began to atrophy in the last third of the twentieth century, they no longer were able to carry out effectively their traditional role of running campaigns for their candidates.[51] Thus these new types of political organizations comprised of individuals with very specialized knowledge and skills—media, polling, opposition research, Get-Out-The-Vote (GOTV), and the like—were created to fill the void. More recently, U. S. Supreme Court decisions[52] which allowed, even promoted, the introduction of "dark money" into political campaigns has contributed another layer, and additional numbers, of political firms and consultants into the campaign landscape.[53] All of this of course cost campaigns a great deal of money—money that enabled the Campaign Industry to develop into the behemoth it has become. And of course once the idea of hiring outside consultants to help with, even run, the business of campaigns caught on, the Campaign Industry's growth was assured: a candidate, learning that his/her opponent had hired a consultant for media, or polling, or fund-raising, was not about to be left behind!

Let us now turn, if only briefly, to the major parts of the Campaign Industry, and the business it is equipped to carry out.

## Fund Raising

The campaign that does not have an individual, or entire teams of individuals spread out over an entire state or nation, whose sole function is to raise money, lots of money, won't get very far. The capacity to raise money for a political campaign is a unique talent, and for some of the largest campaigns—President, Senate, Governor, Mayor of large cities— professionals are often hired to assist, even direct the effort. Fund-raising committees are generally composed of high-powered individuals who are identified with money—if not captains of industry or finance, then persons whom the community, or state, or nation recognize as representatives of a moneyed class. Often, but not always, they are wealthy, because in this country wealth commands respect and social status, and a request from one of these individuals for a maximum donation or large soft money contribution cannot easily be dismissed.

Even at the local level, when a candidate holds so-called "fund raisers," generally a reception at someone's home or rented venue, a "host" committee is often formed for the occasion. Names on the host list will usually consist of prominent business and professional people, community notables whose names lend gravitas, even panache, to the campaign.

What about the candidate? Does not he or she have important fund-raising responsibilities? The answer is yes, and at the local level candidates might well spend upwards of 50 percent of their campaign time seeking funds. But in the largest campaigns, candidates must rely heavily on fund-raising committees and hired professionals, and generally the candidate reserves his/her fund-raising efforts to names of potential deep-pocket donors suggested by his or her fund raising committee and consultants.

## Media

Any campaign that plans to advertise—has there ever been one that did not?—needs media specialists. It is true that anyone can walk into the local newspaper advertising office and place an ad, and often get advice from the people in the office about designing and composing it. But relying on this approach is sure to result in a hopelessly incompetent media campaign and wasted money.

Even a small local campaign with a modest advertising budget needs expert advice about the local market. Which media outlets work best for the kind of voters the candidate needs in order to win? What is the optimum balance among radio, television, online ads, and print ads (even something like bus bench political advertisements, or posters inside the bus, billboards, flyers, campaign signs on major thoroughfares in cities and counties that allow them, yard signs, buttons, tee-shirts and other campaign detritus) to reach and mobilize the candidate's likely voters? Even a small, general-practice local advertising agency should be able to offer guidance about these matters to candidates. And of course for actual production and placement of those ads in appropriate outlets, local expertise is essential.

But, for a presidential campaign, or statewide race, even in a modest size state, matters get more complicated. Examining the reports of both the Obama and Romney campaigns reveals that they each hired a half-dozen and more advertising agencies, specifically ones that specialize in political communications.[54] The design and production of political advertisements, especially in big races, has become so sophisticated (and expensive!) that campaigns must seek out and hire only those with the credentials and skills and record to show that they can do the heavy lifting required of a serious national or state-wide media campaign.[55]

## Data Gathering and Analysis

In the context of political campaigns, readers might think the phrase "data gathering and analysis" refers to polling. That would be correct, but only partially correct. In fact, in modern political campaigns, polling, while essential, is only a part of the need for large, accurate data sets, rigorously analyzed.

Even modest campaigns for local offices need to engage in some form of data gathering and analysis. For example, the best guide to how any given area will vote in the next election is its past voting behavior. How did the voters vote previously? Do they support Republicans or Democrats? What about women candidates or minority group candidates? What is the voter registration in the area and, more importantly, what have been the turnout rates? Is the population primarily young, say, under 35, whose turnout rates are notoriously low, or is there an older population, over 55, who have the highest turnout rates?[56]

Any campaign for public office needs this and similar information as early as possible, so it can define its universe of likely voters and determine a way to reach those who might vote for its candidate. At the local level, these data are easy to secure, as even advanced social science undergraduate students can gather them from local elections officials (even precinct-level data are now available online) and create tables and charts that can aid the campaign in finding its likely voters.

For statewide and presidential campaigns, matters are more complicated but the principle is the same. Modern campaigns at these levels hire firms consisting of skilled statisticians and others able to handle large data sets to slice and dice the electorate to find aggregations of likely voters across the state and nation. Again, a Google search reveals firms that, for a considerable fee, will conduct the kind of statistical analysis and mapping that can show where the campaign can fruitfully spend its resources and what areas/counties/states should be avoided. It is well recognized that, whatever one thinks of his politics and tactics, Karl Rove, the Rasputin of George W. Bush's successful presidential bids, was a master at mining large data sets down to the smallest communities and precincts to find the voters that his candidate needed.[57]

And then of course there are the polls, and pollsters. They are the *sine qua non* of modern campaigns, even small ones, although they have become so prohibitively expensive that they are often, indeed usually, beyond the reach of many local candidates, and unless they can piggyback on a poll paid for by another candidate, or one commissioned and bankrolled by an outside group, or perhaps by the state party, they have to rely on knowledgeable local individuals and pundits, experience, and a lot of time spent out on the street.

But for big campaigns, the polls take center stage. The pollsters themselves have become the rock stars of modern campaigns, the Svengalis without whom no serious campaign will leave the launching pad. And, as the data from the Obama and Romney campaigns show, each hired multiple firms capable of professionally conducting an array of baseline and tracking polls, focus groups, and the like. There are important consequences to the roles that polls and pollsters now play in modern campaigns, a matter to which we will return later in the chapter.

Recognizing how central they are to big campaigns, polling firms advertise aggressively, as a Google search will quickly reveal. While they tend to sort themselves out along partisan lines, there are also highly respected polling firms that proudly wear the mantle, "Independent." The competition is so keen and fiercely fought for the large contracts that big campaigns can tender that they sometimes engage in infighting and "ratings" of one another, to persuade candidates and campaigns that they offer a better and more accurate service than their competitors.[58]

What has also emerged, from inside the campaign, is a kind of politics of pollster selection. Of course the campaign will hire a firm with which it has had success in the past and avoid those with which it has not. And reputation and recommendations count for a good deal. But there is also a practice of hiring a polling firm that the campaign may not need or necessarily even want—because the hire will keep the firm from working with a rival campaign, or even an opponent. The same practice has also been done with media and advertising firms. Wasteful? Perhaps, but as the eminent political scientist E.E. Schattschneider wrote many years ago, the campaign that controls the playing field greatly enhances its chances of success.[59] Hiring additional polling or media firms to keep them off, instead of on, the playing field is one way to do that.

## Campaign Management

The last element of campaign organization or structure that we will discuss is campaign management. All campaigns need it, even the smallest. The reason is that someone has to coordinate and oversee all of the myriad tasks that a political campaign requires, from buying staplers and cartridges for printers, to paying rent and other bills for a campaign headquarters, to meeting with fund raisers to arranging events, to making sure that the candidate is taken to and arrives at the right campaign venue at the right time, to ensuring that campaign financial reports are filed in the correct government office on time, to ensuring that there are volunteers to walk precincts, hand out flyers, and (if it is the local style and custom) arrange for sign-holders at major intersections as election day approaches. And there are hundreds more such tasks; the larger the campaign, the more tasks there are, the more people are needed to carry them out, and the more complex the campaign organization.[60]

Can a candidate serve as his or her own campaign manager or director? The answer comes straight from the old saw about lawyers: "Who represents himself in court has a fool for a client."[61] There are candidates, especially at the local level, who try to manage their own campaigns, but by and large they quickly see the futility and hopelessness of doing so. Their time is better spent campaigning or raising money than setting up a new computer at headquarters, ordering more bumper stickers, or deciding if a luncheon with deep-pocket donors should be at this restaurant, or that one, and on what day and time?

But there is more to campaign management than seeing that fairly low-level tasks are done. Campaign management involves some tasks that are central to the campaign: scheduling appointments, interviews, and events is absolutely critical, for example. For large campaigns, and especially for presidential campaigns, these take on a multi-state dimension, and they have to be coordinated because the candidate cannot be in two states at the same time. On-site field coordinators at state and/or county/local levels and advance men (and women) in charge of setting up events in local venues have to be found and methods of communication assured between on-site personnel and headquarters. Travel has to be arranged, which means chartering airplanes, and buses, and cars, and motorcades; and lodging; and food for the campaign staff—none of this is trivial because, to paraphrase Napoleon, a campaign runs on its stomach, but also its transportation, and its rooms at the Best Western or some comparable inn. If there are debates, practice sessions have to be planned and arranged, and stand-ins for the opponent(s) and interlocutors identified. How are surrogates to be used, if at all? Are members of the family to be involved in the campaign and, if so, how?

But perhaps no aspect of campaign management is more important than designing and implementing campaign strategy and tactics. As the Obama and Romney reports indicate, huge sums were spent for "consultants," the approved euphemism for the strategists who can design what the campaign needs to do in order to win and how to implement its plan. As we saw, the Romney campaign spent more on consultants than Obama's ($25 M to $13 M), but in this regard the Obama campaign had a decided advantage, since it used basically the same team of strategists in 2012 that it had successfully used in 2008, David Plouffe and David Axelrod.[62]

---

### The First Lady Campaigns

In mid-September, 2012, First Lady Michelle Obama made a campaign stop in Gainesville, Florida, where she spoke at a rally organized by students at the University of Florida. By her own account the audience was the largest she had encountered during a number of campaign appearances that she made before the election, nearly 12,000 strong, from the university and surrounding communities. Media accounts were extremely positive about the effectiveness of Mrs. Obama's visit and speech.[63]

Mrs. Obama campaigned assiduously during the summer and fall, 2012. While undoubtedly it was her decision as to whether, or how much, she wished to campaign, it is also true that the Obama brain trust of strategists and consultants who actually designed and ran the campaign wanted to take full advantage of her broad appeal, and very positive polling numbers, among likely voters.[64]

---

## The Internal Politics of the Campaign

But this discussion of the business that a political campaign must undertake to win can only take us so far. Like any complex organization, large campaigns have an internal dynamic and politics that determine how well the tasks of the campaign are, or are not, carried out. There is always internal friction, disputes, rivalries, turf-protection, gatekeeping, personality conflicts, disagreements over strategy and tactics, hurt feelings, and a host of other "office politics" that affect the campaign's ability to operate; indeed, if matters become too conflicted, they can create a train-wreck that derails the whole campaign enterprise.[65]

Small campaigns also have to contend with micro-level versions of these same phenomena. Even if the campaign is composed primarily of volunteers, there can be intra-campaign disputes and rivalries. If a professional media agency is hired, it may be that some of the campaign workers do not like the product being aired, or sent out. Or this volunteer or this committee (fund raising?; event planning?) is, according to others, not working hard enough. And of course the problem with volunteers is exactly that—they are volunteers, free to come and go more or less as they wish. How, then, can the campaign know if the tasks undertaken by volunteers are really being done, until it may be too late?

But it is in the big campaigns that internal politics can cause the most problems. It is not uncommon, for example, for disputes to arise between media agencies and pollsters. Are the pollsters asking the right questions?[66] What do the data that the pollsters and their analysts gather really say? If there are multiple pollsters, are the findings compatible? If not, why not? Are the results from focus groups the same? If there is a message from the polls or focus groups, what is it? How do the media convey that message, or are they doing it the way the pollsters think it should be handled? If there is more than one media agency, as is likely, what happens when there is disagreement? Who becomes the arbiter, or the decider? Which firm's advice will the campaign decide to slight and at what cost?

It is easy to say that it is the job of the campaign manager, and his staff and hired consultants, to resolve such disputes. Ultimately the manager has to make the call. But what if he/she does not? What if the dispute entails end-runs, in which one or another of the parties goes around the manager to appeal to other important players in the campaign (consultants?; a member of the candidate's trusted inner circle?; the candidate him or herself?; a family member?). The result can be chaos.

It is precisely these kinds of issues that form the basis of political scientist Samuel Popkin's important book, *The Candidate*, cited earlier. The thrust of Popkin's book is that organization and management matter, that they are the major determinants of the outcome of the campaign. Popkin has been criticized for placing too much emphasis on management as key in campaign success—other factors are also important, such as public mood and sentiment, economic and other conditions in the larger environment, serendipity and unknown unknowns that happen along the way, for example.[67]

But nonetheless Popkin is on to something important. Relying on an array of data going back to George H.W. Bush's losing campaign in 1992, Al Gore's loss in 2000, through Hillary Clinton's failure to secure the Democratic presidential nomination in 2008, Popkin demonstrates that the commonalties in failed campaigns were those of management and direction. Disputes among the major players—media, pollsters, consultants, state and local field directors, major donors, key constituent groups, the candidate's inner circle—that could not be firmly resolved by the campaign managers almost always meant defeat (Bill Clinton's re-election victory in 1996 appears to be a major exception).

Thus, according to Popkin, the major task of the campaign manager/director is to use a firm hand. The manager, after all, is the major gatekeeper to the candidate (with the possible exception of a spouse/other family members or trusted members of the candidate's inner circle). The manager has to decide who has the candidate's ear last thing at night, and for that first cup of coffee in the morning: those who have his or her ear for the second cup might be too late.

There are of course important ethical issues with this method of handling the internal politics of the campaign. We shall return to them at the conclusion of this chapter.

## Internationalizing the Campaign Industry

By the late1960s, American (and British) political consultants were working with political campaigns in a range of countries. After that, there was a virtual avalanche of American political consultants being exported abroad. In the 1980s, in Great Britain alone, the Conservative Party had called on Americans to assist in its election campaigns; Tony Blair's Labour Party did the same in the 1990s. By that time French and German political consultants had also worked with American colleagues who crossed the ocean to participate in campaigns.[68]

In a self-reported poll of political consultants, Fritz Plasser found that a majority, in some cases a considerable majority, of consultants abroad felt that affiliation or interaction with their American colleagues would be beneficial to the campaigns that they were running: in Eastern and Central Europe, Russia and the Ukraine, South Africa, and Latin America. Only in India did consultants feel skittish about inviting their American counterparts to work with them. By 2008, the journalist Walter Shapiro, reviewing James Harding's new book *Alpha Dogs: The Americans Who Turned Political Spin into a Global Business*, could write of his own experience in Budapest, Hungary, in early 1990:

> It is a truth universally acknowledged that a nation in possession of an upcoming election must be in want of an American political consultant. I learned this iron law of global politics in Hungary in early 1990 while covering the first unfettered campaign in the former Soviet bloc. Budapest, at its glorious dawn of democracy, seemed to boast more Democratic and Republican strategists, pollsters, and media mavens than all the steakhouses in Washington.[69]

Not only in Hungary: American political consultants were and have been busily at work in many countries. Great Britain, France, and Germany, of course, but also Argentina, Bulgaria, Romania, Russia, Israel, Turkey, Brazil, Venezuela, Dominican Republic, Angola, Mozambique, Nigeria, Japan, Serbia, Egypt, Tunisia, and any number of other nations have seen the footprints of American political advisers during their campaigns.[70] But, as any number of commentators listed in the footnote have pointed out, not all of the American political consultants who were brought over to help assured victory for their clients; some, in fact, managed to make a total hash of their campaign.

Indeed, international political consulting has become so common that an organization comparable to the American Association of Political Consultants (AAPC), the International Association of Political Consultants (IAPC), has become a sort of clearinghouse for international consulting firms and information about consulting opportunities across the globe.[71]

And not only American political consulting firms were involved; Brazil, for example, has sent a number of its firms to other nations, including Angola. A quick examination of the IAPC's website reveals just how widespread, and common, international political consulting has become.

Why would this happen? More relevantly for this book, why is it that Walter Shapiro, as early as 1990, could write from Budapest that no campaign in another country is complete without at least some American consultancy involved? While entire books could be written about this question, let us just focus on two reasons.

The first, and most obvious, is expertise. As we have seen, since the 1960s, at least, and probably before, American political consultants have been assiduously at work developing skills and techniques to assist their candidates to win elections.

---

### There Were Campaign Consultants Before There Was a Campaign Industry

William McKinley of course had his Mark Hanna to design and run his campaign. Franklin D. Roosevelt had as leader of his campaign brain trust Jim Farley, who also served as his Postmaster General. It is well understood that Harry Truman's "upset" victory in 1948 was probably not an upset at all, but the product of a brilliant campaign designed by Clark Clifford, a prominent Washington lawyer and advisor to several Presidents. The Gallup Poll first began reporting on presidential campaigns in 1936 and, with the exception of 1948, successfully forecast all of the subsequent presidential elections. Gallup was not the first polling organization, but it early on developed the fundamental techniques that virtually all professional political polling firms still use.

---

Polling, media, fund raising, voter mobilization, negative campaigning, opposition research, data analysis—from very early on these became the stock-in-trade of the American Campaign Industry. Foreign observers, and candidates, could easily see how effective these techniques were, and as the idea, and in some cases the actuality, of democratic elections spread across the globe (especially after the fall of the Soviet Union in the late 1980s), they wanted to utilize American experience, knowledge, and skills for their own political purposes, especially since expert political consulting firms did not necessarily exist in all of the nations that suddenly found themselves engaged in electoral politics.[72]

Second, the employment of American consultants brought a certain *élan* and *éclat* to campaigns abroad: status, if you will. Having prestigious

American consultants as part of a campaign apparatus or retinue in other countries also brought a sense of gravitas, of weight and seriousness to the whole endeavor. Of course much of this was just for appearances; many political consultants abroad were trained in the United States, or had worked on American campaigns with American consultants. None of that mattered. Bringing in American consultants lent respectability and, beyond that, a sense of the inevitability of its success, to the campaign abroad. It's really the same principal behind the choice of some patients to seek admission to the Mayo or Cleveland Clinics for their medical care; the doctors and medical teams at the local hospital may have had the same level of training and experience as those in these famous and prestigious medical centers, but the local hospital does not have the name or same status. Or the same high-powered public relations firm trumpeting its assets and capabilities.

Are there down-sides to the employment of political consultants abroad? At least three come to mind.

The first is that it is not always clear that American-style campaigns are easily adapted to the culture, and laws, of other countries. Turkey, for example, is one of several nations that do not allow political advertisements on television. Given how important TV is for American political campaigns, what role are American media mavens, as Walter Shapiro called them, to play abroad? And many other nations, as we have seen earlier, sharply limit the time of active political campaigns, while American campaigns are essentially endless. Granted, in countries that only allow severely truncated campaigns there might still be a great deal of behind-the-scene planning and preparation that take place over a considerable length of time, but it is not certain that American techniques are always usable in them. And in some nations, Japan for example, the "style" of campaigns and campaign management is so different that American consultants and their often heavy-handed, even pushy, ways have not always been welcome.[73] In short, what works in Chicago or Miami might not work in Mumbai or Istanbul, Kathmandu or Ouagadougou.

Second, the use of American consultants abroad has in some cases become an issue in the local campaigns, disrupting them and blurring the focus from local issues to: What is it exactly that Americans are doing here? The most prominent recent example of this was the spring, 2015 elections in Israel, in which both Prime Minister Benjamin Netanyahu and one of his major challengers, Nimrod Dweck, hired American consultants, which caused a barrage of accusations and counter accusations across the campaign landscape, confusing further the already complicated dynamics of that election cycle.[74]

There is one more issue that the matter of American political consultants abroad raises: what is the message that exporting our campaign professionals sends to other nations about our democratic elections? Readers having just the slightest acquaintance with recent American campaigns and elections are surely aware that increasingly Big Money talks loudest in them, that not all of the money is publicly accounted for, and that the electoral playing field is tilted in favor of wealth. None of this is compatible with healthy democratic elections.

The truth is that, while most of the impetus for this development comes from the U.S. Supreme Court, substantial responsibility also rests on the shoulders of political consultants and the entire Campaign Industry. Money became a powerful determinant of the outcome of elections long before *Citizens United*.[75] Political consultants were instrumental in establishing the centrality of money in our campaigns. But even leaving money aside, political consultants have long been associated with creating and perpetuating some of the ugly, nasty, characteristics of our campaigns: a strong predilection for negativity and character assassination; dirty tricks; lies and fabrications; a "do-anything-ANYTHING-to-win" attitude and campaign culture that has no room for a moral or ethical compass; voter discrimination and suppression. These characteristics are central to the issue of how democratic are our elections. And it is precisely these characteristics that we are exporting to other countries, even as they struggle to establish their own democratic processes and traditions.

Readers need to remember also that exporting American-style campaigns has to be seen in the context of the time-worn American policy of trying to export our democracy abroad. We saw this most clearly after the fall of the Soviet Union, as eastern and central European nations sought to build democratic institutions, including elections, as part of their new governing structures. More recently, we have seen these efforts in the Middle East, especially in Iraq and Afghanistan, but in other nations in that area as well. Not all of these efforts involved military force but, even when the armed forces were not employed, American-style democracy-building was aggressively pushed by the agents and agencies of U.S foreign policy. As scholarly analysts of the "build democracy abroad" initiative have noted, these efforts at creating democratic institutions and processes have not always worked.[76] The formalisms may be put in place, but some of the nations allegedly "building democracy" still look more authoritarian than democratic. Thus, even as we export American-style campaigns abroad, we have to ask if in fact these efforts are really building democratic elections, or only the shell, the meme, of them?

## The Campaign Industry and the Future of Campaigns

This last point in the previous section brings us to the conclusion of this chapter. What exactly is the contribution of political consultants and the Campaign Industry to democratic politics? Without doubt the extraordinarily sophisticated tools that they/it have developed to design and manage campaigns have brought a professional fluidity, a style and sophistication, to the way they go forward, like a well-honed machine when running at its best.

But there is at least one other side to this, one that is much darker. The prominent journalist Joe Klein, in his worthy book *Politics Lost*, discusses it in detail.[77] It is difficult to summarize briefly the argument of this richly textured book, but essentially Klein says that political consultants have taken campaigns away from candidates, voters, and the public at large, literally kidnapped or highjacked them away. Basically, he says, it no longer matters what a candidate or his/her supporters want; the campaign is about what the pollsters and data analysts, and directors of focus groups and media mavens, say it is. He offers example after example of consultants who quite literally tell their clients not to utter what they, the candidates, might want to say, but what is safe, what polls well, what does not offend.[78]

The result, according to Klein, is that campaigns offer nothing but banalities, clichés, insincere rhetoric, pap, words without meaning. Campaign rhetoric, and perhaps our political rhetoric generally, have become so milquetoast and bland as to be soporific; it could well be that one reason why the level of political interest in America is so low is that everyone is asleep because of the "canned", and "robotic," and "pre-tested" language that they are forced to hear. Of course all of this works to the advantage of campaign consultants because, if no one is paying attention, they can do whatever they want. Although he does not say so, we can infer from Klein's argument that campaigns now, instead of offering bold visions of a future intelligently thought out and well articulated, contribute to the "junk politics" so characteristic of our politics generally, not just campaign politics.[79]

Klein pulls no punches. He deeply regrets, rues, this development in his survey of recent presidential campaigns, candidates, and consultants. We the people are the losers, he says, and the candidates themselves, many of whom perhaps started out with clear visions of the future but were forced by their consultants to substitute a fuzzy watercolor portrait for the finely drawn, detailed etching that they originally had in mind.

Even the casual observer of political campaigns and electoral politics can see the clarity of Klein's analysis. It is even picked up in works of popular culture, for example, when campaigns are depicted in such acclaimed television programs as *The Newsroom*, *The Good Wife*, *House of Cards* (the American version, based on the British original), *Alpha House*, *VEEP*, the British-made *In the Thick of It*," and others.[80] Likewise, in movies dealing with political campaigns, the power of political consultants, not of the candidate, or his family, or his inner circle, or even his financiers, to shape the campaign is there for all to see. Not only is this readily apparent in such movies as Robert Redford's *The Candidate*

(1972), *Primary Colors* (1996), based on Joe Klein's novel of the same name, and more recently *The Ides of March* (2011),[81] but in fact in these three prominent films (and there are others) political consultants, and indeed the Campaign Industry as a whole, are shown in much less than a flattering light.

In the end, although Klein does not put it like this, the message of the book is the same as the one attributed to the French statesman Georges Clemenceau, "War is too important to be left to the Generals."[82] It may well be that our political campaigns are too important to our democracy to be left to the political consultants, and the Campaign Industry. But, given the size and power of the Campaign Industry detailed in this chapter, it is not at all clear that a reversal of its influence on our political campaigns will happen anytime soon. We will return to this matter, in a broader context, in the conclusion of this book.

## Notes

1 Only Delaware (219,000) and Rhode Island (598,000) had smaller populations east of the Mississippi in 1916. Source: www.google.com/ ?gws_rd=ssl#q=population+of+Florida+1916; www.google.com/?gws_rd= ssl#q=population+of+Rhode+Island+1916.

2 See David R. Colburn and Richard K. Scher, *Florida's Gubernatorial Politics in the Twentieth Century* (Gainesville, F.L: University Presses of Florida, 1980), pp. 66 69. See also Wayne Flynt, *Cracker Messiah* (Baton Rouge: Louisiana State University Press, 1977).

3 http://uselectionatlas.org/RESULTS/state.php?year=1916&off=5&elect= 0&fips=12&f=0.

4 The online version can be found at www.campaignsandelections.com;

5 George Gao, "The Up and Down Seasons of Political Work," Pew Research Center, FactTank, News in the Numbers, November 17, 2014, viewed online at www.pewresearch.org/fact-tank/2014/11/17/the-seasonal-nature-of-political-campaign-work, July 21, 2015.

6 Pew, November 17, 2014.

7 Pew, November 17, 2014.

8 For example, Rahm Emanuel left his Chief of Staff post in the White House in early October, 2010 to organize his campaign for Mayor of Chicago; that election was held in February, 2011. See Chris McGeal, "Rahm Emanuel Leaves White House to Run for Chicago Mayor," *guardian*, October 10, 2010, viewed online at www.theguardian.com/world/2010/oct/01/rahm-emanuel-leaves-white-house, July 29, 2015. Emanuel already had a well organized campaign in place and working hard in Chicago before he arrived there to campaign full time.

9 Center for Responsive Politics, OpenSecrets.org, "2012 Presidential Race," viewed online at www.opensecrets.org/pres12/index.php, July 19, 2015.

10 The website for followthemoney.org is www.followthemoney.org/ ?gclid=Cj0KEQjw58ytBRDMg-HVn4LuqasBEiQAhPkhuqjgOmjptbsOI2zd TROUgh7yAAn_CRVvpXiGoBFfN6EaAqBE8P8HAQ.

11 Ashley Portero, "Almost Half a Billion Already Spent on 2012 Elections— And That's Just at the State Level," *International Business Times*, June 19,

2012, viewed online at www.ibtimes.com/almost-half-billion-already-spent-2012-elections-and-thats-just-state-level-703462, July 19, 2015.

12  Tarini Parti, "$7 Billion Spent on 2012 Campaign, FEC Says," Politico.com, January 31, 2013, viewed online at www.politico.com/story/2013/01/7-billion-spent-on-2012-campaign-fec-says-87051.html, July 19, 2015.

13  Adam Lioze and Blair Bowie, "Federal Election Spending 2012," *Demos*, November 9, 2012, viewed online at www.demos.org/publication/election-spending-2012-post-election-analysis-federal-election-commission-data, July 19, 2015.

14  Zach Holden, "Overview of Campaign Finances, 2011–2012 Elections," National Institute on Money in State Politics, followthemoney.org, viewed online at www.followthemoney.org/research/institute-reports/overview-of-campaign-finances-20112012-elections July 19, 2015. See also Lauren Feeney, "Dark Money in State and Local Elections," Moyers and Company, June 15, 2012, viewed online at http://billmoyers.com/2012/06/15/dark-money-in-state-and-local-elections July 19, 2015.

15  "Reelection Rates Over the Years," Center for Responsive Politics, opensecrets.org, viewed online at www.opensecrets.org/bigpicture/reelect.php, July 19, 2015.

16  Center for Responsive Politics, opensecrets.org, "Election 2010 to Shatter Spending Records and Republicans Benefit from Late Cash Surge," October 27, 2010, viewed online at www.opensecrets.org/news/2010/10/election-2010-to-shatter-spending-r, July 19, 2015.

17  Editorial Board, "The Worst Voter Turnout in 72 Years," *New York Times*, November 11, 2014, viewed online at www.nytimes.com/2014/11/12/opinion/the-worst-voter-turnout-in-72-years.html, July 19, 2015.

18  Center for Responsive Politics, opensecrets.org, "Estimated Cost of Election 2014," n.d., viewed online at www.opensecrets.org/overview/cost.php, July 19, 2015.

19  The *Fortune* 500, 2012; viewed online at http://fortune.com/fortune500/2012/sempra-energy-266, July 20, 2015.

20  Tess Hoffman, "New Port Authority Bus Terminal Would Cost $10B," *The Real Deal*, March 17, 2015, viewed online at http://therealdeal.com/blog/2015/03/17/new-port-authority-bus-terminal-would-cost-10b, July 26, 2015.

21  Unni Krishnan and Kartikay Mehrota, "Nepal Says Earthquake Rebuilding Cost to Exceed $10 Billion, *Bloomberg*, April 28, 2015, viewed online at www.bloomberg.com/news/articles/2015-04-28/nepal-rebuilding-cost-to-exceed-10-billion-finance-chief-says, July 20, 2015.

22  Mark Arsenault, "Bid Documents Put Cost of 2024 Games at $10b," *Boston Globe*, February 8, 2015, viewed online at www.bostonglobe.com/metro/2015/02/08/nailing-down-cost-boston-olympics/F1m4doCeOi09U8iTcblC5K/story.html#, July 20, 2015.

23  "2015 Legislature—Operating Budget—Statewide Totals—FY16 Post-CC St Structure" (PDF), Alaska State Legislature, Alaska Division of Legislative Finance, 11 June 2015; "Appropriations and Allocations by Department—2014–2015 Biennium" (PDF), Augusta: Maine State Legislature Office of Fiscal and Program Review, 2014, p. 9; Carlson, Amy (2013), "2013 Session Fiscal Report" (PDF), Helena: Montana Legislative Fiscal Office, p. 43; all viewed July 20, 2015.

24  http://cao.lacity.org/budget15-16/2015-16Budget_Summary.pdf; http://chicityclerk.com/wp-content/uploads/2014/10/2015OV.pdf; www.sfmayor.org/modules/showdocument.aspx?documentid=400; all viewed

July 17, 2015.

25 Patrick Ausick, "Why a Boeing 777 Costs $320 Million," *Usa Today*, March 30, 2014, viewed online at www.usatoday.com/story/money/business/2014/03/30/why-a-boeing-777-costs-320-million-dollars/7063805, July 20, 2015.

26 Airbus, "New Airbus Aircraft Prices for 2015," press release, viewed online at www.airbus.com/presscentre/pressreleases/press-release-detail/detail/new-airbus-aircraft-list-prices-for-2015, July 20, 2015.

27 Baizhen Chua, "Maersk Drilling to Spend Much As $6 Billion on Oil Rigs," *Bloomberg*, March 18, 2012, viewed online at www.bloomberg.com/news/articles/2012-03-18/maersk-drilling-to-spend-much-as-6-billion-on-oil-rigs, July 20, 2015.

28 Chavdar Chanev, "Cruise Ship Cost to Build," *Ship Cruise*, May 4, 2015, viewed online at www.shipcruise.org/how-much-does-a-cruise-ship-cost, July 20, 2015.

29 Landon Thomas, Jr., "Dubai Opens a Tower to Beat All," *New York Times*, January 4, 2010, viewed online at www.nytimes.com/2010/01/05/business/global/05tower.html, July 20, 2015.

30 www.stlouis-mo.gov/government/departments/budget/documents/upload/FY15-AOP-Summary-Overview-and-charts-S-1-to-S-82.pdf.

31 www.ci.minneapolis.mn.us/finance/budget/city-budget_index.

32 www.sanantonio.gov/Budget/BudgetFY2015-Adopted.aspx.

33 www.phoenix.gov/budgetsite/Budget%20Books/Summary%20Budget%20 2014-15.pdf.

34 www.freep.com/story/news/local/detroit-bankruptcy/2015/02/24/detroit-budget/23937559.

35 Brent Cox, "How Much More Money Do Presidential Candidates Raise Today?," *The Awl*, November 6, 2012, viewed online at www.theawl.com/2012/11/presidential-fundraising-adjusted-for-inflation, July 20, 2015.

36 Data are from Center for Responsive Politics, opensecrets.org, "The Money Behind the Elections, 1998–2012," viewed online at www.opensecrets.org/bigpicture/index.php?cycle=2012, July 20, 2015.

37 James Heffernan, "Why Does Hillary Need $2.5 Billion for Her Campaign," Huffingtonpost.com, April 13, 2015, viewed online at www.huffingtonpost.com/james-heffernan/why-does-hillary-need-25-_b_7056586.html, July 20, 2015.

38 Russ Choma, "You Won't Believe How Much Money Jeb Bush's Super-Pac Just Raised," *Mother Jones*, July 9, 2015, viewed online at www.motherjones.com/politics/2015/07/jeb-bush-super-pac-right-to-rise-100-million, July 25, 2015.

39 See Albert R. Hunt, "How Record Spending Will Affect 2016 Election," *Bloomberg*, April 26, 2015; Matea Gold, "Bush Blows Away Rivals with 2016 War Chest," *Washington Post*, February 13, 2015, viewed online at www.washingtonpost.com/politics/jeb-bushs-war-chest-far-outpacing-field-of-gop-contenders/2015/02/13/1fd3c076-b2f1-11e4-886b-c22184f27c35_story.h tml; Nicholas Confessore, "Koch Brothers Budget of $889 Million for 2016 is on Par with Both Parties' Spending, *New York Times*, January 26, 2015, viewed online at www.nytimes.com/2015/01/27/us/politics/kochs-plan-to-spend-900-million-on-2016-campaign.html; all viewed July 20, 2015.

40 We will return to this point in Chapter 6.

41 Tory Newmyer, "This Is What It Costs to Run for President," *Fortune*, March 28, 2015, viewed online at http://fortune.com/2015/03/28/campaign-

financing/, July 20, 2015.

42   The data are adapted from "2012 Presidential Race," Center for Responsive Politics, OpenSecrets.org, viewed online at www.opensecrets.org/pres12 July 20, 2015. The author is indebted to Mr. Jose Castaneda for designing and producing the charts.

43   Jen Christensen, "Obama Outspends Romney on Online Ads," CNN online, June 3, 2012, viewed online at www.cnn.com/2012/06/03/politics/online-campaign-spending, July 21, 2015.

44   "But the Republicans Invented It," *New York*, September 18, 1972, viewed online at https://books.google.com/books?id=vVXQxzwsqHgC&pg=PA50&lpg=PA50&dq=republicans+invent+direct+mail&source=bl&ots=LYZ W6Fm94W&sig=2RSQSevmk3xPYbxkJnF_oNmH6Us&hl=en&sa=X&ved=0CCsQ6AEwAWoVChMI-M_ohevsxgIVxaGACh0VngsF#v=onepage&q=republicans%20invent%20direct%20mail&f=false, July 21, 2015.

45   Pew estimates that 84 percent of households in the United States have a computer, and 73 percent an Internet connection. See Lee Rainie and D'Vera Cohn, "Computer Ownership, Internet Connection Vary Widely Across the U.S.," Pew Research Center, FactTank—News in the Numbers, September 19, 2014, viewed online at www.pewresearch.org/fact-tank/2014/09/19/census-computer-ownership-internet-connection-varies-widely-across-u-s, July 25, 2015.

46   Jim Geraghty, "Obama the Campaign Spender," *National Review*, June 25, 2012, viewed online at www.nationalreview.com/article/303854/obama-campaign-spender-jim-geraghty, July 19, 2015.

47   See, for example, Lydia Saad, "TV is America's Main Source of News," *Gallup*, July 8, 2018, viewed online at www.gallup.com/poll/163412/americans-main-source-news.aspx; American Press Institute, "The Personal News Cycle: How Americans Choose to Get Their News," March 17, 2014, viewed online at www.americanpressinstitute.org/publications/reports/survey-research/personal-news-cycle; Amy Mitchell, Jeffrey Gottfried, Jocelyn Kiley, and Katerina Eva Matsa, "Political Polarization and Media Habits," Pew Research Center, Journalism and Media, October 21, 2014, viewed online at www.journalism.org/2014/10/21/political-polarization-media-habits; all viewed July 21, 2015.

48   This is a theme to which we will return later in the chapter, when we discuss Samuel Popkin's book, *The Candidate* (New York: Oxford, 2013).

49   See for example Nate Silver, "When Internal Polls Mislead, A Whole Campaign May Be to Blame," fivethirtyeight.com, *New York Times*, December 1, 2012, viewed online at http://fivethirtyeight.blogs.nytimes.com/2012/12/01/when-internal-polls-mislead-a-whole-campaign-may-be-to-blame, July 21, 2015.

50   Romney's remarks can be viewed at www.youtube.com/watch?v=M2gvY2wqI7M.

51   As Pippa Norris pointed out more than 10 years ago, the rise in the number, use, and cost of political consultants—of all kinds—is a direct result of the decline of political parties and their ability to design and manage campaigns. See Pippa Norris, "The Evolution of Election Campaigns: Eroding Political Engagement," Harvard University, John F. Kennedy School of Government," January 17, 2004, viewed online at www.hks.harvard.edu/fs/pnorris/Acrobat/Otago%20The%20Evolution%20of%20Election%20Campaigns.pdf, July 1, 2015.

52   We will examine these decisions in Chapter 6.

53 See Robert McGuire, "Consultants are Cashing In On Campaigns' New Dark Economics," *The Daily Beast*, February 22, 2014, viewed online at www.thedailybeast.com/articles/2014/02/22/consultants-are-cashing-in-on-campaigns-dark-new-economics.html, July 19, 2015.

54 2012 Presidential Campaign Finance Explorer, *Washington Post*, December 7, 2012.

55 Googling "political communications firms" reveals scores of agencies vying for the lucrative contracts that big campaigns can provide. Reputation, word of mouth, recommendations from other campaigns, and advertisements by the firms themselves are all part of the mix as the campaign chooses which firms will do the media. Architects of major campaigns spend a great deal of time sifting through the array of available talent to choose the right agency; prior experience (pro or con) and recommendations of other campaigns carry a lot of weight in making the final choice(s).

56 See, for example, U.S. Census, 2012 Statistical Abstract, "Elections: Voting Age Population and Voter Participation," viewed online at www.census.gov/compendia/statab/cats/elections/voting-age_population_and_voter_participation.html; Paul Taylor and Mark Hugo Lopez, "Six Take-Aways from the Census Bureau's Voting Report," Pew Research Center FactTank, News in the Numbers, May 8, 2013, viewed online at www.pewresearch.org/fact-tank/2013/05/08/six-take-aways-from-the-census-bureaus-voting-report; "Voter Turnout Rates by Age Cohort," viewed online at www.google.com/search?q=voter+turnout+rates+by+age+cohort&biw=1466&bih=882&tbm=isch&tbo=u&source=univ&sa=X&ved=0CDgQsAR-qFQoTCMq4x5u478YCFULQgAod-osBXw; "Voter Turnout Statistics by Age Group," viewed online at www.google.com/search?q=voter+turnout+statistics+by+age+group&sa=X&biw=1466&bih=882&tbm=isch&tbo=u&source=univ&ved=0CDMQsARqFQoTCN36vdu578YCFceSDQod7a4Jaw; all viewed July 22, 2015.

57 See Wayne Slater's interview with Karl Rove, PBS Frontline, April 12, 2005, viewed online at www.pbs.org/wgbh/pages/frontline/shows/architect/interviews/slater.html; Jeanne Cummings, "Rove's Patented Strategies Will Endure," Politico.com, August 13, 2007, viewed online at www.politico.com/news/stories/0807/5375.html; and Craig Unger, "Boss Rove," *Vanity Fair*, September, 2012, viewed online at www.vanityfair.com/news/politics/2012/09/karl-rove-gop-craig-unger, all viewed July 26, 2015.

58 See, for example, Nate Silver, "Which Polls Fared Best (and Worst) in the 2012 Presidential Race," *New York Times*, November 10, 2012, viewed online at http://fivethirtyeight.blogs.nytimes.com/2012/11/10/which-polls-fared-best-and-worst-in-the-2012-presidential-race/?_r=0, July 22, 2015.

59 E. E. Schattschneider, *The Semisovereign People*, revised edn. (New York: Wadsworth, 1975).

60 In March, 2012, while the Republican primary season was still in high gear, the Romney campaign had a full-time staff of 93, at an average salary of $62,947. See "The Cost of Mitt Romney's Nomination: By the Numbers," *The Week*, April 26, 2012, viewed online at http://theweek.com/articles/476099/cost-mitt-romneys-nomination-by-numbers, July 15, 2012.

61 This is but one version of an oft-heard maxim. Its origin is in doubt, but it first seems to have appeared in print in England early in the nineteenth century. See www.phrases.org.uk/meanings/a-man-who-is-his-own-lawyer-has-a-fool-for-a-client.html, viewed July 22, 2015.

62 David Axelrod left his advisory position in the White House in 2011, to return

to Chicago and begin the process of assembling Mr. Obama's presidential re-election campaign. David Plouffe returned to his position as Obama's campaign manager in 2011. See "David Axelrod Leaving White House in 2011: Will Work on Obama's Re-election Campaign," Huffingtonpost.com, May 25, 2011, viewed online at www.huffingtonpost.com/2010/09/23/david-axelrod-leaving-whi_n_737080.html; Michael Scherer, "Obamaworld 2012," *Time*, May 26, 2011, viewed online at http://content.time.com/time/politics/article/0,8599,2074069,00.html; and "David Plouffe Discusses President Obama's 2012 Reelection Strategy," DailyKos.com, viewed online at www.dailykos.com/story/2011/07/07/992186/-David-Plouffe-Discusses-President-Obama-s-2012-Reelection-Strategy#; all viewed July 23, 2015.

63  Dara Kam and Jason Lieser, "Mrs. Obama Says UF Crowd Her Largest Yet in 2012 Campaign," *Palm Beach Post*, September 17, 2012, viewed online at www.palmbeachpost.com/news/news/state-regional-govt-politics/football-a-theme-as-uf-crowd-readies-for-first-lad/nSDDr; Wade Millward, "Michelle Obama Visits UF," *Florida Magazine*, September 19, 2012, viewed online at http://magazine.ufl.edu/2012/09/michelle-obama-visits-uf; both viewed July 22, 2015.

64  See Lucy Madison, "Can Michelle Obama Help Her Husband Win," *Cbs News*, July 24, 2012, viewed online at www.cbsnews.com/news/can-michelle-obama-help-her-husband-win, July 22, 2015.

65  The notion of "office politics" has been written about so often that it scarcely requires citations. For those not familiar with the idea, two readily accessible and helpful sources are Cheryl Connor, "Office Politics: Must You Play?" *Forbes*, April 14, 2013, viewed online at www.forbes.com/sites/cherylsnapp-conner/2013/04/14/office-politics-must-you-play-a-handbook-for-survivalsucc ess;and Liz Ryan, "How to Win at Office Politics," *Forbes*, January 29, 2015, viewed online at www.forbes.com/sites/lizryan/2015/01/29/how-to-win-at-office-politics, both viewed July 23, 2015. For a slightly different, and both more academic but also more jocular view of how office politics develop, readers might wish to examine the writings of the British organizational theorist C. Northcote Parkinson, especially *Parkinson's Law* (Boston, MA: Houghton Mifflin, 1957).

66  On this very crucial matter, see Jeffrey Lewis, "The Public Opinion Poll as Cultural Form," *Journal Of Cultural Studies*, August, 1999, pp. 199–221.

67  See, for example, Jordan Michael Smith, "What It Takes to Win the White House," *Coolumbia Journalism Review*, May 14, 2012, viewed online at www.cjr.org/critical_eye/what_it_takes_to_win_the_white_house.php; and Nicholas Confessore, "Game Plans: 'The Candidate' by Samuel L. Popkin," *New York Times*, July 27, 2012, viewed online at www.nytimes.com/2012/07/29/books/review/the-candidate-by-samuel-l-popkin.html,    both viewed July 20, 2015.

68  Fritz Plasser, "American Political Campaign Techniques Worldwide," *Harvard International Journal Of Press/Politics*, Vol. 5, No. 4, Fall, 2000, pp. 33–54. The author is indebted to Jose Castaneda for locating this source.

69  Walter Shapiro, "Mad Men," *Democracy*, No. 10, Fall 2008, viewed online at www.democracyjournal.org/10/6650.php, July 24, 2015.

70  See Kenneth P. Vogel and Ben Smith, "President Obama Campaign Consultants Make Mark Overseas," Politico.com, November 18, 2009, viewed online at www.politico.com/news/stories/1109/29410.html, August 4, 2015; Shira Toeplitz, "Consulting in Conflict Zones," *Campaigns and Elections*, February 28, 2010, viewed online at www.campaignsand-

elections.com/magazine/2044/consulting-in-conflict-zones, July 19, 2015; Helene Barthelemy, "Grooming the Globe: Exporting Political Consultancy," *Columbia Political Review*, March 17, 2012, viewed online at http://cpreview.org/2012/03/grooming-the-globe, July 25, 2015; Tyler Harber, "Egypt's Presidential Vote Offers US Consultants Hope," *Campaigns and Elections*, May 25, 2012, viewed online at www.campaignsandelections.com/campaign-insider/619/egypt-s-presidential-vote-offers-u-s-consultants-hope, August 4, 2015; Jean MacKenzie, "US Political Consultants Mucking Things Up Abroad," *Global Post*, February 3, 2013, viewed online at www.globalpost.com/dispatch/news/regions/americas/united-states/130130/foreign-policy-arthur-finkelstein-stanley-greenberg-political-consulting, August; "Political Consultants: Spinning a Win," *The Economist*, March 21, 2015, viewed online at www.economist.com/news/international/21646779-growing-cross-border-trade-campaign-advice-spinning-win, July 24, 2015; and Alexandra Jaffe, "Obama Advisers Coming Up Short in Campaigns Abroad," CNN Politics, May 13, 2015, viewed online at www.cnn.com/2015/05/09/politics/obama-advisers-uk-elections-messina-axelrod, August 4, 2015.

71   The organization's website can be viewed at www.iapc.org.

72   See, for example, Daniella Cheslow, "In Israeli Elections, American Political Consultants Become an Issue," *Mcclatchy Dc*, Middle East, February 17, 2015, viewed online at www.mcclatchydc.com/news/nation-world/world/middle-east/article24780181.html, July 22, 2015.

73   See Plasser (2000).

74   Cheslow (2015).

75   We will look at this matter in Chapter 7.

76   See for example Valerie J. Bunce and Sharon L. Wolchik, *Defeating Authoritarian Leaders in Postcommunist Countries* (New York: Cambridge University Press, 2011).

77   Joe Klein, *Politics Lost* (New York: Doubleday, 2006).

78   Readers may wish to consult the helpful review by Jennifer Senior, "Pollster-Consultant Industrial Complex," *New York Times*, April 30, 2006, viewed online at www.nytimes.com/2006/04/30/books/review/30senior.html?_r=0, July 14, 2015.

79   Benjamin DeMott, *Junk Politics* (New York: Nation Books, 2004).

80   The websites of these programs are, respectively, *The Newsroom*, www.hbo.com/the-newsroom; *The Good Wife*, www.imdb.com/title/tt1442462; *House of Cards*, www.imdb.com/title/tt1856010; *Alpha House*, www.imdb.com/title/tt3012160/; *VEEP*, www.hbo.com/veep; *In the Thick of It*, www.imdb.com/title/tt0459159.

81   Websites for the films are: *The Candidate*, 1972, www.imdb.com/title/tt0068334; *Primary Colors*, 1998, www.imdb.com/title/tt0119942; and *The Ides of March*, 2011, www.imdb.com/title/tt1124035.

82   There are many iterations of this quote, and not everyone agrees that it was Clemenceau who stated it. See "Askville by Amazon," viewed online at http://askville.amazon.com/'war-important-left-generals'/AnswerViewer.do?requestId=3893805, July 25, 2015.

# 5   Political Campaigns and the Media

No one really knows when political journalism, that is, media coverage of politics and political campaigns, actually began. But its origins, if obscure, are worth a little speculation. Possibly, for example, it was in ancient Mesopotamia, when a town chronicler approached local officials, perhaps with clay tablets and cuneiform stick in hand, and began asking pointed questions about strange doings down at the slave market or some other public venue where corruption was rampant.

We know that the ancient Romans relished politics. At one time or another during its long history, the Empire even employed "town criers," who would walk neighborhoods proclaiming the news, or at least what leaders wanted people to know about. While there were no newspapers, sometimes signs were posted in various prominent places, announcing what we would now call the news of the day.

We also know that Americans have long had an uneasy relationship with the media, newspapers in particular. Thomas Jefferson, a staunch defender of freedom of the press, was very suspicious of newspapers.[1] Finley Peter Dunne, the celebrated American satirist of the late nineteenth and early twentieth centuries, made an oft-quoted remark about newspapers—their task is to "comfort the afflicted, and afflict the comfortable"[2]—that is usually taken out of context. But if one looks at the original text, Dunne himself had serious doubts about the role that newspapers played in American society:

> Th' newspaper does ivrything f'r us. It runs th' polis foorce an' th' banks, commands th' milishy, controls th'ligislachure, baptizes th' young, marries th' foolish, comforts th' afflicted, afflicts th' comfortable, buries th' dead an' roasts thim aftherward.[3]

But the media, especially the mainstream print and electronic media, have no doubts whatsoever about the valuable role they play in preserving and strengthening American democracy and protecting Americans from the excesses of politicians, and even, sometimes, from themselves.[4]

Our purpose in this chapter is not to examine how well the media plays their assumed role of Protector of Democracy. Nor is it to take the same path that many "media and politics" or "media and campaigns" discussions do, for example, investigating the relationship between media and readership/viewership that emphasizes different demographic groups, or why viewership/readership of "mainstream" media is declining.[5]

Our task, rather, is to ask several key questions that focus exactly on the relationship between media and campaigns:

- How do the media, reporters in particular, cover campaigns? What pressures and forces shape what and how they present campaigns?
- What is the impact of the ever-increasing distance/gulf/chasm between campaigns and the media?
- How do the new digital media impact coverage of campaigns, indeed, influence campaigns themselves?
- How does the close tie between corporate mainstream media and Big Money affect campaign coverage?
- How does the ability of campaigns to segment voters into ever-smaller slices influence how campaigns are covered?

## Political Campaigns and the Media

Newspapers, as we saw in Chapter 2, have played an important role in American elections since real contests began in 1800. As the Jacksonian era dawned, and political organizations that we now recognize as political parties were created, a close linkage between parties and the media was forged. For much of the nineteenth century, political parties and their surrogates and minions ran campaigns. Presidential candidates, in particular, did little campaigning except to mouth the occasional homily or cliché in the event that a newspaper reporter managed to ask a question; as late as 1896 William McKinley happily sat on his front porch in Ohio, while Mark Hanna ran the campaign for him.

But office seekers at all levels were aided in their task by newspapers. Until well after World War I, at least, mainstream newspapers were openly and proudly partisan. In their coverage of campaigns they wore their political views and preferences loudly on the news pages. Indeed newspapers worked hand in glove with political parties to elect their favored candidates. Even a brief perusal of archives reveals how openly partisan newspaper coverage of presidential, and presumably other, campaigns was.[6]

But it didn't stop there. Newspapers saw themselves as players in the presidential (and other candidates') nominating processes, as party leaders gathered in the "smoke-filled rooms" at conventions and elsewhere to try to assemble winning campaign tickets. Just as William Randolph Hearst and Joseph Pulitzer used their newspapers to shape American foreign policy that culminated in the Spanish–American War (1898), so had newspapers long been in the business of creating and promoting political candidates; it is no exaggeration to say that Andrew Jackson himself, Abraham Lincoln, Ulysses S. Grant, Grover Cleveland and especially William Henry Harrison were in some measure media-created presidential candidates.

Following World War I, seismic changes came to shape how political campaigns were conducted, and these developments hugely affected the relationship between the media and those campaigns. Those changes resulted from a transformation of what "journalism" was supposed to be and from technological changes impacting the nature and conduct of campaigns.

## Objective Journalism

While the idea of "objective" journalism had been discussed during the nineteenth century, its practice did not develop until well into the twentieth. Perhaps it was a reaction to the excesses of yellow journalism, a newspaper and magazine style common in the mid- to late nineteenth century that was characterized by sensationalism, excitement, emphasis on trivialities, and, in politics, overt partisanship with little or no regard for even-handedness or fairness in reporting. Perhaps it was part of the general disillusionment with politics and statecraft that so profoundly permeated Europe and the United States following the Great War. One of the major outcomes of that calamity was to shatter the belief that politics mattered and indeed could be a force for good; the idea increasingly looked like a sham, as evidenced by the catastrophic results of politicians' folly that brought about the carnage.

Journalists, in examining their own role in the war, began to see that being embedded with politicians made them potentially culpable as warmongers; the only real solution was to put distance between themselves and those whose decisions created the world-wide disaster. Perhaps also the change in what journalism was supposed to be grew out of a growing movement in the twentieth century that "rationality," "science," "method," "efficiency," and "objectivity", not politics, were keys to a better future. The work of Frederick Taylor on scientific management in the early 1900s, and re-kindled after World War I, is an example. The idea of rational ordering of all human activity was so powerful and pervasive that it spread to virtually all social endeavors; it even included extensive writings aimed at women, so that they could bring "scientific management" to home making, cooking, and child care.[7]

Whatever its roots, "objective" journalism was the antithesis of yellow journalism. While it was never completely clear what the term meant, it deeply affected how reporters covered campaigns.

## Objective Journalism

In the late 1990s the Pew Research Center's Project for Excellence in Journalism attempted to codify what constituted objective journalism and its practices over previous decades. Its nine-point manifesto included the following:

1. Journalism's First Obligation is to the Truth; 2. Its First Loyalty is to Citizens; 3. Its Essence is a Discipline of Verification; 4. Its Practitioners Must Maintain an Independence From Those They Cover; 5. It Must Serve as an Independent Monitor of Power; 6. It Must Provide a Forum for Public Criticism and Compromise; 7. It Must Strive to Make the Significant Interesting and Relevant; 8. It Must Keep the News Comprehensive and Proportional; 9. Its Practitioners Must Be Allowed to Exercise Their Personal Conscience.[8]

For example, no longer could journalists work hand-in-glove with candidates, politicians, or political parties, or be embedded in their campaigns. Far from being shills for partisan causes, ideological views, or individual candidates/politicians, journalists were expected to stand outside the fray of politics and "report," as directly and objectively as possible, what campaigns were about and what candidates were up to. Their role was similar to that of the scientist in the laboratory, whose feelings and views were supposedly irrelevant to the experiment being conducted; the journalist, whose first responsibilities were to the truth and to the public, was expected to avoid making judgments, in print at least, about what he saw.

There were a number of major consequences for campaign reporting that the rise of "objective" journalism caused, and we will discuss some of them later in the chapter. For the moment, however, we must mention the most important: not only was the journalist no longer a part of the campaign apparatus, but his very access to the campaign itself became much more limited and problematic. Objectivity prevented him from being intimately involved in the campaign; but, more importantly, from the campaign's perspective, why would it allow journalists free and ready access to the campaign, its candidate(s), and its operatives, if the journalists were not going to print what they were told, but instead insisted on ferreting out their own version of "the story?" Clearly it was in the interest of the campaign to provide access to journalists only under carefully structured, orchestrated conditions. In other words, it became the job of the campaign to protect itself from nosy, inquisitive journalists who were trying to find out what was "news," even as the campaign sought to "feed" journalists carefully selected pieces of information about the campaign that they could use in their stories.

The rise of objective journalism, then, exacerbated what had been apparent for decades: the interests of the journalist and the campaign were diametrically opposed. Each needed the other, of course: journalists need a story, and the campaign needs to get its "news" into print or on the air (and, nowadays, into the blogosphere). But the demands of objective journalism, and the protective shell that campaigns created around them to keep out prying eyes and ears, worked in opposite directions. The result of course was a tension, even hostility, that arose between the media and campaigns and which continues to manifest itself today.

The other seismic development following World War I that impacted both political campaigns and their relationship to the media arose from massive technological changes: airplanes and electronics.

## Airplanes

Airplanes, especially jet planes, revolutionized political campaigns and how journalists covered them. It was not so much that they allowed presidential, and U.S. Senate and Gubernatorial, candidates to cover tremendous amounts of territory on any given campaign day, although that was important. More so was the strain in the relationship between candidates and the media that the airplanes exacerbated.

In the old days, when trains were used during campaigns to move the candidate from here to there, journalists could tag along, usually at minimal expense. In the main, there was plenty of room on the train for reporters. Sometimes favored journalists would be invited to join the candidate, or one of the key operatives, in the train's private car, but even for those not so favored access to the candidate was fairly simple.

Not, however, when candidates started flying. For the most part, there was not enough room on the candidate's plane for journalists, given the size of presidential or senatorial campaign retinues; as a result the campaign could totally control who got a seat. Thus the campaign could force journalists to charter their own plane(s) as the price of allowing media coverage. This of course suddenly raised the expense of covering a campaign substantially, since the media (not the campaign) would have to pay. For electronic journalists this cost was non-trivial, because not only the reporter but cameramen and a lot of heavy equipment would have to be accommodated. Even for print journalists, who could travel with less baggage, the cost was substantial. Prestigious national publications like the *New York Times* and the *Washington Post* would of course be expected to bear the cost as part of their reportorial obligations; but was it worth it for regional and essentially state-wide or local publications to buy a seat on the press plane, during a long period of declining revenues and reduced readership?

## Campaigning by Airplane

Politicians, candidates and otherwise, developed an affinity for airplanes very early on. The first American President to ride in an airplane was Theodore Roosevelt, in 1910. In 1932, Franklin D. Roosevelt made history during his political campaign by taking an astonishing step. He flew to the Democratic National Convention in Chicago to accept the presidential nomination; that practice continues to this day. But the first presidential candidate to use airplanes extensively for campaigning was John F. Kennedy; indeed, his father Joseph P. Kennedy bought a Convair CV-240 jetliner in 1959 expressly for the 1960 campaign. Kennedy was the first presidential candidate to use jets exclusively for campaign purposes. But in a historical oddity, the first politician known to have campaigned extensively by air was not an American candidate, but Adolph Hitler, in Germany, in 1932.[9]

Besides the financial burden facing journalists covering the campaign by air, the planes created an even more serious problem for journalists: they limited access to the candidate. Again, sometimes favored journalists might be invited onto the candidate's plane, for exclusive interviews during one of the plane's hops between campaign stops. The others would have to wait until the planes landed, when they were taken to the campaign venue and perhaps had a chance to ask a question or interview a few attendees. Or, perhaps not. Again, the campaign powerfully controlled access, with consequences that Timothy Crouse documented, and which we will discuss shortly.

## The Newsroom

The hit television series *The Newsroom* highlighted the way in which campaigns limit journalists' access to candidates even when they travel by bus. In the show's 2013 second season, Episodes 2–4, a fictionalized portrayal of the Romney campaign bus in New Hampshire dramatically showed how the campaign used access to a seat on the bus—and therefore access to the candidate and senior campaign operatives—to manipulate and try to control journalists and the stories they would tell, especially those viewed as hostile or uncooperative. See *The Newsroom*" Season 2, 2013, produced by HBO. The official website of *The Newsroom* is at www.hbo.com/the-newsroom#.

## Electronic Technology

Early electronic technological changes had been important for political and campaign journalism. The telegraph, for example, allowed reporters to file stories from afar and to report distant campaign events. To be sure, the reporter had to find a telegraph office to file his story. And the technology of the telegraph was slow, awkward, and prone to mistakes. Still, it was a big leap forward over previous reporting capabilities, in which stories had to be written in the newsroom, not in the field. An even bigger leap forward came with the advent of the telephone, through which the reporter could call in stories directly to the newsroom, consult with editors, and so forth. Telephones were rare commodities in small town and rural areas until well into the 1930s, but there was no doubt that they provided the reporter with more opportunity to file more and better stories if he could find a phone, even if it was a laborious process to get a long-distance connection back to New York, Washington, D.C., Chicago, or San Francisco.

## Radio

But the importance of these technologies is tiny when compared to radio, television, and the Internet. Radio of course came first, and it came on like gangbusters. Between 1923 and 1930, 60 percent of all American families purchased a radio. By 1922 there were already 600 radio stations in the United States.[10] In 1921, 75,000 radios were sold in the United States; in 1930, 13.5 million. During the Depression, radio advertising dollars doubled, while newspaper advertising revenues fell by half.[11]

None of this was lost on political campaigns. It was clear from the early 1920s that, by using radio, candidates could communicate with thousands of potential voters—indeed, in cities and metropolitan areas, scores of thousands—at the flick of a switch. Compared to radio, newspapers and magazines were slow, impersonal, and required the involvement of journalists and editors who could obscure or misrepresent or delay what the campaign/candidate wanted to convey. Radio was the opposite: it was immediate, emotional, "hot," and direct. The candidate or his surrogate could speak personally and directly to voters; no journalist was needed to get the message "out." Indeed, the first presidential candidate to campaign over the radio was Calvin Coolidge in 1924; campaigns never looked back, but instead readily embraced every advance in electronic wizardry ever since, including television and the Internet.

Campaigns of course did not abandon newspapers or print journalists. They were still needed to reach the most likely voters (newspaper readers even today are likely voters; and a large percentage of voters continue to read newspapers). They also are needed to reach important opinion leaders; national and large-state campaigns still worry about what the *Washington Post, Wall Street Journal, New York Times,* and similar prestigious print outlets write about them.

And yet it was also obvious to political campaigns, after 1924, that they did not have to rely solely on either print or electronic journalists to reach voters. It is not completely clear when the first truly "political" advertisements aired on radio. But radio programs about politics and campaigns began in June, 1924, when Nelson Poynter broadcast live from the Republican Convention in Cleveland.[12] Shortly thereafter, radio stations began to include political (and presumably campaign) programs among their offerings. These broadcasts could be targeted (it was clear very early on that different radio stations appealed to different demographic groups), the content could be simple and direct, and the "bang for the buck" seemed better than for print outlets; marginally literate voters might not read the papers, but they did listen to the radio.

## Television

But even the potential of radio for campaigns and candidates paled compared to what television offered. First introduced to the public by David Sarnoff at the New York World's Fair in 1939, it was quickly apparent that television did not just offer voters the candidate's voice, but the actual face, even a view of the whole person.

World War II prevented rapid expansion of television but, once hostilities ended, TV exploded. In October, 1950, there were 8 million TV sets in the United States, and 107 stations, most of them in urban areas.[13] By 1960 there were 45,750,000 TV sets in America, with more than 87 percent of homes owning one; in 1978 the numbers jumped to 72,900,000 and 98 percent, respectively.[14]

---

### Television at Conventions and Presidential Inaugurations

In 1940 NBC's experimental television station W2XBS broadcast film from the Republican National Convention in Philadelphia. Harry Truman's 1949 inaugural address was the first to be televised live; John Kennedy's in 1961was the first televised in color.[15]

---

But the sheer number of TV sets is only part of the story of campaigns and television. In the early days, TV cameras were bulky, heavy, unwieldy, immobile. By the mid-1950s they were still awkward to place and use, but some portability was possible. As size reduction of TV cameras continued apace (largely through the replacement of electronic vacuum tubes by transistors), by the mid-1960s their use in the field, if only for limited purposes, was no longer unusual. Later, of course, it became possible to carry TV cameras out of the studio and set them up to broadcast events live (especially after satellites were available commercially in the mid-1960s) or record them for future broadcast.

Enhancing the flexibility of television to broadcast events live was the advent, during the 1950s, of high-speed film-developing techniques and especially video tape, which did not need developing at all; it could be fed directly into a TV broadcast, even from remote locations, via coaxial cable. First used in the late 1940s,[16] coaxial cable was in widespread use by the 1950s and 1960s, and its availability proved highly influential in public perception of unfolding events; for example, during the March, 1965, Voting Rights Campaign in Selma, Alabama, led by Dr. Martin Luther King, Jr. (not all political campaigns are about elective office!), footage captured on film and tape of the mass beatings of demonstrators and seen on national television the same day prompted President Johnson to address the nation on the calamity and propose the Voting Rights Act.[17]

The significance of television and its technological developments for campaigns was prodigious. The idea of reaching voters in "real time," as campaign events unfolded, was within grasp. Once the first commercial satellites were available to receive and re-transmit signals from the field, anything seemed possible. Campaign coverage that showed up on voters' TV sets was fully universalized; anything and everything about the campaign could be broadcast for the immediate consumption of viewers/voters.

---

### More Than Just a Pretty or Handsome Face?

Once candidates could be seen on TV, the "telegenic" quality of a candidate moved to the front burner as a criterion for electability. Candidates from then on would have to "look good" on TV and understand how to speak and act on this new, very "cool" medium, which conveyed a very different impression of the individual than did radio.

---

And, once again, as with radio, campaign coverage by TV was not dependent on the presence or interference of electronic journalists. Campaigns could actually create (stage?) events that could be broadcast directly to voters if the campaign were willing to buy the TV time. Expensive, yes; but highly effective. Not only did campaign commercials become highly sophisticated and targeted,[18] but such made-for-TV events as "debates" became popular campaign devices for reaching voters.

## Campaign Debates—Made-for-TV Gimmickry

The first "modern" debates took place in 1960, between Vice President Richard Nixon and Senator John F. Kennedy. But these were essentially donations of time and place by TV networks. Later, especially during presidential primary season, the candidates themselves created and paid for "debates." Perhaps the most famous was in 1980, when Ronald Reagan, in a moment of frustration, reminded his rivals that "I am paying for this microphone, Mr. Green." During the 2012 primary period, paid-for campaign "debates" reached epic proportions among Republicans, who staged some 26 between 2011 and early 2012.[19] As of mid-summer 2015, there were 17 announced or soon-to-announce GOP candidates, and party leaders began to worry about how to fit all of them into debates already being planned.[20]

There were other made-up campaign events that also suited broadcasts by TV: examples include "photo-ops," in which candidates could be shown in real time acting presidential, or senatorial, or gubernatorial, or mayoral, and the images conveyed directly to viewers. Photo-ops allowed the campaign to carefully limit the type of participation allowed by the media; for example, questions to candidates or campaign operatives by journalists might not be permitted before, during, or after the photo-op. Other common made-for-TV events were interviews with selected (presumably friendly) journalists, the latter being especially useful for local television, since the positive electoral impact of a sitting but campaigning President, or other prominent candidate, in a key local media market could be substantial, because local media were often shut out of national coverage.

And both commercials and staged events were under the full control of the campaign. Journalists may or may not have been invited to whatever the campaign occasion or event happened to be, but it was always very clear who was running it, just as it was very clear that practicing journalists or their editors had no role in creating TV ads, except to the extent that a campaign might wish to hire a journalist to "consult" on what the ads should be like.

Whatever leverage radio gave candidates over journalists, whether print or electronic, television expanded exponentially. Indeed, while volumes and volumes have been written about the impact of television on campaigns, it is perhaps possible to summarize much of it in two ways.

First, television (more so than radio) provided an immediate, tight connection between candidate/campaign and voters. While that connection could not reach the levels of live, face-to-face, in-the-living-room closeness, as TV pictures became sharper, as color became more life-like and realistic, and especially as HD television sets were developed, that connection became closer and more intimate. Consider the voter sitting at home, watching and listening to a candidate on his/her 50-inch HD television, in which a larger-than-life, finely detailed picture of the candidate leaped from the screen: was that not a more immediate and powerful connection than standing 100 rows back at a political rally, sitting in the rafters in a town auditorium, trying just to see the candidate, or—and this was the crucial power of television—reading about the candidate's appearance and speech in the paper the next morning?

Second, television (again, more so than radio) allowed the campaign to control media coverage. Accepting E.E. Schattschneider's oft-referenced discussion of the importance of controlling the rules and scope of political conflict in determining its outcome,[21] candidates and campaigns quickly saw, assuredly by the 1960s, that they held better cards than electronic journalists and their stations in determining what would be broadcast. If the campaign were well organized, and recognized that electronic journalists, needing footage to broadcast nightly, were heavily dependent on them for information and access, then the power of the campaign to determine what viewers saw on their sets during the morning and evening "news" broadcasts was extraordinary.

### The Professor Becomes a Reporter

The author once had the opportunity to attend both the Democratic and Republican conventions as a working journalist. His credentials were supplied by the Florida News Network, in exchange for which twice a day he did on-the-scene "standup" reports for local television stations. At first, other broadcast journalists who used the same TV pool cameras and who were, in the main, from smaller, regional TV markets, were distant and somewhat suspicious: Who was this guy and why was he taking up time on the pool cameras? But, when they learned he was an academician knowledgeable about the dynamics of political conventions, he rapidly became a resource for them: What meetings and caucuses should they attend to get the "story?" What speeches should be covered and which could be ignored? Whom should they interview for their stories? The author found that many of the local and regional journalists, while professionally able and anxious to do their best, were not well prepared for their assignments, had not been briefed on what to look for and seek out, and were very appreciative of any direction and advice that this outsider-professor could offer. In exchange, many offered him tips on how to be more effective on camera.

And print media? Their journalists were really in no stronger a position than their electronic colleagues. Print journalists may have had the luxury of a little more time than their radio and TV colleagues, but not much. In any case, as Timothy Crouse points out, by the 1970s, campaigns were sufficiently well organized that they could control print media access to information just as they could electronic media access. True, there was the occasional aggressive, capable investigative journalist, such as Seymour Hersh and Tom Fiedler, among others, who could discover and write something damaging. And the campaign itself, or the candidate, could do or say something sufficiently bone-headed that it derailed the whole enterprise: George Romney's famous remark in 1968 that he had been brainwashed by the North Vietnamese, or Ed Muskie's breakdown in front of TV cameras in 1972, which caused his campaign to crash and burn, or John McCain's 2008 ignorance of how many houses he owned, or Mitt Romney's disparaging remark in 2012 about the derelict 47 percent who didn't pay income taxes, are all examples of this happening.[22] Campaign moments such as these are, for the media, like blood in the water for sharks, and the feeding frenzy that they create is damaging to the campaign.

But these kinds of things notwithstanding, technological advances provided campaigns with powerful leverages to use against the media and gave them ample, if not total, control over the campaign "news" that was conveyed to viewers and readers.

## The Internet

The last electronic development that we will discuss that impacted how political campaigns are conducted, and that influenced their relationship to the media, is the Internet, and digital communications more generally. Indeed, so much has already been said and written about this topic that our discussion can be brief.[23]

Although digital political campaigns were used in local races as early as the late 1990s, the first national one is generally considered to have been Dr. Howard Dean's in 2004, run by Matt Taibbi.[24] From there, digital campaigns exploded and were used extensively and well by any number of successful candidates, most especially Barack Obama in 2008 and 2012. It is no exaggeration to say that the sophistication of Obama's digital campaigns overcame the power of Hillary Clinton, to wrest the 2008 Democratic nomination from her grasp, and overwhelmed the traditional, stodgy, analog presidential campaign of Republican John McCain in the November, 2008, General Election. Even 4 years later, the GOP presidential campaign, headed by Mitt Romney, could not keep up with the Obama digital onslaught and, while there were any number of reasons for Mr. Romney's defeat, one of the most prominent is thought to have been its failure to engage digital resources more thoroughly and effectively.[25]

Indeed, it is no exaggeration to say that all political campaigns, even small local ones, will now be heavily digital. The Internet and the panoply of available digital communications have completely transformed how campaigns will be designed and conducted, at all levels.

We need not spend time on how the Obama and other effective digital campaigns used electronic communications in the form of social media, e-mail networks, Twitter, Tumblr, instant messaging, and the like to identify voters, raise money, organize events, and mobilize get-out-the-vote campaigns. These have all been thoroughly documented.[26]

---

### Does Social Media Really Help Political Campaigns?

Much has been written about the alleged effectiveness of social media for mobilizing voters (indeed, a good deal was written about its effectiveness in mobilizing street demonstrations in the so-called "Arab Spring" of 2010–2011[27]). But much of the writing, while interesting, is heavily anecdotal and assertive.

In *Presidential Campaigning and Social Media*, edited by political scientists John Allen Hendricks and Dan Schill, empirical data and rigorous analysis are brought to bear on just what social media accomplished, and did not accomplish, in the 2012 presidential election. Some 35 contributors in 17 chapters actually paint a mixed picture of results, most of which are not surprising. For example, even young people obtained most of their information about the campaign on television (still the most important source for political/campaign news) or from the Internet. And there was little evidence that social media, by itself, mobilized people to vote. Another chapter argues that young people, particularly, who rely primarily on social media for political information are actually less knowledgeable about politics than those who use a variety of sources.

Most of this has been well known for some time, demonstrated by other studies. In addition, the "mythology" of the power of social media has, according to this volume, been too much overstated.

Nonetheless nothing in the book suggests that social media is anything less than a force to be reckoned with in future political campaigns, that candidates and their campaign consultants do believe it can work and advance the campaign (which in a sense makes it important), and that future campaigns will not use social media in ever greater quantities, not less.[28]

Instead, we can point to the major consequences of digital campaigns, including how they have transformed campaigns' relationship to other forms of media. Three, in particular, are worth mentioning.

The first is that, to a degree that even television cannot reach, digital campaigns personalize the relationship between candidates and voters. As realistic and effective as is the image of that candidate leaping from a 50-inch HD TV screen in a voter's living room, the candidate must still address voters *en masse*. Viewers may *think* the candidate is talking directly to them, and effective TV campaigners (one thinks of Ronald Reagan and Bill Clinton in this regard) can assuredly convey the impression that they are *directly* addressing individual voters, but, in fact, they are not. They may be sincere, they may be appealing, they may be convincing. But they cannot speak personally to individuals.

But digital campaigns can and do. An email message, an instant message, a text message, a tweet, a Facebook message will be aimed at very specific individuals, complete with name ("Richard: I need you to ....."). How much more personal can the campaign get? True, old-fashioned snail mail can be personalized, but it lacks the immediacy and intimacy—the *urgency* and *pop*—of an electronic message that suddenly appears on a smart phone or iPad or inbox. Perhaps sophisticated recipients of such instant messages or tweets will be aware that thousands, perhaps millions, of other supporters are receiving the same message at the same moment. But so what? All recipients, from the most naïve to the most knowledgeable understand that the message was sent only nano seconds before, directed specifically at him or her (because the name is on it), and its emotional impact, if not its cognitive one, is powerful. It can, and does, serve to energize and mobilize the recipient into action. When the multiplier effect of the messages is assessed, it is clear that thousands, or millions, of potential voters are suddenly engaged, mobilized, ready to act.

There is an additional important feature of the personalization of the digital campaign. It is highly cost effective and efficient. Radio, television, and newspaper campaigns are expensive and wasteful. Their messages reach far beyond targeted voters, to those not registered, not eligible, not interested, even those opposed.

Not so digital campaigns: they *only* reach those voters whom the campaign has identified and targeted. There are of course costs associated with assembling the various list serves and social networks needed to reach supporters, but those costs pale in comparison to the wastefulness of TV and newspaper advertisements.

A second consequence of the advent of digital political campaigns is that they have put further distance between the campaign and the traditional, analog media. Bluntly, a digital campaign does not need the traditional media. A digital campaign communicates virtually instantly,

---

### The Inefficiency of Broadcast Messages

Campaign messages broadcast over radio are actually reasonably efficient, as radio stations keep careful demographic data on their listeners, and campaign messages can be specifically tailored to individual groups. And, of course, compared to television, radio ads and spots and very cheap. Cable TV networks also help keep ads more demographically focused than those broadcast on general network TV but, even so, there is considerable waste; an advertisement on ESPN or the Food Network is still going to reach many non-voters, or hostile voters. Campaign ads broadcast over national networks are both expensive and, arguably, the least efficient because they reach so many non-voters and those having no intention to vote for the candidate or cause being espoused.

---

personally, and directly with voters, both *en masse* and individually. Absolutely no intervention or mediation by a reporter, TV camera, news anchor/talking head, TV screen, or printed page (even a digitized version of a printed page) is needed.

Indeed, a print or electronic reporter who is not plugged into a candidate's digital campaign may know virtually nothing about it. How could he or she? All of the communication with voters bypasses reporters completely. Unless the reporter is hooked into the campaign digital networks (of whatever kind they may be), or has a source who is, and is willing to share the information received, the reporter may very well spend a lot of time in the dark. And this increasing distance between campaign and journalists strengthens the latter's dependence on campaign "handouts" for preparing stories and broadcasts. We shall return to this point shortly.

Does this mean that political journalism is becoming extinct? Of course not, in fact there may be more of it now than ever before because of blogs and blogging. And, as noted above, campaigns will still want and need coverage from the *New York Times* and other major print outlets, including important regional and local ones; it is how they reach opinion leaders and important elites with whom it is important to stay in contact. And candidates, or their surrogates, will still want to be on the evening network news, FOX, CNN, MSNBC, and other major cable outlets, and of course the Sunday morning "news" programs. How important these are is a matter of debate; what is clear, however, is that the major campaign that ignores Big Media outlets, whether print or electronic, cedes the territory to opponents, with potentially disastrous results.

A third consequence of the digital campaign is that it has created a kind of fourth dimension about it, in which time and space become irrelevant. Because of digitization, information to supporters, appeals to their pocketbooks and loyalty, and efforts to mobilize them into action (including voting) can go forward any time, any place. Campaign functionaries are able to program computers, or sit at keyboards, and send out whatever they wish, whenever they want.

Television, while far more universal than radio, cannot do this. TV sets have to be turned on; advertising slots arranged and paid for; the "cost" of interrupting favored TV shows considered before the message can be heard by voters. The universality of TV campaigns cannot be denied, especially when compared to radio or print. But, compared to digital campaigns, TV seems slow, inefficient, wasteful.

One of the points made earlier in the book is that, in modern times, the distinction between "campaigning" and "governing" has largely broken down. There are many reasons for this, and consequences of it. But a prime force behind this development is the rise of digital politics. Digital campaigns can be, and are, carried out 24/7/365, literally non-stop. Depending on one's point of view, the non-stop, perpetual campaign can be a positive or negative development. But, unless candidates and sitting politicians decide to jettison digital technology, a highly unlikely development, we can expect that the future will bring even greater avalanches of emails, tweets, instant messages, text messages, Facebook communications, and the like than exist now. It will be harder and harder to tell, indeed it already is, when a politician is in campaign or governing mode.

Finally, digital campaigns serve to fragment the electorate into much smaller and smaller components than has been the case in the past. Under more traditional forms of media campaigns, candidates carefully tailor a message that has broad appeal, because it will reach a broad audience; a TV commercial or a made-for-TV event will touch thousands, perhaps millions of viewers/potential voters. The media themselves can, if paying attention, note even subtle changes in the campaign message, as it orients itself to appeal to relevant groups of voters. And it was not unusual to read a newspaper story, or hear and see a TV reporter note, that a candidate may have said very different things, and sent different messages, to voters depending on where he was, or who was the audience; sometimes conflicting messages could create a firestorm of media attention, much of it unfavorable.

Now, it doesn't matter. Because of the way campaigns "slice and dice" groups of voters, the message sent to each can be very different. Reporters and "fact checker" organizations can be slow to discover discrepancies in messages being transmitted; if they are not well plugged into the digital campaign, they may never find out.

But the campaigns care little about any of this. Their goal is to tailor messages to the groups whom they need to mobilize to assemble a winning coalition.[29] If it looks as though blog or printed stories or TV reports about "saying different things to different people" seem to be gaining traction, it is a relatively small matter for the campaign press team to issue "clarifications" about what was said or meant, or claim that the reports were taken "out of context." It is also true that the campaign knows that it will trump the media whenever this happens. Most people, as it turns out, are not paying attention and, of those who are, very few care. Nor does it affect what the campaign will do: digital messages are designed primarily to preach to supporters, to their choirs, and any campaign (even at the local level) has different choirs; if one choir is receiving a message different from that of others, then that is simply a result of the need to reach and mobilize different choirs of voters in different ways.

And of course one of the characteristics of digital communications is the speed with which the message appears, and then disappears just as fast. So it matters very little to the campaign if it says different things to different constituencies. Once it gets the message(s) out to the targeted groups, it doesn't matter what the media, or opponents, or anybody else thinks. Here suddenly, gone just as suddenly: the lack of permanence gives campaigns maximum flexibility to do and say what they want.

## Fighting Back?

Could not the media fight back? Do they have no options to counter the increasing wall of separation between journalists—print and electronic—and candidates/campaigns? They really only have two. One is to boycott the campaign, decide not to play, and claim that they refuse to be victimized by the candidate/campaign. But, while tempting, undoubtedly, this is not a realistic strategy. Print and electronic media cannot just ignore political campaigns, even local ones. To do so would be folly, as they would lose already declining credibility and probably advertising revenues and readership, and increase the rate of their descent into irrelevance and oblivion.

The only other serious resource the media have to counter the power of the campaign is to use effectively their ability to decide which stories to print or broadcast, when, and how to frame them. At this point in time, this capacity of the media is probably their strongest asset. They can determine what they want to print or broadcast daily, even hourly. They can, if they so choose, do so in ways which can potentially embarrass, even damage, a campaign and candidate; the media have vast latitude to decide what words and pictures to use and are fully aware of the impact their choices will have. And in many ways the media, regardless of which type, have the last word; as a distinguished long-time newspaperman, recently deceased, often told the author, newspapers buy ink by the barrel and can outlast any politician, or any candidate, or any campaign. They see them come and go; there will be others next year, or in 2 years, or in 10. The same would be true of electronic outlets; they can, if they wish, pound on a campaign by portraying it repeatedly in the most unfavorable light possible, until it is moribund. Whether or not they choose to do so is another matter entirely.

But to use this strategy effectively would require that both print and electronic media move towards much more aggressive coverage and reporting than exists now. They would have to find, and finance, independent sources of information about the candidates/campaigns and not rely so heavily on "canned" information or "fact sheets" provided by the campaigns, but instead would have to go out and secure information on their own. As the next section of this chapter will show, there is very little chance that this will happen.

## Covering and Reporting Campaigns

How are campaigns covered and reported? We can rapidly skip over many of the usual criticisms of campaign coverage: it focuses on the "horserace" of who seems to be ahead on any given day, instead of focusing on the broader picture of where and how the campaign is going; coverage of issues is skimpy; reporting, especially in broadcast journalism, tends more towards "human interest" approaches than in-depth analysis of what a campaign is about, or not about; the rise of "celebrity journalists" (especially on national and prominent cable news networks) means that face time on TV for the reporter is as important as the substance of what is reported, perhaps more so. At the local level, especially, news media— both print and electronic—are so fearful of offending advertisers and readers/viewers by overplaying political coverage that they often ignore campaigns altogether, or report in such a bland manner that readers have to wonder if they are reading or watching a review of a highly stylized Kabuki play rather than a report on a political campaign.

These are all important criticisms and deserve the reader's serious consideration. But they pale in comparison to the staggering burden that all media are facing: declining credibility. In one of the most authoritative of surveys, Pew has shown that, in the period 1985–2011, Americans' trust in news organizations[30] fell precipitously. Its research reveals that only 25 percent of Americans believe that they get the facts right, while 66 percent say the stories are inaccurate, and 60 percent say the news organizations are politically biased. Some 77 percent of respondents say news organizations favor one side over another, and 80 percent think that they are too influenced by powerful individuals and other organizations (money?).[31]

Some readers might object that these data refer to media coverage of politics generally, not just campaigns. Correct, but so what? Are not political campaigns part and parcel of American politics generally? That message is central to this book and it is not an idiosyncratic view. More to the point, is there any reason to think that there is a qualitative difference between the way in which the media cover political campaigns and, say, Congress and the President, state legislatures and the Governor, or the mayor, county commission, and school board?

How, or whether, the media will be able to regain the trust and confidence of the American public is a serious topic, but one beyond the scope of this book. Instead, we can examine the territory in which campaign journalism takes place. To do so, we shall briefly consider two books that largely define that territory. Both were written about the same presidential campaign (Nixon–McGovern, 1972), roughly at the same time. They could not be more different. But they not only help us understand the territory or landscape of campaign reporting, then and now; they are also as powerful and relevant reading today as when they were first published.

Timothy Crouse's now classic book *The Boys On The Bus* burst onto the political scene like a bombshell.[32] Far from glorifying campaign coverage or the journalists (including many nationally prestigious ones) who covered campaigns, Crouse was one of the first journalistic analysts to uncover the fundamental weakness of campaign reporting.

In particular, Crouse used the phrase "pack journalism" to show how too much campaign reporting took place.[33] Crouse found that the world of journalism on the press plane was completely insular, and isolated. Journalists spent their time talking with one another, rather than seeking stories from the campaign or the candidate. As a result, not only was there a sameness to campaign reporting—whether print or electronic—their stories too often were based on fantasy, on impressions of what was happening, perhaps on wishes rather than "facts." As Yardley quotes Crouse,

> The fact that [some reporters] thought that McGovern had a chance to win showed the folly of trying to call an election from 30,000 feet in the air .... The reporters attached to George McGovern had a very limited usefulness as political observers, by and large, for what they knew best was not the American electorate but the tiny community of the press plane, a totally abnormal world that combined the incestuousness of a New England hamlet with the giddiness of a mid-ocean gala and the physical rigors of the Long March.

But matters did not stop there, according to Crouse. Journalists became far too dependent on press sources within the campaign for their stories. Rather than seeking out their own material, they took campaign handouts and treated them as "news." Again, quoting Yardley,

They all fed off the same pool report, the same daily handout, the same speech by the candidate; the whole pack was isolated in the same mobile village. After awhile, they began to believe the same rumors, subscribe to the same theories, and write the same stories.

The danger in all of this is apparent, and requires little elaboration. Where is the independent journalist? What happened to his/her obligation as an objective journalist, to find out, to ferret out information, to inform the public, to seek the truth? Sadly, they largely disappeared. And, as Yardley as well as other commentators have noted ever since, pack journalism, at least as far as campaign coverage (and, many would also hold, political coverage of Washington, D.C., as well), remains the norm.

And yet, based on our previous discussion in this chapter, it should surprise no one that this happened. As the creed of objective journalism required, reporters had to observe a distance, a detachment, from the campaign. Taking full advantage of this, campaigns themselves forced a physical separation as well: a separate airplane, limited access to the candidate even at campaign stops, hotel accommodations where candidates, campaign operatives, and functionaries on the one hand, and journalists on the other, were not likely to encounter one another, even in the bar. The exhausting physical rigors of multi-venue campaign stops every day; living out of a suitcase for weeks at a time; bad food; limited time to talk with editors let alone family and friends—how could the result be otherwise for the stories printed and broadcast?

The other side or territorial boundary of campaign coverage, we can assert, was defined in the same year by Hunter S. Thompson, who may or may not have created "gonzo" journalism.[34] His book on the 1972 presidential campaign, called *Fear And Loathing On The Campaign Trail '72*,[35] could not be more different from Crouse's, and yet each speaks to the other in very meaningful ways.[36] If Crouse's book appeared on the political and journalistic scene like a bombshell, Thompson's was like a thermonuclear blast.

As Tom Seligson points out in his review, Thompson's book has to be read on two levels. On the one hand, he is a journalist trying to cover the presidential campaign much like his colleagues.[37] But then he takes a very different step from Crouse. Rather than pointing out the deficiencies of objective journalism and its restrictions on the way the campaign was being covered, Thompson unloads. He hesitates not in the least to offer his feelings and views about what was happening. Judgments, opinions, acerbic put-downs of colleagues and candidates abound. He himself assumes the role not simply of reporter, but of active participant in the campaign circus, leaving no doubt about his reactions to the zaniness he saw all around him.

Even more importantly, Thompson makes very clear that he views the whole campaign as nothing but smoke and mirrors, deception and pandering, as fundamentally dishonest, as the candidates sought votes. The loser, in his view, was the American people, because they were being duped into thinking that the candidates actually cared about them, or about American democracy. He loathed Nixon, and while he thought McGovern was basically a decent man (unlike Hubert Humphrey, the losing Democratic nominee 4 years earlier, whom he despised[38]), he felt that McGovern had sold his soul to try to get elected. And as hard as he was on the candidates, he was equally critical of his fellow journalists, whom he felt were afraid to tell the truth about the deceptions and illusions that the candidates and their campaigns were creating for the public. He was, explicitly, very concerned that the phoniness of our political campaigns would ultimately undermine Americans' belief in their democracy.

What, then, can we say about the territory of campaign reporting that Crouse and Thompson map? They share a very critical view of how it was being done and they put the blame squarely on journalists, whom they felt could do better. Crouse thought they were not living up to the obligations, and the promise, of the journalism profession, because they were allowing themselves to be used by campaigns by uncritically accepting what was being fed to them as newsworthy. Thompson of course agreed, but he was adamant that journalists who saw the dishonesty of candidates, their willingness to sell out for votes, and their pandering to special interests, but who did not write or speak up, were doing a disservice, to themselves, their profession, and the public.

What does this have to do with contemporary campaign reporting? Everything. The pictures that these two astute observers painted of the campaign journalism scene have not gone away. Indeed, journalists, their editors, and journalism watchdog groups must decide if they will be satisfied both with the status quo of pack journalism and their unwillingness to address questions of campaign values and ethics that could potentially damage the health of democracy. If they choose to continue present practices, undoubtedly public confidence in news organizations will decline further. So, too, will public confidence in democratic campaigns and elections.

What about the Internet? Is it a salvation for some of these problems? It seems unlikely. Clearly the Internet provides far greater access to information about politics and campaigns than has ever existed before. And clearly it allows that access in real, even nano-second time.

But the question is, how good is the information? Does it fill in the yawning gaps in coverage by the traditional print and electronic media? The answer, sadly, is probably not.

There are of course innumerable digital sources on the Internet which anyone can access. The major print outlets, both newspapers and magazines, have digital versions. Even network and cable TV news organizations have websites that carry news in real time. And then there are the blogs, perhaps thousands of them, ranging from highly professional and thoughtful to worthless bloviation and fear-mongering. Undoubtedly somewhere in the cacophony that is Internet journalism are crusading, investigative reporters who can break through the superficiality and irrelevance of so much "traditional" reporting.

But how is that occasional voice to be heard and attended to? It doesn't simply have to swim upstream; it is, on an ongoing basis, overwhelmed by the daily tsunami of unmonitored, largely un-self-regulated, verbiage of which so much political "reporting" on the Internet consists. To say that the occasional pearls of insight that undoubtedly are being produced in blogs simply get swamped is to understate the obvious.

And of course the information that bloggers have to work with is limited in the same way that traditional reporters face. Granted, blogs do not have to adhere to any kind of journalistic standards, and "information" can be faked, made up, misused, and misstated, largely without fear of sanction or retribution. But, unless there is a blogger inside a campaign willing to be unusually candid—and chances are he or she will quickly be found out—then what the blogs are reporting about campaigns is not much different than what readers will find in the *New York Times* or on FOX News. Or, perhaps, they are nothing more than speculations and even delusions about whatever the blogger wants to think about the campaign. One wonders, in that sense, if blogs, and the Internet generally, are really enhancing our knowledge and understanding of campaigns. Fun, yes. Informative? Not so much.                                    .

## Structural Constraints on Media Coverage of Campaigns

Crouse and Thompson offer deep insight into the constraints that the media have in covering campaigns and tell us a great deal about why contemporary reporting of them is wanting. There are many other reasons why reporting on campaigns so frequently disappoints, but space allows a discussion of only the most important, the structural constraints that even the best journalists face: beside-the-point reporting; the 24-hour news cycle; who owns and runs the media; the interest of the media in campaign outcomes; and the communications linkages that the media provide among campaigns and among political elites.

## Beside-the-Point Reporting

Because of changes in the way modern campaigns view the electorate, the news media cannot keep up. The result is that campaign "reporting" increasingly appears to be on sideshows and irrelevancies. And, as methods of viewing and analyzing the electorate become more sophisticated, campaign coverage is likely to be more beside-the-point than ever.

In a very real sense, campaigns do not think of the voting public as a whole, nor do they even think in large blocs of voters. Rather, modern campaigns rely heavily on "slicing and dicing" the electorate, using a microtome to make finer and finer cuts to examine its likely voting propensities. Only, in this case, the microtomes are statistical models—extremely sophisticated statistical models.

What a number of observers have recently pointed out is that most reporters, and their employers, lack the statistical skills to understand what campaigns are really doing as they take ever finer cross-sections of the electorate. True, they might be able to discern that a campaign may be saying different things, and sending different messages, to different groups of voters. But why, and how it is done, escapes them.

The result, as has been noted,[39] is that reporters are slow to keep up with the campaign. As the *New York Times* reported, "There's a lot that goes on in a campaign that reporters never really get at .... There are a lot more things at play." To the extent that journalists can understand how the statistical models are constructed and used, so they may at least follow the basics of campaign strategy. But to the extent that they do not, their reporting is increasingly irrelevant, because it is not about the fundamental focus and allocation of resources of campaigns.

Of course, there is nothing to prevent media outlets—print, electronic, blogosphere—from hiring their own statisticians to try to make inferences about the models being used by the campaigns.[40] But at best they would

---

### The Demise of Nate Silver at the *New York Times*

Nate Silver, the statistician who developed models used by campaigns (and baseball teams) for identifying likely voters (and players) and whose blog fivethirtyeight.com was carried by the *New York Times* throughout the 2012 campaigns, was consistently the most accurate forecaster of the final presidential and Congressional elections. Indeed, his accuracy was almost uncanny. Eventually however he was dismissed by the *Times*, allegedly for being a "disruptive" force in the organization, according to Michael Calderone.[41] Other analysts claimed that he was forced out because the reporters did not like him, especially his insistence that they stop reporting the "horserace" and focus on more substantive issues.[42] The entire episode is important because it illustrates the tensions and disagreements that take place in the media about how campaigns are to be covered and reported, and indeed their ability to do so.

be making guesses; campaigns keep their statistical models for making strategic resource allocations as deeply guarded secrets. And of course hiring a statistical team to track campaigns would add to the already increasing financial burden of covering campaigns that afflicts major media outlets; minor, regional, and local outlets probably could not even begin to think of hiring such resource personnel.

## The 24-Hour News Cycle

The 24-hour news cycle is also highly influential in how campaigns are reported, and therefore what voters know about them.

It is generally agreed that the 24-hour news cycle was created by the advent of cable news networks—at first CNN, to be joined by a host of others.[43] Continuous news reporting that was the hallmark of early cable news networks required not only speed but freshness. A story could only be cycled and recycled so many times before viewers tuned out; something new was needed every day.

The 24-hour news cycle is highly controversial; there are many who argue that it has been the downfall of professional journalism, because it allows little opportunity for in-depth reporting that includes serial or follow-up stories. The "once over lightly" approach to reporting that seems to characterize much of cable (and even network) news stories— and it has spilled over into print media—has been criticized for perpetuating superficiality, half truths, and misinformation.[44]

Our concern here is not to enter this debate, but to emphasize that the 24-hour news cycle gives campaigns extra license to do and say whatever they want. The "news" reported about the campaign is not only not permanent, it is not tested or examined. It cannot be; the pressure of time and the need to produce "stories" insure that whatever is reported today is gone today.

Compounding all of this is digital speed. While it allows for virtually instantaneous dissemination of whatever message the campaign may wish to put forward, it also vanishes just as fast. The idea is to put the campaign message "out there," let the point fill the print and electronic media and the blogosphere, and then let the "story" vanish, to be replaced by something else. The 24-hour news cycle insures that all traces of it will disappear.

Thus in a very real sense the 24-hour news cycle works to the advantage of campaigns and puts further distance between them and the media. Campaigns can put out whatever message and information they choose; reporters, hungry for stories, will gobble them up. But since there is almost zero chance that there will be follow-up stories (unless the campaign wants them), there is also almost zero chance that the campaign will be held accountable for what it said or did. The message is already gone, almost the moment that it appears in some media outlet.

## Why Cover Campaigns? What's in it for the Media?

The questions introducing this section might strike some readers as odd. Why *not* cover campaigns? Why wouldn't the media cover them? Isn't that its job?

If covering campaigns is one of the media's obligations, it is a self-imposed one. There is no requirement—Constitutional or legal—that they must. In spite of the increasing costs of covering and reporting campaigns, and declining revenues/viewerships/readerships, the fact that the media continue to cover them suggests that media may have an interest, and anticipate certain benefits, in doing so. What are those interests?

## Money

The media makes money from political campaigns. For some races, a staggering amount of money. True, it is costly for mainstream media to cover campaigns; but they more than recoup their outlays through the money that campaigns pay the media. *Forbes* reported that, in the 2007–2008 election cycle, about $2.7 B was spent on political advertising, eclipsing earlier totals. But, in 2011–2012, largely because of the introduction of so-called SuperPacs, that figure topped $5 B.[45] Other analysts thought the total figure approached $8 B.[46]

Of course, not all of this money went to the media. But a great deal of it did.[47] The *Washington Post*, surveying the campaign expenditures of President Obama and Mr. Romney, revealed that together they spent over $1 B just on campaign advertising: $580 M, and $470 M, respectively. In both cases money spent on media constituted the lion's share of campaign expenditures: 55 percent for Obama and 54 percent for Romney. In addition, as PBS reported, Obama outspent Romney 10:1 on social media, a figure that demonstrates the centrality of digital media to the successful Obama campaign.

---

### Campaign Media Expenditures Are Not Distributed Evenly, Nor Are They Always Disclosed

Not all media outlets shared equally in the avalanche of campaign money. As the *Washington Post* showed, media in the swing, battle-ground states of Florida, Virginia, and Ohio received the preponderance of media buys, $173 M, $151 M, and $150 M, respectively, followed rather distantly by North Carolina, Colorado, Iowa, Nevada, Wisconsin, New Hampshire, and Michigan. As Tim Dickinson noted in *Rolling Stone*, it is not always possible to determine which media outlets in individual states and cities receive the bulk of ad buys. Beginning in 2012, the FCC ruled that outlets of ABC, CBS, NBC, and FOX in the nation's 50 largest media markets had to disclose political media buys, but the networks continue to fight this ruling and have not complied. In addition, as the 2012 election drew closer, many of the buys, according to Dickinson, were in smaller markets exempt from the FCC rules. Thus, for example, while it might be a reasonable supposition that much, perhaps most, of the GOP media buys were placed at FOX outlets, it really is not possible to say so with certainty until and when all media buys are fully disclosed.[48]

## Choose the Players! Play Favorites! Back the Winner!

But covering campaigns is more than just a matter of raking in the cash that the candidates throw at the media for advertisements. The media play a major role in determining who are the real candidates and who are just spear-carriers and extras in the campaign opera. It does this by playing favorites. The media covers some candidates more than others; indeed, it ignores some almost completely.

The Republican presidential nominating/primary season began seriously sometime in late 2010/early 2011. There were nearly 20 declared or nearly declared candidates. From the outset some were hopeless unknowns going nowhere. The media ignored them or gave them short shrift, and they quickly retired from the scene. But even among those who received media attention, coverage and reporting were never equal. As front-runner Mitt Romney's fortunes ebbed and flowed, the media showcased now this candidate—Michele Bachmann—and now that one—Herman Cain—and then another—Rick Perry—still someone else—Rand Paul—then Newt Gingrich—and next Rick Santorum. And, just as quickly as these individuals attracted media attention, so just as quickly did their coverage fade. Why? In retrospect it is even more clear than it was at the time: the media had recognized Mr. Romney as the inevitable nominee even before the primary season ended, while the others were entertaining sideshows designed to attract an audience and sell advertising.

### Who Are the Candidates? Who Are the Real Candidates?

On August 6, 2015, FOX News sponsored two debates of Republican candidates for their party's presidential nomination. The first, held late afternoon in Cleveland, was comprised of the seven candidates who, at that moment, ranked lowest in national opinion polls. The second, held during prime television time in the same Cleveland forum later that day, was for the 10 candidates who ranked highest in the polls.

FOX claimed that it decided to hold two debates because it was impractical to try to have 17 candidates on the same stage at the same time trying to debate, a not unreasonable point. But FOX also chose how to divide the candidates—not through a random drawing or other process in which each candidate had the same chance as everyone else of being in either the first or second debate, but through its own choice and interpretation of national polls.[49] In other words, there was no consideration of fairness or equity.

The episode is an example of how the media chooses who are the real candidates, and who are the also rans.

It follows from this discussion that determining the real candidates is not enough for the media: they want to identify the winner, as well. Of course everybody wants to back a winner; there is no comparable slogan for losers. But, for the media, the stakes are high: the media have taken it on themselves to identify the real players in the campaign game because they want to limit the choices that voters actually have. Beyond that, if the media can successfully identify the winner(s), they assure themselves of a place at the table as political games unfold; what candidate, or office holder, would shut out the media outlet that favored, even anointed, him or her?[50]

## Owning the Media: Circle the Wagons, Preserve the System

Some years ago, Bernard Herman and Noam Chomsky published a book called *Manufacturing Consent: The Political Economy Of The Mass Media*.[51] Their message is that the media must be seen as part of what American capitalism has become: dominated by Big Money. Big Media, according to Herman and Chomsky, is not interested in democracy any more than its allies in Big Money are; its interest is in continually expanding its share of power, influence and profitability.

The message of Herman and Chomsky created a firestorm of controversy, producing avalanches of criticism and defenses. In fact, however, it turned out that the authors were onto something important.[52] As gigantic American corporations had clearly taken over the American economy, so had their role in American politics turned from a major influence into something of a stranglehold.[53]

Big Money is also very careful about the kind of candidate whom it will legitimize for a campaign; oddballs, loose cannons, freethinkers, populists, members of "marginalized" or "minority" groups who aren't sufficiently white or Anglo, the working poor, progressives, and other such subversives and fifth columnists will not be annointed. Big Money does *not* want to take the chance that voters might choose someone who could threaten "the system."

Big Media is a powerful contributor to and player in circling the wagons. It wants to dominate—even control—what the public "learns" about what government decision makers—at all levels—are doing or not doing. It's no wonder that media reports on campaigns are really about the horserace and not what the candidates are *not* saying; it is counter to their interest to do otherwise.[54]

And so it is no wonder that Big Media wants to identify and promote a winner. "Winner" for Big Media means one of its own, not someone who does not play the political game by its rules. What if Americans elected a Hugo Chavez or Alexis Tsipras as President? Or even— *horreurs!*—a centrist Socialist like President Francoise Hollande of France? Circle the Wagons, Protect the System, Don't Upset the Applecart—at all costs.

---

### The "Liberal" *New York Times*?

In the 2013 contest for Mayor of New York City, the *New York Times*, perhaps the archetype of the so-called "liberal media" in America, endorsed Christine Quinn in the Democratic primary, not the eventual winner Bill de Blasio. Quinn was very much the establishment candidate, a moderate former City Council Speaker. Mr. de Blasio was the outspoken progressive/populist in the primary, something of which the *Times* never ceased to remind voters. The *Times* did endorse de Blasio in the general election over Republican Joseph Lhota; de Blasio won the general election with over 73 percent of the vote, suggesting that the *Times* may have read the post-primary tea leaves and chose to back a winner, even if not enthusiastically.[55]

---

### Who Owns the Media? And What Does That Have To Do With Political Campaigns?

This section will present evidence that supports the argument in the preceding one. Two sources can be marshaled to do so.

The Pew Research Center's Project for Excellence in Journalism not long ago published its finding on "Who Owns the News Media?"[56] It examines, in summary fashion as well as in detailed databases, media ownership. Even a cursory glance at the summarizing "Dashboard" reveals how much of the newspaper, network TV, local TV, radio, magazine, and ethnically oriented markets is dominated by 5 or 6 large corporations in each category.

These findings are supplemented by earlier studies that show how much control over all media markets is held by just 6 conglomerates: Time-Warner, Walt Disney, Viacom, The News Corporation, CBS, and NBC Universal.[57] As several commentators have pointed out, these organizations control about 95 percent of what Americans watch, read, and hear. It is indeed a near monopoly. The result is that there is not much diversity in American news reporting, including of political campaigns. Limited corporate ownership and the lack of alternative voices are a powerful constraint on the scope and depth of campaign coverage offered to American voters.

## Inter-Campaign Communications

The last structural element influencing campaign coverage that we shall discuss is the media's role in inter-campaign communications. As a general rule, rival campaigns don't talk to one another; and even campaigns from the same party but for different offices (say, mayor and county commission, or U.S. Senate and U.S. House) usually don't communicate directly.

But they do send signals to one another through the media. Just as political elites in America talk to one another through Sunday morning talk shows, or evening political shows on cable TV, or op-ed pieces in prestigious newspapers, so do campaigns send messages to other campaigns using these same media channels. These messages might be about reactions to what opposing candidates are saying or doing, or ads that they are airing, or even might be trial balloons for changes in strategy or message that one campaign is contemplating, to see what the opposing campaign's reaction might be.

But the media channels, as we have seen, are not neutral. Through their invitations to certain campaigns, but not necessarily all, to have a representative on a talk show on a given day, an interview on a news broadcast, or to prepare an op-ed piece, they advantage one campaign but not others. The questions asked, the follow-up talking heads afterwards, the topics encouraged in op-ed pieces put the media's slant on messages which the campaigns send out.

Thus, far from being passive conveyors of information from one campaign to another, or one elite to others, the media actually shape that communication by choosing how, when, and in what format the messages will be transmitted. But of course much of this is beyond the ken of the public, whose trust in and willingness to engage with the media has been in serious decline for decades. It is rather the media's attempt to play a central role in shaping developments in the world of political campaigns, indeed of the larger political universe beyond them.

## Waning Public Interest in Mainstream Media

The number of Americans who regularly read a newspaper or watch TV news—network or cable—had declined significantly over the past decade. Pew reports that, as of 2012, only 23 percent of people report that they had read a newspaper the previous day; this is a drop of 18 percent in a decade.[58] Pew also reports that, while 71 percent of Americans watch some kind of local news broadcasts, and 65 percent network news, the amount of time that cable news viewers (38 percent of the viewing public) spend watching is twice as much as those viewing the other platforms. But viewership among younger audiences of any kind of news has declined precipitously.[59] More generally, analysts report that TV viewership of all types, including cable, is declining rapidly in favor of watching on mobile and other digital devices.[60]

At the end, we can return to where we began. From our discussion, it should be clear why Finley Peter Dunne may be endlessly thrashing in his grave. The media, in covering political campaigns, probably long ago stopped comforting the afflicted and afflicting the comfortable. Its interest, rather, is in comforting itself and pushing its favored candidates onto the electorate. If the public is afflicted, no longer is that the media's problem. Instead, it will have to live with the judgments of a very few huge corporate conglomerates, who share everything in common with one another and nothing with the body politic, about who are acceptable candidates and what are the acceptable limits of campaign discourse.

But what is also clear is that political campaigns and the media now operate in very different universes. What the media learns, and reports, about campaigns is almost entirely what campaigns want them to know; the gulf between campaigns and media is not easily breached. Yet Big Media still wants to be players in the campaign game, anointing candidates, seeking to influence campaign discourse, and trying to affect the electoral outcome. Given how far and how fast public trust in the media has declined, one can only speculate how long their efforts will continue.

## Notes

1  See, for example, "Thomas Jefferson on Politics and Government," viewed online at www.famguardian.org/Subjects/Politics/ThomasJefferson/jeff1600.htm, June 30, 2013.
2  The line is perhaps most famously used in the movie *Inherit the Wind*, in which Gene Kelly, playing an H. L. Mencken-type character, recites a version of it. Indeed, the line is often incorrectly attributed to Mencken, the influential

Baltimore editor, essayist, and social critic of the early twentieth century.

3   See Poynter.org, March 2, 2011, viewed online at www.poynter.org/archived/ask-dr-ink/1298/afflicting-the-afflicted, September 25, 2013.

4   The theme was an old one even at the time de Tocqueville wrote *Democracy in America*. For a thoughtful recent restatement, see "US: Surveillance Harming Journalism, Law, Democracy, *Human Rights Watch*, July 28, 2014, viewed online at www.hrw.org/news/2014/07/28/us-surveillance-harming-journalism-law-democracy, July 6, 2015.

5   See, for example, Shanto Iyengar, *Media Politics, A Citizen's Guide*, 3rd edn. (New York: W. W. Norton, 2016).

6   See, for example, Roger Butterfield, *The American Past* (New York: Simon and Schuster, 1957); Eugene H. Roseboom, *A History of Presidential Elections* (New York: Macmillan, 1957); Keith Melder, *Hail To The Candidate* (Washington, D.C: Smithsonian Institution Press, 1992); *New York Times*, *Campaigns: A Century Of Presidential Races* (New York: DK Books, 2001).

7   See, for example, Laura Shapiro, *Perfection Salad* (New York: Modern Library, 2001). More generally, see "Who Made America?, Frederick Winslow Taylor, Scientific Management," PBS, n.d., viewed online at www.pbs.org/wgbh/theymadeamerica/whomade/taylor_hi.html, July 6, 2015.

8   See Pew Research Center's Project for Excellence in Journalism, Journalism.org, 2013; viewed online at www.journalism.org/resources/principles, July 4, 2013.

9   James Sullivan, "On This Day," Finding Dulcinea, August 22, 2011, viewed online at www.findingdulcinea.com/news/on-this-day/Aug/Theodore-Roosevelt-Becomes-First-President-to-Ride-in-a-Car.html; "In Roosevelt History," FDR Library, September 6, 2012, viewed online at https://fdrlibrary.wordpress.com/tag/democratic-national-convention; Joe Sharkey, "Campaigning by Private Jet," *Business Jet Traveler*, June, 2011, viewed online at www.bjtonline.com/business-jet-news/campaigning-private-jet; all viewed August 2, 2014.

10   See "Radio in the 1920s," May 1, 2000, viewed online at http://xroads.virginia.edu/~ug00/3on1/radioshow/1920radio.htm, July 4, 2013.

11   See "Media in the 1930s," Oracle ThinkQuest Educational Foundation, viewed online at http://library.thinkquest.org/27629/themes/media/md30s.html, July 4, 2013.

12   See David Shedden, "The First Convention Broadcast: Radio at the 1924 Conventions," Poynter.org, March 2, 2011, viewed online at www.poynter.org/uncategorized/25177/the-first-convention-broadcast-radio-at-the-1924-conventions;

13   "Television History—The First 75 Years," n.d., viewed online at www.tvhistory.tv/1950%20QF.htm, July 4, 2013.

14   www.tvhistory.tv/Annual_TV_Households_50-78.JPG, viewed online July 4, 2013.

15   Shedden, 2011; see also Brian Wolly, "Inaugural Firsts," Smithsonian.com, December 17, 2008, viewed online at www.smithsonianmag.com/history-archaeology/Presidential-Inauguration-Firsts.html, September 18, 2013.

16   See "Cable Television History," About.com/inventors, viewed online at http://inventors.about.com/library/inventors/blcabletelevision.htm, October 5, 2013.

17   See for example David Garrow, *Protest at Selma* (New Haven: Yale University Press, 1980); "Bridge to Freedom," *THE AMERICAN EXPERIENCE: Eyes*

*On The Prize: America's Civil Rights Years, 1954–1965*, disc 3, PBS, 1986; the 2014 film *Selma* (www.imdb.com/title/tt1020072; and Richard K. Scher, *Politics in the New South*, 2nd edn. (Armonk, N.Y: M. E. Sharpe, 1997).

18  Readers are invited to examine the rich archive of presidential TV commercials available at the Museum of the Moving Image, *The Living Room Candidate*, which covers 1952–2012. It is available online at www.livingroomcandidate.org, viewed July 4, 2013.

19  Mr. Reagan's testy remark can be seen online at www.youtube.com/watch?v=OO2_49TycdE, viewed July 4, 2013. See also Linton Weeks, "6 Reasons We're Feeling Debate Fatigue," NPR Election 2012, February 22, 2012, viewed online at www.npr.org/2012/02/22/147187228/6-reasons-were-feeling-debate-fatigue, July 4, 2013.

20  See Wilson Andrews, Alicia Parlapiano, and Karen Yourish, "Who is Running for President (and Who's Not)," *New York Times*, July 2, 2015, viewed online at www.nytimes.com/interactive/2016/us/elections/2016-presidential-candidates.html?_r=0; Zake J. Miller, "The GOP's First Big 2016 Test: Fitting Candidates on the Debate Stage," *Time*, May 14, 2015, viewed online at www.nytimes.com/interactive/2016/us/elections/2016-presidential-candidates.html?_r=0; and 2016 Debate Schedule, *Election Central 2016*, viewed online at www.uspresidentialelectionnews.com/2016-debate-schedule; all viewed July 6, 2015. There were some GOP strategists who felt that the party hurt itself in 2012 by having too many televised debates and should not make the same mistake in 2016. See Jonathan Martin, "Republicans Tighten Grip on Debates in 2016 Race," *New York Times*, May 9, 2014, viewed online at www.uspresidentialelectionnews.com/2016-debate-schedule, July 6, 2015.

21  E. E. Schattschneider, *The Semi-Sovereign People* (New York: Cengage Learning, 1975).

22  George Romney's famous remark, made during a television interview, can be seen on YouTube, www.youtube.com/watch?v=t5dSiBehQpI; Ed Muskie can be seen crying on YouTube also, www.youtube.com/watch?v=LiLL8ZAXGys; McCain's house blunder also, www.youtube.com/watch?v=K4I881MTWEs; and likewise Mitt Romney's remark at www.youtube.com/watch?v=XnB0NZzl5HA; viewed July 6, 2013 and August 13, 2013.

23  See, among other sources, Eric Boehlert, *Bloggers On The Bus* (New York: Free Press, 2010); Hyatt, "Internet Tools in Digital Campaigns," *Politics And The New Media*, February 25, 2011, viewed online at http://politicsandthenewmedia.commons.yale.edu/2011/02/25/internet-tools-in-political-campaigns, July 6, 2013; Seema Mehta, "The Rise of the Internet Electorate," *Los Angeles Times*, April 18, 2011, viewed online at http://articles.latimes.com/2011/apr/18/nation/la-na-social-media-20110418, July 6, 2013; CNN Wire Staff, "Obama Campaign More Active Online, Pew Says," *Cnn Politics*, August 25, 2012, viewed online at www.cnn.com/2012/08/15/politics/presidential-campaign-web, July 6, 2013; Steve Lohr, "The Obama Campaign's Technology is a Force Multiplier," *New York Times*, Bits, November 8, 2012, viewed online at http://bits.blogs.nytimes.com/2012/11/08/the-obama-campaigns-technology-the-force-multiplier, July 6, 2013; Aaron Smith, "Civic Engagement in the Digital Age," Pew Internet, Pew Internet and American Life Project, April 25, 2013, viewed online at www.pewinternet.org/topics/Politics.aspx?typeFilter=5, July 6, 2013.

24  See, for example, Matt Taibbi, *Spanking The Donkey* (New York: Three Rivers Press, 2005).

25  See, for example, Molly McHugh, " How Social Media is Sinking Mitt

Romney," digitaltrends.com, September 27, 2012, viewed online at www.digitaltrends.com/social-media/how-social-media-is-sinking-mitt-romney; Nick Judd, "For Romney's Digital Campaign, A Second Place Finish," techpresident.com, November 7, 2012, viewed online at http://techpresident.com/news/23106/romneys-digital-campaign-second-place-finish; and Sean Gallagher, "How Team Obama's Tech Efficiency Left Romney IT in Dust," arstechnica.com, November 20, 2012, viewed online at http://arstechnica.com/information-technology/2012/11/how-team-obamas-tech-efficiency-left-romney-it-in-dust; all viewed August 14, 2013.

26  See for example Alex Fitzpatrick, "4 Reasons Why Obama's Digital Effort Was a Success," mashable.com, December 26, 2012, viewed online at http://mashable.com/2012/12/26/obama-digital-success; and Jim Rutenberg, "Data You Can Believe In," *New York Times Magazine*, June 20, 2013, viewed online at www.nytimes.com/2013/06/23/magazine/the-obama-campaigns-digital-masterminds-cash-in.html?pagewanted=all; both viewed August 14, 2013. See, very importantly, John Allen Hendricks and Dan Schill, *Presidential Campaigning and Social Media* (New York: Oxford University Press, 2014).

27  Catherine O'Donnell, "New Study Quantifies Use of Social Media in Arab Spring," *UW Today*, September 12, 2011, viewed online at www.washington.edu/news/2011/09/12/new-study-quantifies-use-of-social-media-in-arab-spring, and "Social Media Arab Spring," Huffingtonpost.com, n.d, viewed online at www.huffingtonpost.com/news/social-media-arab-spring; both viewed July 9, 2015.

28  John Allen Hendricks and Dan Schill (eds.), *Presidential Campaigning and Social Media* (New York: Oxford University Press, 2014; see also Karl Heim, review, *Presidential Campaigning and Social Media*, ed. by John Allen Hendricks and Dan Schill, *Presidential Studies Quarterly*, Vol. 5, No. 2, June, 2015.

29  See Sasha Issenberg, *The Victory Lab: The Secret Science of Winning Campaigns* (New York: Broadway Books, 2013).

30  Pew includes both print and electronic media in the term "news organizations."

31  Pew Research Center for People and the Press, "Press Widely Criticized, But Trusted More Than Other Information Sources," September 22, 2013, viewed online at www.people-press.org/2011/09/22/press-widely-criticized-but-trusted-more-than-other-institutions/?src=prc-headline, July 7, 2013.

32  Timothy Crouse, *The Boys On The Bus* (New York, Ballantine, 1973).

33  Readers are urged to examine Crouse's text, and also to consult Jonathan Yardley's helpful essay, "'Boys on the Bus': Pack Journalism at Unsafe Speeds," *Washington Post*, August 27, 2004, viewed online at www.washingtonpost.com/wp-dyn/articles/A37323-2004Aug26.html, September 1, 2012.

34  See Dr. Gregory Borse, "Hunter S. Thompson: The Death of Gonzo Journalism," *Chronwatch.Com^*, February 22, 2005, viewed online at www.freerepublic.com/focus/fr/1348762/posts, July 7, 2013.

35  Hunter S. Thompson, *Fear And Loathing On The Campaign Trail '72* (New York: Popular Library, 1973).

36  See for example Tom Seligson, "*Fear and Loathing on the Campaign Trail '72*," *New York Times*, July 15, 1973, viewed online at www.nytimes.com/1973/07/15/books/thompson-1973-trail.html?_r=0; Eric Sundermann, "Q&A: Matt Taibbi on the 40th Anniversary of *Fear and Loathing on the Campaign Trail '72*," *Village Voice*, June 27, 2012, viewed

online at www.villagevoice.com/2012-06-27/books/q-a-matt-taibbi-on-the-40th-anniversary-of-fear-and-loathing-on-the-campaign-trail-72-hunter-s-tho mpson-s-influence-and-why-barack-obama-isn-t-a-great-shark; and Matt Taibbi, "*Fear And Loathing* 40 Years Later," Slate.com, June 29, 2012, viewed online at www.slate.com/articles/news_and_politics/books/2012/06/ hunter_s_thompson_fear_and_loathing_on_the_campaign_trail_72_review_b y_matt_taibbi_.html; all viewed July 7, 2013.

37  Interestingly, both Thompson and Crouse wrote campaign articles for *Rolling Stone* magazine, and each transformed them into their respective books.

38  "There is no way to grasp what a shallow, contemptible and hopelessly dishonest old hack Hubert Humphrey is until you've followed him around for a while on the campaign trail," quoted in Seligson.

39  The best article describing what is happening, and the increasing inability of journalists to grasp the essence of campaign strategy, is Sasha Issenberg, "Why Campaign Reporters Are Behind the Curve, *New York Times*, September 1, 2012, viewed online at http://campaignstops.blogs.nytimes.com/2012/09/01/ why-campaign-reporters-are-behind-the-curve/?hp, September 1, 2012. See also Emily Steel and Robert Cookson, "Tracking Technology Catches U.S. Voters," *Financial Times*, October 20, 2012, viewed online at w w w . f t . c o m / i n t l / c m s / s / 2 / d e 9 e b b 3 e - 1 a 0 8 - 1 1 e 2 - a 1 7 9 - 00144feabdc0.html#axzz2YOTRiWy4, October 22, 2012; and Michael Scherer, "Inside the Secret World of the Data Crunchers Who Helped Obama Win," *Time*, November 7, 2012, viewed online at http://swampland.time.com/ 2012/11/07/inside-the-secret-world-of-quants-and-data-crunchers-who-helped-obama-win, July 13, 2015. See also David W. Nickerson and Todd Rogers, "Political Campaigns and Big Data," Harvard University, John F. Kennedy School of Government, February, 2014; viewed online at https://research.hks.harvard.edu/publications/getFile.aspx?Id=1040, July 24, 2015. For a different view of how data crunching during campaigns takes place, and its prospects for the future, see John Sides and Lynn Vavreck, "Obama's Not-So-Big-Data," *PS—Pacific Standard*, January 21, 2014, viewed online at www.psmag.com/books-and-culture/obamas-big-data-inconclusive-results-political-campaigns-72687, July 13, 2015; and see Issenberg's recent book, cited earlier in this chapter.

40  The idea is not quite as absurd as it seems; during World War II the British, apparently, hired astrologers to develop strategies against Hitler, who allegedly consulted them often. See "British Used Astrologer Against Hitler," UPI.com, March 4, 2008, viewed online at www.upi.com/Top_News/2008/03/04/ British-used-astrologer-against-Hitler/UPI-27671204642203, July 8, 2013.

41  Michael Calderone, "Nate Silver, 'Disruptive' Force at the *New York Times*, Joins ESPN," Huffingtonpost.com, July 22, 2013, viewed online at w w w . h u f f i n g t o n p o s t . c o m / 2 0 1 3 / 0 7 / 2 2 / n a t e - s i l v e r - e s p n - n e w - y o r k - times_n_3636035.html, August 7, 2014.

42  See Margaret Sullivan, "Nate Silver Went Against the Grain for Some at the Times," *New York Times*, July 22, 2013, viewed online at http://publiceditor.blogs.nytimes.com/2013/07/22/nate-silver-went-against-the-grain-for-some-at-the-times, August 17, 2013.

43  CNN first broadcast on June 1, 1980; see www.youtube.com/ watch?v=dqDopY5dMD8, viewed online August 22, 2013.

44  See the collection of articles elaborating on this sentence in "24 Hour News Cycle," Huffingtonpost.com, September 4, 2013, viewed online at www.huffingtonpost.com/tag/24-hour-news-cycle, September 4, 2013.

45    Charles R. Taylor, "Five Reasons Why 2012 Will Be A Banner Year for Political Advertising," *Forbes*, January 10, 2012; view online at www.forbes.com/sites/onmarketing/2012/01/10/five-reasons-why-2012-will-be-a-banner-year-for-political-advertising, May 23, 2012.

46    Open Secrets estimated the total for presidential, U.S. Senate, and U.S. House at more than $6.2 B (www.opensecrets.org/bigpicture); Politico.com reported FEC figures at $7 B (www.politico.com/story/2013/01/7-billion-spent-on-2012-campaign-fec-says-87051.html); both viewed online July 9, 2013. If one adds expenditures for state and local races, $8 B is not out of the question.

47    See "2012 Presidential Campaign Finance Explorer," *Washington Post*, December 7, 2012, viewed online at www.washingtonpost.com/wp-srv/special/politics/campaign-finance. See also "Mad Money: TV Ads in the 2012 Presidential Campaign," *Washington Post*, November 14, 2012, viewed online at www.washingtonpost.com/wp-srv/special/politics/track-presidential-campaign-ads-2012; and PBS Newshour, "Daily Download: Obama Spent 10 Times as Much on Social Media as Romney," November 16, 2012, viewed online at www.pbs.org/newshour/bb/media/july-dec12/download_11-16.html; all viewed July 9, 2013.

48    Tim Dickinson, "Guess Who's Profiting Most from Super PACs?," *Rolling Stone*, August 6, 2012, viewed online at www.rollingstone.com/politics/news/guess-whos-profiting-most-from-super-pacs-20120806, August 11, 2014.

49    Kevin Quealy and Amanda Cox, "The First GOP Debate: Who's In, Who's Out and the Role of Chance," *New York Times*, July 29, 2015, viewed online at www.nytimes.com/interactive/2015/07/21/upshot/election-2015-the-first-gop-debate-and-the-role-of-chance.html?abt=0002&abg=1, August 7, 2015.

50    Perhaps the classic example is the iconic photograph of incumbent President Harry S. Truman holding up a copy of the *Chicago Daily Tribune* on November 3, 1948; the newspaper headline read, "Dewey Defeats Truman." The actual outcome of the election was exactly the opposite; the headline is an archetypal example of poor journalism and editorial wishful thinking, as the paper had supported Dewey. The photograph can be seen at www.chicagotribune.com/news/nationworld/politics/chi-chicagodays-deweydefeats-story-story.html.

51    Edward S. Herman and Noam Chomsky, *Manufacturing Consent: The Political Economy of the Mass Media* (New York: Pantheon, 1st edn. 1988, 2002).

52    A Canadian documentary of the same title has become a mainstay of conferences and roundtables on alternative media, criticism of mainstream media, and many college classrooms. See *Manufacturing Consent: Noam Chomsky And The Media*, directed by Mark Achbar and Peter Wintonick, Humanist Broadcasting Foundation, National Film Board of Canada, 2002.

53    For an elaboration of this point, see Robert Reich, *Beyond Outrage* (New York: Vintage, 2012) and Hedrick Smith, *Who Stole the American Dream* (New York: Random House, 2012).

54    For a revealing look at how corporate influence over reporting affects the kind of questions that journalists are willing to ask, see Alex Pareene, "How I Botched It on CNBC," Salon.com, September 30, 2013, viewed online at www.salon.com/2013/09/30/how_i_botched_it_on_cnbc, September 30, 2013.

55    See Editorial, "Bill de Blasio for Mayor," *New York Times*, October 26, 2013, www.nytimes.com/2013/10/27/opinion/sunday/bill-de-blasio-for-mayor.html, July 3, 2014.

56    Pew Research Center's Project for Excellence in Journalism, "Who Owns the

News Media," *The State Of The News Media 2011*, viewed online at http://stateofthemedia.org/media-ownership, May 24, 2012.

57 Data on these and other media giants can be readily found; a few readily accessible sources are: http://theeconomiccollapseblog.com/archives/who-owns-the-media-the-6-monolithic-corporations-that-control-almost-everythin g-we-watch-hear-and-read; www.freepress.net/ownership/chart/main; www.cjr.org/resources; www.pbs.org/wgbh/pages/frontline/shows/cool/giants; www.leechon.com/media-conglomerates-who-owns-what-325.htm.

58 "Number of Americans Who Read Print Newspapers Continues Decline," Pew Research Center, October 11, 2012, viewed online at www.pewresearch.org/daily-number/number-of-americans-who-read-print-newspapers-continues-decline, August 5, 2014.

59 Kenneth Olmstead, Mark Jurkowitz, Amy Mitchell, and Jodi Enda, "How Americans Get TV News at Home," Pew Research Journalism Project, October 11, 2013, viewed online at www.journalism.org/2013/10/11/how-americans-get-tv-news-at-home, August 5, 2014.

60 Jim Edwards, "TV is Dying, and Here Are the Stats to Prove It," Business Insider, November 24, 2013, viewed online at www.businessinsider.com/cord-cutters-and-the-death-of-tv-2013-11, August 5, 2014. See also the telling graphs at Google Search, "Decline of TV News Watching," www.google.com/ search?q=decline+of+tv+news+watching&tbm=isch&tbo=u&source=univ& sa=X&ei=jOrfU-zSEJLcoATR-YCYDA&ved=0CEEQsAQ&biw= 1704&bih=824.

# 6   Money and Political Campaigns

A recurring theme of this book is that, in the past, our political campaigns were a source of embarrassment, but not terribly injurious to our democracy. But, as we saw in the last two chapters, the growth of the Campaign Industry and changes in the way in which the media covers campaigns very much call that view into question.

But, in the case of money and political campaigns, a real threat to the health of our democratic elections has been created. Since the author's earlier version of this book, there has been a convulsive change in how money enters and impacts political campaigns. It is not just the amount involved, although it has risen almost exponentially. Part of the money problem in campaigns is that too much of it comes from too few people and groups. But the single greatest problem now is the non-transparent source of massive infusions of campaign dollars. Much of it is completely unregulated, and the level of accountability of so much of it is too often zero. Money has, in fact, become the single greatest potentially corruptive force in modern political campaigns.

## Money, Legality, and Ethics in Political Campaigns

Money has been a problem in political campaigns in America since the early nineteenth century, at least. Illegal donations—including those from non-citizens and other foreigners, expressly forbidden by federal law, to campaigns at any level[1]—under-the-table payments, efforts to "buy" elections, outright bribery, "pay-to-play" schemes, currying favors and purchasing politicians, all of these and other unsavory practices—are part of the not-so-grand American tradition of funding campaigns. During the period of the Great Immigration to the United States following the Civil War and continuing until World War I, it was not unusual for state and urban political bosses to cajole/manipulate/demand that immigrants whom they had taken under their wings, "vote" as the machines wanted. Often this meant casting pre-marked ballots and, sometimes, following this charade, there were small cash payments and/or "refreshments" at the local tavern run by the machine for the "vote" which was cast. The whole business of course was totally corrupt, but "good government" groups were powerless to stop it until reforms eventually weakened the power of the bosses.

Even after World War I and continuing to the present, money was used to buy and determine the outcome of elections. One thinks, for example, of Boss Ed Crump of Memphis, Tennessee, who from the 1920s until the 1940s dominated local and state politics in the Volunteer State by flagrantly buying votes from African-Americans whom he "imported" from Arkansas across the Mississippi River and arranged to be transported to polling stations.

Later, as the more overt, egregious forms of voter and voting fraud became more subtle, new techniques were devised to inject money illegally into campaigns and elections to influence, if not always directly purchase, the outcome. For example, there are many accounts of political operatives using "walking around" money to pay off precinct captains and other local political functionaries, advertisers, even editorial boards of small local papers to favor their particular candidate. It was also common, especially in African-American precincts, to offer "walking around" money as so-called "roof money," whether or not the churches in black precincts actually needed roofs; they were in fact "donations" to influence ministers—often powerful mobilizers of their congregants to vote—to endorse their candidate.

---

### "Walking Around" and "Roof" Money .

The terms "walking around" money and "roof money" have been used for generations. And it has long been noted that black ministers have been very influential in steering their congregants' votes towards one candidate rather than another. In one very famous example, Dr. Martin Luther King, Sr., minister at Ebenezer Baptist Church in Atlanta, endorsed Senator John F. Kennedy for President on the Sunday before the election, 1960. Dr. King was thought to favor Vice President Richard M. Nixon, but the Senator called personally to express concern about the health and safety of King's son, at the moment incarcerated in one of Georgia's notorious jails into which many black prisoners were taken and never seen again. Any number of observers thought Dr. King's endorsement may have helped Kennedy carry the state. It is not clear if any "walking around" or "roof" money was involved on this occasion.[2]

---

And the presence of illegal campaign donations continues to the present day. In late May, 2012, the FBI began an investigation of questionable contributions to two campaigns in Ohio,[3] and other illegal uses of campaign money have been reported in the media during recent years.[4]

Indeed, there continues to be a very gray area between "illegal" and "legal" when it comes to money in political campaigns. There are of course Federal Election Commission (FEC) rules and regulations about proper and improper campaign donations in federal elections. Every state also has its own set of laws and administrative decisions about what is the difference between a proper and improper campaign contribution; so do at least some counties and cities around the country.

But the legalisms and administrative rules are not really the point, although they are certainly not trivial either. The real issue is the use of private money in what is a public enterprise: a political campaign.

It potentially undermines democratic elections when the public forgets, or fails to recognize, that campaigns are not simply playgrounds in which political contributors can act however they want, making up the rules to benefit themselves as they go along. And it further undermines democratic elections if we fail to remind ourselves that elections are a true manifestation of the health of democracy. To the extent that they are taken over by private interests, and the rules allowing private money into campaigns favor those interests, then our elections become less democratic because they are less transparent and less accountable. They further become examples of how our campaigns become more exclusionary, less inclusive, less responsive to the public voice, and less fair. And third, they raise the very troubling issue of whether in fact our elections are for sale.

---

### Elections for Public Office Are Public Activities

There is nothing original or even new in the observation that elections for public office are public activities or endeavors. Writing in the first decade of the twentieth century, Perry Belmont, scion of the wealthy Belmont family of New York and later a Congressman and Ambassador, wrote that "contributions and expenditures in elections are public acts for public purpose." The first serious scholar of money in elections, especially presidential elections, Louise Overacker, noted during the 1930s and 1940s that "once we have real publicity [transparency] the question of 'how much' [money] is 'too much' may safely be taken out of courts of law and left to courts of public opinion." The context of Overacker's comment was that campaigns and elections are the public's business, and the public has a right to know who is paying for them, how much they are paying, and when the money becomes too much money.[5]

But matters run even deeper. Even if all of the legal niceties and formalities are observed, and the election "looks" democratic on the surface, the uneasy relationship between "money", on the one hand, and "candidate" and "campaign", on the other, remains. That relationship can be characterized in several ways: superordinate–subordinate; independent–dependent; manipulative–manipulated are all possibilities.

It is not just the money in itself that causes the imbalance in the relationship between contributor and candidate. It is what the money represents and means that is far more important. A donation or contribution of money by necessity raises the possibility—likelihood—that a non-equal influence/power relationship develops between the one giving the money and the candidate receiving it. Of course, every candidate in history, most likely, has made some sort of speech or produced some kind of press release that says, in effect, "I cannot be bought! I am a candidate of integrity, and when I am in office I will not allow these donations to influence my decisions one whit!"

Bunkum, all of it. And hypocritical as well. Candidates need money, increasingly lots of it. The very act of giving and accepting money creates a bond between donor and recipient, a bond which says, "We both know that by my giving and your accepting this donation, even $1.00, I have some access to you, some say in what you do and how you act, some expectations for you once you are in office." Or indeed, just for the duration of the campaign itself, in case it is an unsuccessful one. Only the most naïve observer would ever assume that the fact of a political donation has no consequences. In America, there is no such thing as a fiscally or politically neutral campaign contribution.

Indeed, this is the heart of the matter. Defenders of the campaign-contribution system as it presently exists in America like to point out that candidates get lots of contributions, from all sorts of people, who want different things. The candidate is thus the center of a field of vectors converging on him, pushing/pulling him in many different directions, thus allowing him flexibility, even freedom, to maintain his independence.

Bunkum, again. Donations are not of equal size ($1.00 is not the same as $1,000). People give money for all sorts of reasons, not all of them involving an immediate *quid pro quo*. But many do have such an expectation and do not wish to wait a year or two or four to cash in their chips. And donations are rarely if ever spread equally across the ideological/policy spectrum; people donate money to candidates and causes they agree with, not ones they don't, or candidates likely to support views they don't like. The larger the donation, and the more powerful, keenly felt, and expressed are the views and political preferences of the donors, the greater the influence will be on the candidate. The impact of donations on a candidate is not a matter of vector or cost/benefit analysis; it is a very human matter of political pressure, power, and built-up sense of obligation.

---

### Congressmen and Nascar Drivers

Journalist Carolyn Baum once pointedly, even sardonically, wrote, "Members of Congress should be compelled to wear uniforms like NASCAR drivers, so we could identify their corporate sponsors." It is exactly the power relationship between donor and recipient and built-up sense of obligation caused by campaign donations from private interests to which she was referring.[6]

---

In the end, as anyone who has engaged in a "money and politics and campaigns and candidates" discussion, whether in a college classroom or the office canteen or neighborhood bar, knows that eventually someone will (correctly) ask, "What is the ethical difference between a campaign contribution (even $1.00) and a legal bribe?"[7] Very, very little: painfully little, as it turns out.

Of course there are any number of counter-arguments that try to sweep the ethical issues under the carpet: "Money contributions to a campaign are a form of political speech, protected by the First Amendment!," cries the U.S. Supreme Court.[8] "Good citizens practice good citizenship and are involved in their communities, and making donations to favored candidates is one way to do this!," declared our grade school teachers. "Making a donation increases the citizen/voter sense of efficacy, that he/she is not just contributing money but internalizing a feeling of 'making a difference' to the community/state/nation!," declare the political scientists. "Giving campaign contributions makes for likely voters, since they develop a sense of ownership, a stake, in the outcome; those who don't contribute, don't have the same stake, and aren't as likely to vote!," intone the political consultants. "The size and number and breadth of campaign contributions demonstrate candidate appeal and strength!," argue the editorial boards, as they debate which candidate, if any, to endorse. "Follow the money, it's the best guide/predictor as to who will win!," yell the bookies and traders.[9] We hear this and other sloganeering in America, time and again. Some of it may even be true.

But essentially the sloganeering is all irrelevant, because it begs the question of what happens when private money, especially in unequal amounts, enters the public square of the political campaign/election process in the first place. At a minimum, contributions are a way to influence, even indirectly, the behavior and speech of candidates. At the more extreme end, contributions allow corruption, favoritism, under-the-table deals, putting private interests before the public interest and public good. Even if none of this happens, the possibility of behavior counter to democratic norms and standards exists. The fact that it is not manifest at any point in time in no way diminishes the chance that it will appear, as it has too often in the past. In campaign politics, as in law, the *appearance* of a violation, or the *possibility* that wrongdoing may occur, is as important as if it actually happens.

---

**Conveying Favors to Donors**

The *Guardian* reported that companies which donated to the Republican Governor's Association, when led by New Jersey Governor Chris Christie, and other Republican causes/campaigns during that time, received some $1.25 B in state contracts and other deals from his administration.[10] This is but a recent example of spoils system politics, which can be found from the earliest days of our Republic onward to the present.

---

## Two Axioms of Campaign Finance

The old days of ethics in campaign finance were not good, but compared to the post-*Citizens United* world,[11] they look pretty appealing. This was especially true after the passage of the *Bipartisan Campaign Reform Act*, the so-called McCain-Feingold law, in 2002.

Before surveying this effort at campaign finance reform and moving on to *Citizens United* and subsequent cases, we need to remind or inform readers that any understanding of campaign finance rules and requirements must keep two separate but related distinctions—axioms, really—in mind.

The first is that campaign finance illustrates the most basic element in our federal system: there are federal (national) laws and regulations about campaign finance, and there are state (and sometimes local) campaign finance laws and regulations. It's the same principle behind our legal system: there are federal civil and criminal laws, and 50 state sets of civil and criminal laws. The two seldom meet or intersect, unless a case arises which involves both a federal question and a violation of state law. The same point is even more true of campaign finance: federal requirements have virtually nothing to do with state requirements except under very narrow circumstances, to be highlighted later. In other words, FEC guidelines and requirements are not relevant to state campaign finance laws and practices; and those at the state level have virtually no bearing on federal elections.

---

### Elections in Our Federal System

Readers are reminded that there are really only three kinds of federal elections in this country: President/Vice-President; U.S. Senate; and U.S. House of Representatives. The 50 states are responsible for running these elections through state and local elections officials, not the FEC, which has no authority to administer elections. However, FEC rules on campaign finance do govern these three categories of federal elections. State and local elections are governed and regulated by state authorities in their respective states, not the FEC.

---

On the other hand, both McCain-Feingold and *Citizens United* have some bearing on state campaign finance, as we will see, but only because, in the case of the former, the law specifically covers a narrow portion of state campaign finance practices; and the latter primarily because of the floodgates that it opened, which at least potentially swamp state and local campaign finance practices (there were 24 states which limited or outlawed corporate and union involvement in certain types of campaign activity and, following *Citizens United*, 17 of them moved to bring their requirements in line with the U.S. Supreme Court decision).[12]

But in the main the distinction between federal practice and state/local procedures on campaign finance is axiomatic. It is unfortunate that too often media stories, and even otherwise learned commentators and pundits, are confused if not outright wrong, because they fail to note that campaign finance rules at the two levels really operate in very different universes, and any overlap is quite minor.

The second axiomatic distinction that readers need to keep in mind is that between so-called "hard money" and "soft money" campaign contributions. The distinction exists at both federal and state/local levels.

Hard money consists of donations given directly to a political campaign. What does that mean? Every campaign—whether for a cause or for a candidate—is required to have its own treasury. That treasury— usually it takes the form of a bank account—exists as an independent depository for contributions; it cannot be connected to any other account. It is usually called or labeled something like, "Campaign Account of Suzy Smith for County Commission," or "Campaign Account of Citizens for a Better City." All contributions given directly to a campaign must—MUST—be deposited in the campaign account or they cannot be used. A candidate who is funding his/her own campaign must *still* move personal funds into the campaign account; spending personal dollars on the campaign without depositing and reporting them is illegal, at any level.

Why is this important? Because hard money donations are carefully regulated and examined, by the FEC at the national level, or by state and local officials in those jurisdictions. Limits are imposed on how much can be contributed directly to campaigns. At the federal level it is currently $2,600;[13] at the state level the range is enormous, from $41,000 for gubernatorial elections, and $10,000 in statewide elections in Wisconsin, down to $500 per candidate per election[14] in a few states.[15] Alabama, Indiana, Iowa, Mississippi, Missouri, Nebraska, North Dakota, Oregon, Pennsylvania, Texas, Utah, and Virginia impose no limits; literally it is the sky.[16] But, whatever the limit, if any, of donations, all hard money donations *must* be reported to the FEC or state election officials within an allotted time frame. Failure to do so can result in fines or, at a minimum, embarrassment to the campaign.

Thus hard money contributions are generally transparent and accountable. The FEC and state election agencies continually publish (nowadays, online as well) which individuals or PACS make hard money donations and how much they gave.[17] In many states, contributions of $100 or over must also list the occupation of the donor (for the FEC a contribution of even $1.00 imposes this requirement, and donors must affirm a number of other stipulations as well, such as not serving as a contractor for the federal government, or making a contribution from a corporation or union. *Citizens United* did *not* lift the ban on union or corporate direct, hard money contributions to campaigns. This point is frequently missed).

There are also a number of good-government watchdog groups that monitor and publicize on their websites campaign contributions; among the most readily accessible of these are CQ Money Line; Open Secrets (The Center for Responsive Politics); The Center for Public Integrity; Common Cause; Public Campaign; Follow the Money; and Campaign Finance Information Center, among others.[18]

The point of all this is that if one wishes to follow campaign contributions, it is relatively easy to view those given as hard money donations directly to the campaign. They are generally well documented, overseen by the FEC and states, and publicly reported, and they represent by far the most transparent part of campaign finance.

The opposite is true of "soft" money contributions. These are moneys spent by outside individuals or groups on behalf of a campaign, but are (at least supposedly) completely separate from it.[19] Whether at the federal or state level, soft money donations are supposed to be kept at arm's length from the campaign, each operating in separate universes and with no knowledge of or coordination between or among them. Bunkum, of course.

## Who Knew and What Did They Know?

The George H.W. Bush presidential campaign in 1988 was adamant that it had no prior knowledge of the infamous "Willy Horton" ad, a mean-spirited and likely racist attack on Michael Dukakis (it can be viewed at www.youtube.com/watch?v=Io9KMSSEZ0Y). However, in the documentary *Boogie Man: The Lee Atwater Story* (www.imdb.com/title/tt1262863, 2008), Atwater clearly states that the campaign, of which he was the manager, knew all about it. In addition, the Bush campaign never repudiated or abjured the ad. More recently, a federal investigation into the campaign finances of Governor Scott Walker of Wisconsin alleged that members of his campaign staff actively worked with independent groups to raise and spend money in conjunction with fighting efforts to recall him.[20]

Soft money has three features that render it a direct danger to democratic elections: there are virtually no limits on how much money can be raised and spent for soft money campaigns; the money is basically unregulated by the FEC or state election officials; and much—but not all—of soft money is unaccounted for, essentially given anonymously, that is, it is "dark" money. Some qualification will be put on these bold assertions below, but in the main they hold true. But, even with minor modifications, they represent political activity directly counter to fundamental principles of democratic elections: transparency, accountability, and basic standards of fairness, meaning the playing field is reasonably level.

Much of the complaining about soft money began with PACs, political action committees that are legalized fictions. They pretend to be separate organizations from their parent institutions, and legally that is true. From a functional and ethical standpoint, however, one can and should question just how "separate" separate really is. This simply deepens the ethical dilemma created when parent organizations are forbidden from making hard money political contributions, but their PACs can.

PACS of course can and do give hard money contributions and are subject to the same limits and reporting requirements as individuals. At the federal level, corporate and labor PACs have been able to make campaign contributions, whereas the parent organizations were forbidden to do so. There was and is some range of variation at the state level. In some states corporations and unions can make contributions; in others they cannot. And in some states both corporations/unions *and* their PACs are able to contribute separately, which represents for campaigns a legalized form of double-dipping and a state-sanctioned evasion of campaign finance donation limits. Matters become more egregious in those jurisdictions that allow PACs to breed "sub-PACS," which are just other channels through which the "parent" PAC can donate still more funds.

Another, even more important cause for concern with soft money began in the early 1980s, but really did not gather steam until the mid-1990s. As a result of changes in federal requirements, PACs and individuals could donate *unlimited* amounts of money to the national parties (and there were few if any limits on donations to state parties). These donations were supposed to be for "party-building" activities such as voter education, get-out-the-vote, and "issue ads," which did not name candidates, but which made very emphatic statements about what was the "right" side of an issue, presumably the side party-favored candidates were to hold.[21]

The whole thing was a ruse, a subterfuge, a sham. It was a way of getting around contribution limits and reporting requirements; and as long as the money was donated to party "soft money" accounts, it was not even necessary to account for the origin of the funds. The names of donors giving to parties for "issue ads" were protected, and they could donate as lavishly as their wishes and checkbooks would allow. By the early 1990s matters were spinning out of control. In the 1992 presidential election cycle, the two national parties raised about $86 M for soft money, issue-based advertising campaigns. By 1996 that figure rose to nearly $120 M a 40 percent increase.[22] And the upward acceleration of party spending on behalf of presidential candidates continued through 2000; by that time, also, state parties were paying for their own "issue ads," many of which were poorly disguised endorsements of candidates, even though the soft money expenditures were supposed to be separate from those of the actual candidates and their campaigns.

Indeed by the late 1990s, early 2000s, matters had become more complicated. While PACs more or less (there were exceptions) limited their work to publicizing their endorsement of candidates and making hard money contributions, lawyers and campaign finance experts stumbled upon a new possibility: "527" organizations. The term comes from their origin in the Internal Revenue Code (§ 527); they are tax-exempt organizations that generally are issue advocacy groups, but which can also engage in activities that are directed at the election or defeat of actual candidates, at any level.[23] In general, those that are strictly advocacy groups need make only the most rudimentary reports to FEC or state officials; those playing hardball politics, naming names for example, have more stringent reporting requirements, such as reporting donors, than those just advocating "issues."[24]

Nonetheless, what is important is that besides parties running "issue" campaigns, increasing numbers of 527s were also getting involved in "issue" advertisements on their own, and as long as they did not *specifically* advocate the election or defeat of a candidate, they could pretty much do whatever they wanted. Readers with long memories will recall the infamous "Willy Horton" ad of 1988, held by some to be decidedly racist; while they showed Democratic candidate Michael Dukakis in a profoundly unflattering light, they never said anything about electing George H.W. Bush or defeating Dukakis.[25] Other readers will recall the 2004 independently sponsored ads against John Kerry, the so-called "Flip-Flop" wind-surfing ad, and the "Swift-Boat" ads on his Vietnam service. Both were examples of soft money ads paid for by independent 527 groups; some regarded them as vicious and unfair, even though they never advocated Kerry's defeat, or the election of his opponent George W. Bush.[26]

By the late 1990s and early 2000s there were increasing calls to get rid of PACs and 527s, or at least emasculate them in such a way as to limit their involvement and power in political campaigns. But most of the voices advocating such ideas were crying in the wilderness, not necessarily unheard but certainly unheeded. There were many problems associated with efforts to regulate PACs and 527s, the most important of which were Constitutional: the First Amendment protected both their right of speech *and* their right to petition the government.[27] And from a political standpoint, trying to get rid of them was harder than the task of Sisyphus pushing his boulder up the hill: there was no incentive for members of the Congress, in either chamber, almost all of whom had benefitted from PAC and/or 527 organizations, to eliminate or even restrain them. The same was true at the state level.

## Reforming Campaign Finance: Two Opposing Cavalry Charges

The increasing activism of PACs and 527s in the campaign arena, and the massive dollars that political parties were pouring into alleged "issue" campaigns, set off warning sirens among watchdog groups, good-government types, and editorial boards. Beating up on second- and third-party expenditures in campaigns became a serious industry by the late 1990s. One could hardly pick up a newspaper or magazine covering politics without seeing a piece on how alarmingly dangerous our campaign finance system had become and how it was falling into the hands of wealthy contributors to parties, PACs, and 527s. The term "fat cats," not heard in political circles since the campaign excesses of 1972, became a short-cut way of complaining about how wealth was buying American elections.[28]

In retrospect it all seems very naïve, compared to what was coming. But there was no doubt about the good faith and determination of those who called the massive infusion of campaign dollars into question; they saw very black clouds on the horizon if nothing was done. By the mid-1990s political parties and other groups were throwing money into "issue" advertisements in support of or opposition to causes (and, in reality, candidates) in record amounts. There seemed to be no limit, and traditional ways of running and financing campaigns appeared as outdated as hula hoops or disco suits or 8-track tape players. The time seemed ripe for "reform" of campaign finance and some campaign practices.

Leading the cavalry charge was the unlikely duo of Senator John McCain, a maverick, centrist/right Republican from Arizona and later 2008 Republican nominee for President, and Senator Russ Feingold, an old-fashioned populist Democrat from Wisconsin. After many skirmishes, some pitched battles, and years of hard work, Congress passed the *Bipartisan Campaign Reform Act* (BCRA), more commonly known as the McCain-Feingold bill, on March 27, 2002; it was one of the last times the term "bipartisan" showed up in the title of a major piece of Congressional legislation.

BCRA was not universally loved when it was passed. Opponents of the bill, such as Senator Mitch McConnell of Kentucky, thought it was an unconstitutional violation of First Amendment rights. Others were certain that it did not go far enough in blocking the use of second- and third-party money in campaigns. Even President Bush expressed doubts about the bill when he signed it into law.

But BCRA did take a number of important steps which should be noted here:

- It prohibited the national parties from engaging in soft money campaigns, by denying parties the ability to solicit "non federal" money.
- It limited the amount of money that individuals and PACs could donate to parties at national and state levels.[29]
- It limited the use of federal moneys at the state and local levels to campaign activity carried out in association with federal campaigns.
- It created the requirement, by now familiar to everyone who has heard on TV or the radio a campaign ad, that the candidate state something like "I am _____, and I approve this message," forcing the candidate to acknowledge and take ownership of the ad.
- And last, but by no means least, McCain-Feingold created limits of when political advertisements paid for by "outside" groups could be aired: not within 30 days of a primary election and not within 60 days of a general election; and McCain-Feingold also imposed limits on the kind of groups that could pay for such ads.[30]

As anyone who follows campaign politics knows, McCain-Feingold did not get rid of Big Money in campaigns. It did, however, get political parties out of the "issue" campaign advertising business, because there were limits on what they could spend money on besides candidates for federal office. And it prevented "fat cats" from throwing unlimited money into party accounts at national and state levels, earmarked to be spent in conjunction with particular campaigns. It insured that national parties could not simply bankroll favored state and local candidates; and dollars from national parties could only be used on federal elections, not state/local ones. And of course it opened the door to *Citizens United*, by attempting to restrict the kind of organizations that could sponsor political advertisements in conjunction with soft money campaigns, and when they could do so.

It was in fact this latter stipulation that essentially brought down the entire campaign finance edifice, or most of it anyway, in *Citizens United*, a matter to which we will now attend. However, before doing so, it is well to make another observation about McCain-Feingold: it was undoubtedly a blow in favor of strengthening democratic elections, even if a tentative and halting one, because it restricted the use of private money in political campaigns, which is a public enterprise. That particular topic had been ignored for years. And it was an honest attempt at bipartisanship, an idea that now, a decade and a half later, looks more like a subject suitable for archeologists and paleontologists than students of contemporary American politics.[31]

The facts behind *Citizens United vs. FEC* are straightforward.[32] In January, 2008, a non-profit corporation called Citizens United "released a documentary ... critical of then-Senator Hillary Clinton, a candidate for her party's [Democratic] presidential nomination." It was in fact a hatchet job. Citizens United produced ads so that the documentary could run on cable TV within 30 days of the primary election (readers will remember that BCRA rules *prohibited* such broadcasts within 30 days of the primary). Citizens United requested a ruling in Federal District Court which would have held that the BCRA rules concerning its sponsorship of the film and the reporting/disclosure rules were unconstitutional violations of its First Amendment, free speech rights. The District Court declined to offer Citizens United what it wanted and in fact granted the FEC summary judgment.

---

### Summary Judgment

Summary judgment is a legal device in civil law whereby a matter can be resolved without need of a trial; to win a summary judgment there can be no dispute about the facts of the case, and one of the parties is entitled to a favorable judgment as a matter of law.[33]

---

Citizens United then appealed; the U.S. Supreme Court first heard oral arguments on March 24, 2009 and again on September 9, 2009. The case was decided on January 21, 2010, by essentially a 5:4 majority that gave Citizens United what it wanted.

The line-up on the decision was so complicated, however, that one needed a scorecard to keep up; Justice Kennedy was joined in the majority by Chief Justice Roberts and Justices Scalia and Alioto; Justice Thomas also joined, but not for Part IV, although Justices Stevens, Ginsburg, Breyer, and Sotomayor did join in that Part. There was a concurring opinion by Chief Justice Roberts and one by Justice Scalia; there was one by Justice Stevens which concurred in part and vigorously dissented in another. Justice Thomas filed his own, separate opinion.

It is worth mentioning the entangled web of opinions because it points to a very crucial issue. It is not just that the Court was sharply divided—that happens regularly on the Roberts Court—but it is an indication of a) just how opaque and incomprehensible FEC rules on campaign finance had become in the years following BCRA; and b) the depth of the political waters which the case plumbed, and which clearly troubled some of the Justices.

Indeed, this is the heart of the matter. *Citizens United* is not just—or even mainly—a legal decision. It is a deeply political one. To be sure, it is dressed up with all of the legalese and formulaic language one would expect in a Supreme Court decision. At heart, however, the ultimate decision—which struck down FEC and BCRA provisions against corporate sponsorship of outside, soft money campaign advertisements—was a victory for those advocating a political agenda that wanted to break the dam blocking them since *Buckley vs. Valeo* in 1976.[34]

A partisan agenda? Perhaps so, because the decision does acknowledge and reward what had become Republican mantras over the years, namely that preventing corporate resources (a major source of GOP funds) from directly entering the campaign arena was unfair, unwarranted, and a violation of First Amendment rights; and that reporting and disclosure of names would cause major discomfort and embarrassment to wealthy donors, and even possibly retribution against them. Or so the tune went, year after year.

But there is a deeper, more significant thrust of the decision. It was a victory for Big Money. Indeed, just as McCain-Feingold led a cavalry charge in favor of democratic (that is, transparent and accountable) campaign finance practices, so *Citizens United* was an even more powerful counter-attack against these practices.

In the text of the decision there is some high-minded window dressing. The Court observes, for example, in a now famous sentence, "Because speech is an essential mechanism of democracy ... political speech must prevail against laws that would suppress it by design or inadvertence." In other words, government cannot pick and choose who gets to have free speech, because that would raise issues of fairness and equity. True enough. And, the Court continued, it did not matter that the resources used by some groups (corporations in particular) to practice political speech are gained in the "marketplace" (the Court's word). Here of course matters start to get a little dicey, because the Court deliberately passed over what has become all too apparent since the mid-to-late 1970s, namely, that big corporations have become so dominant in the marketplace as to cause serious market distortions and eliminate competition.[35]

But irrespective of the legal merits of the Court's decision, in Section 2(c) it opened the doors to avalanches of money into campaign finance. The Court said:

> this Court now concludes that independent expenditures, including those made by corporations, do not give rise to corruption or the appearance of corruption. That speakers may have influence over or access to elected officials does not mean that those officials are corrupt. And the appearance of influence or access will not cause the electorate to lose faith in this democracy.

It's hard to know if the Court, in publishing this language as a (more or less) majority opinion, is being disingenuous, or something else.

First and most obviously, it is wrong. In the history of this country, corporations have often been prosecuted for having corrupted American politics. The so-called Gilded Age of the late nineteenth century, the Age of the Robber Barons, when railroads and banks, and big steel and big mining, and other large aggregations of capital simply bought state and local officials, is well known.[36] It took the Populists, the Progressives, the muckrakers, Teddy Roosevelt, and a host of others to start rooting out the cancers and corrosiveness and corruptions that they caused our democracy.

---

### Montana Dissents

In a courageous decision flying right in the face of *Citizens United*, the Supreme Court of Montana, a decidedly red-leaning state, chastised the U.S. Supreme Court for its historical ignorance. Residents of that state know all too well, the Court said, of the damage caused by corruption that huge corporations, especially but not only mining, wreaked on Montana in the past. The U.S. Supreme Court later rejected the Montana Justices' view of their history.[37]

---

More recently, one need only consider the disastrous impact of the now-defunct corporation Enron and its disgraced chief managers on national and California politics. It's so-called "independent" expenditures manufactured a phony power "crisis," brought down a Governor (Gray Davis) who had had the temerity to stand up to the company, and caused massive hardships to millions of California residents. This is not simply the appearance of corruption; it is the very essence of corruption.[38]

Not all corporations are corrupt, of course; and the Court correctly noted that not all elected or public officials are corrupt. But the Court gave too little attention to its own observation about the appearance of corruption. In a democracy, people's faith and trust in the system rests on its axiomatic belief that not even the *appearance* of corruption can be tolerated. Corruption is insidious, like the camel's-nose-under-the-tent in the old cliché, or two fleas on a dog, or one drink for an alcoholic; left unchecked, the situation can quickly spiral out of control and turn hopeless. It's exactly for this reason that, as our grade-school teachers used to tell us, *appearances* of wrongdoing and corruption are every bit as important as their actual presence.

It is this last thought that was one of the guiding principles behind both the *Buckley* decision and the McCain-Feingold Act. They were just as much concerned with the *possibility* of wrongdoing, corruption, and other forms of behavior subversive to democratic elections by corporations (and unions) that might take place as the actual fact of it. In a very real sense, both *Buckley* and McCain-Feingold should be viewed as much as prophylactics against political corruption in campaign finance as antidotes for its presence. Interestingly, the decision in an important and controversial U.S. Supreme Court Case involving state voter ID laws, a few years before *Citizens United*, rested not on evidence shown of voter fraud, but on the possibility that it might take place.[20] In *Crawford*, the possibility of corruption motivated a majority of the Justices to uphold draconian voter ID laws; in *Citizens United*, they simply dismissed the possibility of corruption out of hand.

The evidence of corruption or the potential for corruption was all there for the Court to see. It preferred instead to allow basically unlimited independent, soft money campaign contributions by Big Money to run roughshod over the campaign landscape. By so doing, it destroyed any semblance of a fair or level campaign finance playing fields and essentially changed the campaign and elections game to favor money over voters.

Much has been written about *Citizens United*, almost all of it critical. Instead of re-plowing already well-tilled ground, let us address just a few of the most central points of *Citizens United*, as they highlight both the major thrust of the decision and allow a word or two on how it leads in a direction inimical to democratic elections.

The first point comes not from *Citizens United* but *Buckley vs. Valeo* (1976): money given for a political cause, including money spent independently on a campaign, is speech protected by the First Amendment. It is this point which provides the entire structural foundation for *Citizens United* because, without it, the case collapses completely. Whatever are the merits of the legal arguments made on behalf of protecting money as speech, from a political standpoint the position is injurious to democratic elections. Why? Because it denies the fundamental tenet that, in democratic elections, every vote is equal, and every voice is equal. Once money is introduced into the mix, because it is unequally distributed throughout the population, some voices will be more equal than others, that is, those with more money will have more voice. If money were equally distributed throughout the population, then there would be no problem about equality or fairness, because each voice would have the same resources behind it. But money is not equally distributed, never has been, and most likely never will be. So, by inviting an unequally distributed resource into political campaigns, the Supreme Court has institutionalized inequality and unfairness into how campaigns are funded, and therefore whose voice is stronger and whose is weaker—unless that money is strictly regulated in its use.

But this brings us to the second point. *Buckley* and McCain-Feingold recognized, even if in limited ways, that money in political campaigns has to be regulated. *Citizens United* swept away one of those important regulations: corporations could now pour vast funds into independent expenditures in a completely unregulated, and in some cases a completely unaccountable, way. In a subsequent decision, to be discussed shortly, the Supreme Court eliminated another important regulation, allowing even greater sums to be donated to political campaigns.[40] The effect of *Citizens United*'s removal of just one set of regulations was to turn political campaigns into playgrounds for rich corporations and wealthy donors who can use as much of their resources as they wish, free and clear of any regulation.

There is a third point. Many commentators have noted that to equate corporations with people, natural persons, is preposterous on the face of it. We need not explore this idea further; readers are encouraged to do so themselves. But what is crucial is that the formation of a corporation requires state action; in other words, the state has the power to authorize, or not authorize, the formation of a corporation. They must be chartered by the state to become "fictitious persons" (as any first-year law student knows) in order to do business. Therefore they are accountable to the state, and indeed are required to file reports with the chartering agency as a way of being held publicly accountable.

Humans are not created by state action, but by a biological process called procreation. No state action is required or necessary for conception. While humans have an obligation to the state—they must obey the law, for example, and pay taxes—the accountability of humans to the state, and their relationship to state authority, is much different from that of corporations; filing an annual state income tax form in those states that require it, for example, is hardly the same as the annual reports required of corporations. The fundamental difference of state action being required for one entity to exist, and none whatsoever on the other, is enough to render attempts to equate the two as sophistry.

And finally, in democratic elections all eligible persons are guaranteed an equal, single voice. But in trying to equate corporations with humans, the Supreme Court has ensured that corporations have two: the entity called the corporation can enter the political fray through donations of campaign money, and its managers and owners/stockholders can also do so as private individuals. Thus they have an extra voice, one denied individual humans who are not part of corporate ownership or management. The result is a further tilting of the playing field of campaigning and democratic elections to favor money over votes.

But the U.S. Supreme Court chose not to stop the deregulation of independent campaign expenditures with *Citizens United*. Four years later, in a case called *McCutcheon vs. FEC* (April 2, 2014, cited above), the Court removed another set of regulations in campaign finance.

The case dealt with both hard and soft campaign donations. In the hard money category, donors have been limited to $2,600 per candidate, per election (these limits are for candidates for federal offices, not those in state or local races). In a 2-year election cycle, donors were further limited to a total donation to individual candidates of $48,600; this means that, in any given cycle, a donor could give to approximately 18 different candidates. *McCutcheon* removed those limits. While no single candidate for federal office can receive more than $2,600, there is no limit to the number of candidates to whom a donor can now give.[41]

In addition, donors were limited to $32,400 for national party committees, $10,000 to state and local party committees, and $5,000 to any other political committee, up to a maximum total donation of $74,600 in a 2-year cycle. These individual limits still apply, but there is no limit on how many committees a donor can contribute to. In sum, before *McCutcheon* donors were limited to a total of $123,200 in donations to candidates, parties, and other political groups per cycle ($48,600 + $74,600 = $123,200); now, there are no limits. Indeed, the *New York Times* noted that a donor wishing to give to every single candidate, party committee, and other political committee that he/she could find could spend about $3.6 M dollars every election cycle on party committees, Congressional candidates, and presidential candidates.[42]

It seems hardly necessary to observe that, in giving its *McCutcheon* ruling, the Supreme Court has enormously broadened and deepened the opportunity for money—Big Money—to be donated to political campaigns. But it must be noted that *McCutcheon* did not eliminate the limits on the *amount* of money that could be donated to candidates, parties, and committees; it instead eliminated the *number* of donations that could be made. Nor are unions and corporations now allowed to donate directly to federal candidates in the form of hard money contributions; *McCutcheon* did not address that limitation, and corporations and unions wishing to donate on behalf of candidates must do so through independent expenditures, à *la Citizens United.*

One of the possible outcomes of *McCutcheon* could well be a strengthening of party coffers. The reason is that all parties need do is create an abundance of political committees, and donors are free to contribute as much as they like to any and all of them.[43] This may, but not necessarily, make contributions to independent groups less desirable, since donors can give to as many committees, and candidates, as they choose. On the other hand, the contributions to party committees have to be reported, meaning that the names of donors will become public. Not all donors want their names made public and, as we will see in the next section, there is an exquisite way in which anonymous donations can be made, all perfectly legal and with no dollar limits at all, so it is not likely that party committees will pre-empt donations to particular kinds of independent groups.

Finally, *McCutcheon* raises the question of whether the Roberts Court will take the next step and eliminate limits on direct contributions to candidates, parties, and political committees. Justice Thomas, in his more-or-less concurring opinion in *Citizens United*, indicated that he would favor such a step. And as the distinguished legal scholar Charles Fried, Professor of Law at Harvard University and former Solicitor-General in the second Reagan Administration, noted even before the *McCutcheon* decision was announced, the Court has in effect eliminated donation limits to candidates because donors can contribute to every single federal candidate they wish.[44] But there remains the open question of whether or not the Supreme Court will remove all limits on donations, including direct contributions to candidates. Full deregulation of that sort will foster even greater avalanches of Big Money into political campaigns.

## What Have We Done?

Campaign finance is a mess. The complexities of reporting funds and expenditures, disclosing (or not) donors, determining whether a particular organization involved in independent expenditures is a PAC, or 527 or 501(c)(4), (5), or (6), or not[45]—these are just the beginning. The traditional categories of hard money donations, in-kind contributions, and soft money independent expenditures have, at the margins, gotten so blurred as to make the distinctions virtually meaningless.

The U.S. Supreme Court has created these problems on its own. Hearing and deciding cases post-*Buckley* and pre-*Citizens United* on what is or is not permissible in campaign donations caused immense confusion: *Bellotti*, *Austin*, and *McConnell*, among others, all seem to go in different directions.[46] One can legitimately say that *Citizens United* created still further problems because it paid no attention to the social and political consequences of its decision.

But the FEC is also to blame. From its origins in the 1970s, it has never been certain of its role. It has very few powers of enforcement, yet it is the author of rules and regulations of federal campaign finance and the arbiter of many disputes that occur under that umbrella. It is deeply, deeply affected by the partisan politics of the moment in Washington, D.C., and by the far-reaching impact of U.S. Supreme Court decisions. Given how slowly regulatory agencies move and act at the federal level, the FEC had barely settled into BCRA/McCain-Feingold (2002) when it took a major hit because of *Citizens United* (2010).

Confusion also reigns across the United States, at the state level. As we saw with the relatively simple matter of limits on campaign donations, the rules and requirements of reporting and disclosure across all 50 states are not easily grasped. However, we can say that the themes that will immediately strike any interested observer will be: enhanced power of big money in campaigns and decreasing levels of transparency and accountability as well.

But if we focus just on *Citizens United* and its aftermath, there are additional consequences that are so significant that the chapter would be incomplete without at least some discussion. The most important might seem surreal, were it not so serious: the creation of SuperPacs. Strictly speaking, SuperPacs are not a result of *Citizens United* but of an ensuing case in a lower court: *SpeechNow.org vs. Federal Election Commission*.[47] It allowed certain types of 527 organizations to collect and spend campaign money freely and without limits. Technically, they are known as "independent expenditure-only committees."[48]

*SpeechNow.org* went well beyond *Citizens United*, insofar as the Supreme Court in that case noted that no evidence was offered to support the claim, articulated by plaintiffs in the case, that disclosure of names can have a "chilling" effect on donations, as potential contributors might not wish to face the publicity, let alone the reprisals, that donating might bring. The disclosure requirements of McCain-Feingold were upheld in *Citizens United*.

But *SpeechNow.org* was a game-changer.[49] It essentially created two kinds of SuperPacs.[50] The "regular" SuperPacs could collect and spend as much money as they wished on a "soft" money basis. And they could attack or promote candidates and causes overtly, mentioning names if they so chose. But they would have to report their donors on either a monthly or quarterly basis, as they chose.[51] They could not, however, make "hard money" direct contributions to campaigns as "regular" PACs can. On the other hand, hard money contributions are strictly limited in amount (*Buckley*) if not in the number donated (*McCutcheon*), so the prohibition against SuperPacs making them was hardly a burden, given their unlimited ability to raise and spend "soft" money outside of a campaign.

But, as a result of new FEC rules and interpretations of "non-profit" organizations under other portions of IRS rules besides 527, it became possible to create another type of SuperPac organization that did not have to disclose donors. So-called 501(c)(4) tax-exempt organizations have actually existed for a long time.[52] According to the IRS they are supposed to be "social welfare" organizations; the National Rifle Association and the Sierra Club have long operated under this umbrella. Their primary purpose was to be non-political, but beginning in 1959 the IRS relaxed the rules to allow limited political activity. Theoretically the organization was not to spend more than 50 percent of its operating budget on political activity, a rule which has essentially proven meaningless and unenforceable.[53]

Immediately political operatives and consultants across the country saw the virtues of creating 501(c)(4) SuperPacs, freed from the disclosure requirements of "regular" SuperPACs (527s). The appeal to many wealthy potential donors was obvious. They could drop unlimited amounts of money into a 501(c)(4) SuperPac, and their names would never come forward or be publicized.[54]

---

### How To Hide Donors' Names

ProPublica illustrates how the 527 SuperPac and the 501(c)(4) groups can work together:

> "Say some like-minded people form both a Super-PAC and a nonprofit 501(c)(4). Corporations and individuals could then donate as much as they want to the nonprofit, which isn't required to publicly disclose funders. The nonprofit could then donate as much as it wanted to the Super-PAC, which lists the nonprofit's donation but not the original contributors."[55]

---

The floodgates opened. The sums involved are staggering. To cite the most prominent example, Karl Rove, the former advisor to President George Bush and master of his election and re-election campaigns, established two major SuperPacs—one a "regular" 527 SuperPac, which has to disclose donors, called America Crossroads, and the other a 501(c)(4) called Crossroads GPS.[56] *Forbes* reported that, as of late May, 2012, Rove's SuperPacs had raised over $100 M, and planned to spend over $240 M in an effort to defeat President Obama.

But other SuperPacs have also had astonishing success at raising money. The Center for Public Integrity reported that, by May 29, 2012, a SuperPac supporting Mr. Romney had raised over $56 M; President Obama's own

SuperPac—he was slow to form one, after first claiming he would not because he opposed the whole idea, but then became aware of the avalanche of Koch-Rove-Romney money facing him—only raised about $11 M, although he was well funded from other sources, as he was in 2008. In late May, 2012, the online newsletter "Politico.com" reported that GOP SuperPacs planned to spend in the neighborhood of $1 B on advertisements to oust Mr. Obama from the White House.[57]

In September 2013, published reports appeared that an organization closely allied with the Koch Brothers called "Freedom Partners" donated some $256 M—a quarter of a billion dollars—to an array of conservative groups in 2012.[58] Freedom Partners was not a 501(c)(4) organization but rather a 501(c)(6),[59] regarded by the IRS as a sort of Trade Association or Chamber of Commerce. Under IRS rules, Freedom Partners was not required to reveal the list of those donating money, although of course it was required to specify to which groups it made donations. Once again, anonymity of donors ruled.[60]

---

### SuperPacs on Campus

In October, 2013, one of the author's students was approached by a conservative organization that targeted students at colleges and universities. His investigation revealed that it was a 501(c)(3) organization, another kind of non-profit group which, according to IRS rules, is not supposed to engage heavily in political activity. But, as the student reported, the whole idea of the group approaching him was to create and enhance support for right-wing causes on campus—a very political activity.[61]

---

And the avalanche of money into SuperPacs continues even as this book is written. The Center for Responsive Politics reported that, as of June 24, 2014, 1,075 SuperPacs had raised $234,169,364 and spent $73,980,739 for the 2014 campaign cycle.[62] How much of this is "dark" money, that is, money from undisclosed sources, is not always clear.[63] But the Center for Responsive Politics tracks the expenditures of "dark money" groups (mainly 501(c)(4) and 501 (c)(6) organizations) and reported that in 2006 they spent under $5.2 M, but in the 2012 presidential year, over $300 M, an increase of 5,700 percent![64]

What has happened since 2012? The answer is that more and more money, more and more SuperPac money, and more and more dark money has entered political campaigns. The Center for Responsive Politics reported that, in 2014, an off-presidential year, the "one percent of the one percent" of the U.S. total population, some 31,976 donors, gave $1.18 B in *disclosed* monies for federal elections. This was about 29 percent of all donations reported to the FEC for that campaign cycle.[65] The Center also estimated that, while in the 2010 election cycle dark money accounted for about $127 M, it rose to over $300 M in 2012, fell to just over $120 M in the non-presidential year of 2014, and for the 2016 elections is tenfold greater than at the same period in the 2012 cycle.[66]

Since the 2014 cycle the floodgates have opened to allow seemingly limitless donations, both dark and reported. By midsummer, 2015, presidential Republican candidate Jeb Bush had already raised over $114 M.[67] By comparison, Democrat Hillary Clinton raised "only" $45 M.[68] The Koch brothers, major donors to right-wing candidates and causes, announced early in 2015 that they planned to spend close to $1 B on 2016 elections.[69] Many analysts were already observing that the 2016 election cycle would be overwhelmed by SuperPac money, both dark and reported.[70] In addition, as we noted in Chapter 3, 2015 has seen the rise of billionaire patrons of individual candidates, any one of whom has the personal resources to comfortably bankroll an entire presidential campaign for his chosen favorite.

Some readers might object that this discussion overstates the danger of money in campaigns, SuperPac money in particular. After all, they might point out, in spite of the vast amounts of SuperPac money—dark and otherwise—spent in 2012, the return on the "investment" was unimpressive: President Obama was handily if not easily re-elected, and several Senators or Senate candidates targeted for defeat by right-wing SuperPacs actually won.[71] These observations are correct, but they miss two important points. The first is that one election cycle doesn't prove anything; as a number of spokesmen for right-wing groups pointed out, they may not have spent their money wisely. Second, and more importantly, whether the right-wing SuperPacs won or lost is not the point. What is the point is that the rules under which they are allowed to operate are subversive of the democratic tenets of transparency, accountability, and fairness.

---

### The Personal SuperPac

The *New York Times* in early August, 2014, reported and editorialized on the creation of a new kind of SuperPac, the "Personal SuperPac." It is one that is created exclusively for the benefit of a single candidate. While disclosure of donors is required, there is no limit on how much money can be raised, or spent, on behalf of the favored candidate. So much for the idea that "soft money" expenditures are to be independent of, and at arm's length from, the candidate's actual campaign structure. Indeed, such an idea now seems hopelessly naïve and ingenuous.[72]

And other readers might continue the objection by saying, So what? Why is money a problem? Why should not wealthy people use their vast resources to fund and further their political purposes?

When one donor can simply outspend others by many orders of magnitude other legitimate voices are shut out.[73] While we know that the equal-voice principle is often violated in the political arena, attaching a dollar sign to it raises the concerns beyond just fairness, it denies the very fundamental tenet of democratic elections that everyone, no matter how poor or modest, has an equal say, an equal voice.

And there is a practical side to an excess of money from too few sources. It not only shuts out other voices, it crowds them out as well. There are only so many media buys to be made, only so many ads and sites that can be put on the Internet. Allowing billionaires to dominate the campaign ad marketplace doesn't simply distort it, it destroys it by creating a monopoly. The "The Public Be Damned" attitude that Gilded Age industrialists and Robber Barons articulated in the late nineteenth century shows every evidence of reappearing in campaign finance, as billionaires create their own kind of monopolies to dominate the campaign market.

The other major problem about SuperPacs is one we have met before: disclosure of donors is not always required, and thus there are vast amounts of "dark money" at play in our political campaigns. This is troubling for democratic elections. Besides level playing fields, they demand full disclosure: a little sunlight shined into dark corners can root out not simply wrongdoing, but the impression that wrongdoing and corruption are present.

Disclosure also means letting people know who are the players. The public has a right to know who are funding our campaigns. This is not a criticism of anyone's politics; donors have a right to believe in and fund anything they want. But they need to do so in full view of the public. To do less, to keep things secret, is all too reminiscent of shady deals made without the public's knowing until it is too late.

In the end, we return to a point made earlier in the chapter. What is wrong with *Citizens United* and subsequent developments in campaign finance is that they all fail to come to grips with a central point: What happens when unequally distributed private resources take over a public enterprise? The possibility of further corrupting our democratic elections increases sharply as the playing field tilts in favor of a few at the expense of the many. We shall return to this point in the next, concluding chapter.

## Notes

1   The prohibition is not Constitutionally based, but rather comes from 1966 amendments to the Foreign Agents Registration Act and is now part of the Federal Elections Commission rules and regulations. See FEC, "Foreign

Nationals," July 2003, viewed online at http://usgovinfo.about.com/gi/ o.htm?zi=1/XJ&zTi=1&sdn=usgovinfo&cdn=newsissues&tm=27&f=20&su =p284.13.342.ip_&tt=2&bt=0&bts=0&zu=http%3A//www.fec.gov/pages/br ochures/foreign.shtml, May 27, 2012. Foreigners with a permanent residency status in the United States. (that is, those with a green card) are permitted to make campaign contributions.

2   See, among many possible examples, William Safire, "Ed Rollins, Reformer," *The Baltimore Sun*, November 16, 1993; viewed online at http://articles.baltimoresun.com/1993-11-16/news/1993320233_1_heaven-forfend-ed-rollins-compulsion, May 27, 2012.

3   Laura A. Bischoff, "FBI Looks at 'Illegal' Campaign Donations," *Dayton Daily News*, May 22, 2012; viewed online at www.daytondailynews.com/ news/election/fbi-looks-at-illegal-campaign-donations-1379332.html; a recent survey suggests that illegal corporate campaign contributions are up by as much as 400 percent, see Alex Seitz-Wald, "Survey: Illegal Corporate Campaign Contributions Up 400%," *Think Progress*, January 12, 2012, viewed online at http://thinkprogress.org/justice/2012/01/12/403738/survey-illegal-corporate-campaign-contributions-up-400; and iWatch News, "Koch Fined for Making 12 Illegal Campaign Contributions that It Self-reported," *Center For Public Integrity*, July 1, 2011, viewed online at www.iwatchnews.org/2011/07/01/5105/koch-fined-making-12-illegal-campaign-contributions-it-self-reported; all viewed May 27, 2012.

4   See, for example, Scott Hiaasen and Patricia Mazzei, "U.S. Rep. David Rivera Won't Face Criminal Charges in State Investigation, Sources Tell Miami Herald," *Miami Herald*, April 17, 2012; viewed online at www.miamiherald.com/2012/04/17/2754216/us-rep-david-rivera-wont-face.html, June 1, 2012; and *Miami Herald*, "David Rivera Investigation Leaves Behind $50,000 Mystery," Huffingtonpost.com, May 30, 2012, viewed online at www.huffingtonpost.com/2012/05/30/david-rivera-investigation-50000_n_1555464.html?ref=miami&ir=Miami, June 1, 2012.

5   The Belmont quote is from Louise Overacker, *Presidential Campaign Funds* (Boston, MA: Boston University Press, 1946), p. 20; and the Overacker quote from her book at page 47. See also Perry Belmont, *The Recollections of Perry Belmont* (New York: Columbia University Press, 1940, reprinted 1967); and Louise Overacker, *Money in Elections* (New York: Macmillan, 1932). I am grateful to Roger Austin, attorney and senior Ph.D. student, Department of Political Science, University of Florida, Gainesville, for bringing the Belmont and Overacker comments to my attention.

6   See Carolyn Baum, "Congress Should Wear T-Shirts With Endorsements," *Bloomberg*, March 26, 2009, viewed online at www.bloomberg.com/apps/ news?pid=newsarchive&sid=aAFgqtwU4K2Y, June 16, 2014.

7   See the comment of Robert Reich, quoted in "Corruption, American Style," by Michael Maiello, *Forbes*, January 2, 2009, viewed online at www.forbes.com/2009/01/22/corruption-lobbying-bribes-biz-corruption09-cx_mm_0122maiello.html, October 1, 2013.

8   Noted importantly in *Buckley vs. Valeo*, 424 US1(1976).

9   Intrade.com was one of the most consistently successful predictors of the outcome of the 2012 Presidential election (as well as other elections in prior years), along with Nate Silver, the former political data analyst of the *New York Times*. In early 2013, however, Intrade went out of business because of "financial irregularities." See John Cassidy, "What Killed Intrade?," *The New Yorker*, March 11, 2013, viewed online at www.newyorker.com/online/blogs/

johncassidy/2013/03/whatever-happened-to-intrade.html, August 24, 2013.

10 See Jon Swain, "New Jersey Grants $1.25bn in Public Funds to Firms That Back Republicans," July 2, 2014, viewed online at www.theguardian.com/world/2014/jun/26/new-jersey-chris-christie-republican-backers, July 2, 2014.

11 *Citizens United vs. FEC*, 558 US _____ (2010), Docket No. 08-205); 130 S. Ct. 876.

12 See National Conference of State Legislatures, "Life After *Citizens United*," updated January 24, 2011; viewed online at www.ncsl.org/legislatures-elections/elections/citizens-united-and-the-states.aspx, May 28, 2012.

13 Federal Election Commission, "Contribution Limits 2013–2014," n.d., viewed online at www.fec.gov/pages/brochures/contriblimits.shtml, June 21, 2014.

14 Primaries and the general election are considered separately; thus, for candidates surviving the primary, the effective limit is double the maximum contribution for an election. Some states, however, impose a total on how much can be contributed per person, or per family.

15 A number of states have recently raised campaign donation limits. Florida, for example, which previously had a $500 limit, increased it to $1,000 for legislative races and $3,000 for statewide offices. See Adam Wollner, "Florida Among States that Increased Campaign Contribution Limits," Florida Center for Investigative Reporting, July 1, 2013, viewed online at http://fcir.org/2013/07/01/florida-among-states-that-increased-campaign-contributions-limits, August 24, 2013. See also Amy Myers, "Contributions at Risk in States Thanks to Supreme Court," The Center for Public Integrity, June 27, 2012, viewed online at www.publicintegrity.org/2012/06/27/9230/contribution-limits-risk-states-thanks-supreme-court, August 24, 2013.

16 National Conference of State Legislatures, "State Limits on Contributions to Candidates, 2011–2012 Election Cycle," updated September 30, 2011, viewed online at www.ncsl.org/Portals/1/documents/legismgt/Limits_to_Candidates_2011-2012.pdf, May 28, 2012.

17 Campaigns at all levels must also report their expenditures, although there is no limitation on what they can be used for. See *Buckley vs. Valeo*, 424 U.S. 1 (1976).

18 See Who Rules?, Money and Politics, An Internet Guide to Power Structure Research, "Sources of Information on Campaign Finance 2010," viewed online at http://darkwing.uoregon.edu/~vburris/whorules/money.htm, May 28, 2012.

19 See Ashley Parker, "Outside Money Drives a Deluge of Political Ads," *New York Times*, July 27. 2014, viewed online at www.nytimes.com/2014/07/28/us/politics/deluge-of-political-ads-is-driven-by-outside-money.html?hp&action=click&pgtype=Homepage&version=HpSum&module=first-column-region&region=top-news&WT.nav=top-news, August 6, 2014.

20 See Monica Davey and Nicholas Confessore, "Wisconsin Governor at Center of a Vast Fund-Raising Case," *New York Times*, June 19, 2014, viewed online at http://mobile.nytimes.com/2014/06/20/us/scott-walker-wisconsin-governor.html?smid=fb-share&_r=0&referrer=, June 22, 2014.

21 See, for example, *Washington Post*, "Campaign Finance, Overview Part 4, Soft Money, a Look at the Loopholes," 1998, viewed online at www.washingtonpost.com/wp-srv/politics/special/campfin/intro4.htm, May 28, 2012.

22 *Washington Post*, 1998.

23 See "Types of Advocacy Groups, 527 Organizations," Center for Responsive Politics, OpenSecrets.org, n.d., viewed online at www.opensecrets.org/527s/types.php, May 28, 2012.

24 Not all 527s are PACs, but those engaged in political activity at the federal level must register with the FEC as political committees and are subject to FEC rules and regulations.

25 The ad was paid for by the National Security PAC, not the Bush/Quayle campaign. Viewed online at www.youtube.com/watch?v=Io9KMSSEZ0Y, May 28, 2012. The ad can be seen on YouTube at www.youtube.com/watch?v=Io9KMSSEZ0Y or on The Living Room Candidate 1988 Bush vs. Dukakis, www.livingroomcandidate.org/commercials/1988/willie-horton.

26 See "The Living Room Candidate, 2004 Bush vs. Kerry," www.livingroom-candidate.org/commercials/2004/windsurfing; and Swiftboat Veterans Ads on John Kerry—Sellout 2004, www.youtube.com/watch?v=phqOuEhg9yE and www.youtube.com/watch?v=ngjUkPbGwAg; all viewed May 28, 2012. See also Michael Hyman, "Ads by 527 Groups and the 2004 Presidential Elections," November 11, 2013, viewed online at www.academia.edu/5136591/Ads_by_527_groups_and_the_2004_US_presidential_election, June 21, 2014.

27 Readers should be reminded that the U.S. Supreme Court, in *Buckley vs. Valeo* (1976), declared that money spent independently was the equivalent of speech in the campaign arena.

28 For a brief overview, see Federal Election Commission, "The FEC and the Federal Campaign Finance Law," February 2004 and updated February 2011, viewed online at www.fec.gov/pages/brochures/fecfeca.shtml, May 28, 2012. In brief, in 1971 Congress passed the *Federal Election Campaign Act* (FECA), and strengthened it in 1974, when limits were imposed on campaign contributions by individuals, parties, and PACs; it also increased reporting requirements, and established the FEC. The Act was again amended in 1976, to take account of rulings in *Buckley vs. Valeo*.

29 The original limit on donations to national parties was $20,000/year. By 2014, it had been raised to $32,400, although as the *Washington Post* noted, there were so many loopholes that in fact it was possible to donate 10 times that amount. See Matea Gold, "Spending Deal Would Allow Wealthy Donors to Dramatically Increase Giving to National Parties, *Washington Post*, December 9, 2014, viewed online at www.washingtonpost.com/blogs/post-politics/wp/2014/12/09/spending-deal-would-allow-wealthy-donors-to-dramatically-increase-giving-to-national-parties, July 12, 2015.

30 See, among many other sources, Kathy Gill, "McCain-Feingold Campaign Finance Reform," About.com US Politics, 2012; viewed online at http://uspolitics.about.com/od/finance/a/mccain_feingold.htm; Federal Election Commission, "Campaign Finance Law Quick Reference for Reporters, n.d., viewed online at www.fec.gov/press/bkgnd/bcra_overview.shtml; Adam Liptak, "Justices Seem Skeptical of Scope of Campaign Law," *New York Times*, March 24, 2009, viewed online at www.nytimes.com/2009/03/25/washington/25scotus.html?hp; all viewed May 28, 2012.

31 See, for example, John F. Harris and Jonathan Allen, "Death of Bipartisanship Has Killed the Washington Deal," Politico.com, January 30, 2012, viewed online at www.politico.com/news/stories/0112/72132.html, June 22, 2014.

32 The author wishes to make clear that the following analysis is a political one, not legal. He has no qualifications to offer the latter. All quotations are from the text of *Citizens United* as found at www.law.cornell.edu/supct/html/08-205.ZS.html unless otherwise noted.

33  See, for example, http://legal-dictionary.thefreedictionary.com/
Summary+Judgment, viewed online May 29, 2012.

34  424 US 1 (1976); the case will be discussed later in the chapter.

35  This point has been incontrovertibly documented by two Nobel Prize-winning
economists, Joseph Stiglitz and Paul Krugman, as well as by a host of other
eminent economists such as Noriel Rubini, Robert Reich, Jared Bernstein, and
Robert Kuttner, among others. A thoughtful study of what happened that is
approachable for the general ruler is Hedrick Smith, *What Happened to the
American Dream* (New York: Random House, 2013). More recently, see
Robert Reich, "American Democracy is Diseased," Alternet.org, August 20,
2014, viewed online at www.alternet.org/economy/robert-reich-american-
democracy-diseased?akid=12147.1898446.HZQMWO&rd=1&src=newslette
r1016239&t=3, August 21, 2014.

36  The literature on the Gilded Age and Age of the Robber Barons is well known,
and it started early. See for example Frank Norris, *The Octopus* (1901), about
the Union Pacific Railroad; Matthew Josephson, *The Robber Barons* (New
York: Mariner Books, 1962); Charles R. Morris, *The Tycoons: How Andrew
Carnegie, John D. Rockefeller, Jay Gould and J. P. Morgan Invented the
American Supereconomy* (New York: Times Books, 2005); and more recently
Michael Kazin, "How the Robber Barons Railroaded America," *New York
Times*, July 15, 2011, viewed online at www.nytimes.com/2011/07/17/
books/review/book-review-railroaded-by-richard-white.html?pagewanted=all,
June 22, 2014.

37  See Dahlia Lithwick, "In Montana, Corporations Aren't People," *Slate-
Jurisprudence*, slate.com, January 4, 2012, viewed online at
www.slate.com/articles/news_and_politics/jurisprudence/2012/01/montana_su
preme_court_citizens_united_can_montana_get_away_with_defying_the_supr
eme_court_ html, June 3, 2012,

38  Readers seeking support for this point of view should watch "Enron: The
Smartest Guys in the Room," a documentary directed by Alex Gibney and
written by staffers from *Fortune* magazine (2005),
www.imdb.com/title/tt1016268.

39  *Crawford et al. vs. Marion County Election Board et al.*, No. 07-21, April 28,
2008.

40  *McCutcheon vs. FEC*, No. 12-536, April 2, 2014, viewed online at
www.fec.gov/law/litigation/mccutcheon_sc_opinion.pdf, June 23, 2014.

41  See "Before and After the Supreme Court's Ruling," *New York Times*, April
2, 2014, viewed online at www.nytimes.com/interactive/2014/04/02/
us/politics/supreme-court-ruling-campaign-finance.html, June 23, 2014.

42  Editorial, "The Court Follows the Money," *New York Times*, April 2, 2014,
viewed online at www.nytimes.com/2014/04/03/opinion/the-court-follows-
the-money.html, June 23, 2014. See also "Before and After the Supreme
Court's Ruling," cited above; Chris Cillizza, "Winners and Losers from the
*McCutcheon vs. FEC* Ruling," *Washington Post*, April 2, 2014, viewed online
at www.washingtonpost.com/blogs/the-fix/wp/2014/04/02/winners-and-
losers-from-the-mccutcheon-v-fec-ruling; and The Brennan Center for Justice,
"*McCutcheon vs. FEC*," viewed online at www.brennancenter.org/legal-
work/mccutcheon-v-fec, both viewed June 23, 2014.

43  See Adam Liptak, "Supreme Court Strikes Down Overall Contribution Cap,"
*New York Times*, April 2, 2014, viewed online at www.nytimes.com/
2014/04/03/us/politics/supreme-court-ruling-on-campaign-contributions.html,
June 23, 2014.

44  See Charles Fried, "It's Not Citizens United," *New York Times*, October 1, 2013, viewed online at www.nytimes.com/2013/10/02/opinion/its-not-citizens-united.html?nl=opinion&emc=edit_ty_20131002, October 5, 2013.

45  501 (c)(4), (5) and (6) organizations will be explained shortly.

46  *First National Bank of Boston vs. Bellotti*, 435 U.S. 765 (1978); *Austin vs. Michigan Chamber of Commerce*, 494 U.S. 652 (1990); and *McConnell vs. Federal Elections Commission*, 540 US 93 (2003).

47  See the discussion of SpeechNow.org in Federal Election Commission, "Ongoing Litigation—*SpeechNow.org vs. FEC*," 2010, viewed online at www.fec.gov/law/litigation/speechnow.shtml, May 29, 2012.

48  Center for Responsive Politics, "OpenSecrets.org.—Super Pacs," May 19, 2012, viewed online at www.fec.gov/law/litigation/speechnow.shtml, May 29, 2012.

49  See Editorial, "When Other Voices are Drowned Out," *New York Times*, March 25, 2012, viewed online at www.nytimes.com/2012/03/26/opinion/when-other-voices-are-drowned-out.html, June 6, 2012.

50  Readers are urged to examine ProPublica's *Pactrack* and its other research to keep up with, and try to make sense of, developments in campaign finance. Two excellent places to begin are Al Shaw and Kim Barker, *Pactrack*, ProPublica, updated daily, viewed online at http://projects.propublica.org/pactrack/#committee=all, June 6, 2012; and Kim Barker and Marian Wang, "Super PACs and Dark Money: ProPublica's Guide to the New World of Campaign Finance," ProPublica, July 11, 2011, viewed online at www.propublica.org/blog/item/super-pacs-propublicas-guide-to-the-new-world-of-campaign-finance, June 6, 2012.

51  Center for Responsive Politics, May 29, 2012.

52  The IRS established them in 1913.

53  See Center for Responsive Politics, "Outside Spending: Frequently Asked Questions about 501(c)(4) Groups," n.d., viewed online at www.opensecrets.org/outsidespending/faq.php, June 23, 2014. See also Center for Responsive Politics, "Political NonProfits," June 23, 2014, viewed online at www.opensecrets.org/outsidespending/nonprof_summ.php?mv; Center for Responsive Politics, "Types of Advocacy Groups," n.d., viewed online at www.opensecrets.org/527s/types.php; both viewed June 23, 2014.

54  See, for example the Editorial, "Rise of SuperPacs," *Gainesville Sun*, March 31, 2012, viewed online at www.gainesville.com/article/20120331/OPINION/120339980; and Editorial, "End of the Charade," *New York Times*, May 28, 2012, viewed online at www.nytimes.com/2012/05/29/opinion/end-of-the-charade.html?_r=1&hp; both viewed May 29, 2012.

55  Barker and Wang, ProPublica, 2011.

56  See Claire O'Connor, "How Karl Rove's Billionaire-Backed Super PAC Will Be Election Game Changer," *Forbes*, April 27, 2012, viewed online at www.forbes.com/sites/clareoconnor/2012/04/27/how-karl-roves-billionaire-backed-super-pac-will-be-election-game-changer, May 29, 2012.

57  See the report on Talkingpointsmemo.com, viewed online at http://livewire.talkingpointsmemo.com/entries/gop-super-pacs-plan-to-spend-1-billion, May 30, 2012.

58  The *Washington Post* reported that Koch-backed independent groups raised over $400 M for the 2012 elections. See Matea Gold, "Koch-Backed Political Network, Built to Shield Donors, Raised $400 Million in 2012 Elections," *Washington Post*, January 5, 2014, viewed online at www.washingtonpost.com/politics/koch-backed-political-network-built-to-

shield-donors-raised-400-million-in-2012-elections/2014/01/05/9e7cfd9a-719b-11e3-9389-09ef9944065e_story.html, June 24, 2014. The *Post* research was conducted with the collaboration of The Center for Responsive Politics.

59  501(c)(5) organizations are essentially unions.

60  See Eric Lach, "Revealed: The Secret Koch Group That Gave Conservatives $236 M in 2012," in Muckraker, TPM.com, September 12, 2013, viewed online at http://tpmmuckraker.talkingpointsmemo.com/2013/09/freedom_partners_koch_brothers.php, September 12, 2013.

61  See IRS rules, online at www.irs.gov/Charities-&-Non-Profits/Charitable-Organizations/Exemption-Requirements-Section-501(c)(3)-Organizations, viewed October 1, 2013.

62  Center for Responsive Politics, "SuperPacs," June 24, 2014, viewed online at www.opensecrets.org/pacs/superpacs.php, June 24, 2014.

63  For discussions of "dark money," see for example the range of articles in Huffingtonpost.com, "Dark Money," n.d., viewed online at www.huffingtonpost.com/tag/dark-money/1; Mother Jones, "Dark Money," n.d., viewed online at www.motherjones.com/topics/dark-money; and Julie Patel, "IRS Chief Promises Stricter Rules for 'Dark Money' Nonprofit Groups," Center for Public Integrity, June 18, 2014, viewed online at www.publicintegrity.org/2014/06/18/14960/irs-chief-promises-stricter-rules-dark-money-nonprofit-groups.all, viewed June 24, 2014.

64  Center for Responsive Politics, "Political Nonprofits, June 24, 2014, viewed online at www.opensecrets.org/outsidespending/nonprof_summ.php, June 24, 2014. Union 501(c)(5) organizations peaked in their expenditures in 2008, at $17 M, and since then have declined precipitously to almost nothing in 2014; but 501 (c) (4) and (6) organizations have risen steadily, each at about $13.5 M in 2014.

65  Peter Olsn-Phillips, Russ Choma, Sarah Bryner and Doug Weber, "The Political One Percent of the One Percent in 2014: Mega Donors Fuel Rising Cost of Elections, Center for Responsive Politics, OpenSecrets blog, April 30, 2015, viewed online at www.opensecrets.org/news/2015/04/the-political-one-percent-of-the-one-percent-in-2014-mega-donors-fuel-rising-cost-of-elections, July 11, 2015.

66  Russ Choma, "Money Won on Tuesday, But Rules of the Game Changed, Center for Responsive Politics, OpenSecretsblog, November 5, 2014, viewed online at www.opensecrets.org/news/2014/11/money-won-on-tuesday-but-rules-of-the-game-changed, July 11, 2015; Robert Maguire, "A New Low in Campaign Finance," *New York Times*, October 27, 2015, viewed online at www.nytimes.com/2015/10/27/opinion/a-new-low-in-campaign-finance.html?action=click&pgtype=Homepage&module=opinion-c-col-right-region&region=opinion-c-col-right-region&WT.nav=opinion-c-col-right-region; and Center for Responsive Politics, OpenSecrets.org, "Outside Spending by Disclosure, Excluding Party Committees," October 31, 2015, viewed online at www.opensecrets.org/outsidespending/disclosure.php?range=tot, both viewed October 31, 2015.

67  Steve Holland and Michelle Conlin, "Bush 2016 Campaign for White House Rakes in Record $114 M, Reuters, July 9, 2015, viewed online at www.reuters.com/article/2015/07/09/us-usa-election-bush-fundraising-idUSKCN0PJ29U20150709, July 11, 2015.

68  Denise Hassanzade Ajiri, "Hillary Clinton Has Raised $45 M in Campaign Contributions So Far," *The Christian Science Monitor*, July 1, 2015, viewed online at www.csmonitor.com/USA/Politics/2015/0701/Hillary-Clinton-has-

raised-45-million-in-campaign-contributions-so-far-video, July 11, 2015.

69  See Kenneth P. Vogel, "The Kochs Put a Price on 2016: $889 Million," Politico.com, January 26, 2015, viewed online at www.politico.com/story/2015/01/koch-2016-spending-goal-114604.html, July 12, 2015.

70  Fredereka Shouten, "SuperPacs Move to Forefront of 2016 Campaigns, *Usa Today*, April 10, 2015, viewed online at www.usatoday.com/story/news/politics/elections/2015/04/09/super-pacs-forefront-of-presidential-campaigns/25522659, July 11, 2015.

71  See Michael Isikoff, "Karl Rove's Election Debacle: Super PAC's Spending Was Nearly for Naught," NBC News, November 8, 2012, viewed online at http://investigations.nbcnews.com/_news/2012/11/08/15007504-karl-roves-election-debacle-super-pacs-spending-was-nearly-for-naught, August 6, 2014.

72  See The Editorial Board, "The Custom-Made Super PAC," editorial, the *New York Times*, August 3, 2014, viewed online at www.nytimes.com/2014/08/04/opinion/the-custom-made-super-pac-.html?hp&action=click&pgtype=Homepage&module=c-column-top-span-region&region=c-column-top-span-region&WT.nav=c-column-top-span-region&_r=1, August 6, 2014.

73  See the *New York Times* editorial, "When Other Voices Are Drowned Out," cited above.

# 7 Conclusion

## Political Campaigns and Democratic Elections in the United States

The discussions in the previous six chapters of this book all lead to an inevitable conclusion: changes in American political campaigns are actually serving to erode our democratic elections. If left unchecked, these changes and trends and developments could ultimately reduce them to just the shell of democratic elections: the formalisms of meaningful elections, but not the substance.

But how to justify this point of view? How can we tell when democratic elections are at risk? We can do so by looking at three very crucial axioms of democratic governance as they apply to political campaigns: transparency, accountability, and fairness, along with its corollary, responsiveness. The healthier and more robust and vital each of these is, so can elections be thought of as more resiliently democratic.

### Transparency

Transparency may be the most fundamental axiom of democratic elections. For political campaigns, transparency means what it says: doing things out in the open, in full view. It requires that the public's business be conducted in front of the public's eyes.

Transparency insists that hidden agendas be tucked away for good; there are no circus magic tricks or sleights of hand or *trompe l'oeil* as the public's business is carried out. Nothing destroys transparency as much as smokescreen politics, secret codicils, unseen transactions at back tables in expensive restaurants or in automobiles with smoked glass windows circling the block, shady deals done under the table or in the men's room, "funny business" that cannot be explained away. Sunshine, of course, is the best way to promote transparency. There is nothing like a little light shined into dark corners to make the cockroaches scamper away. Everything that is done by, for, or to the public must be done in full view of anyone or any group who cares to look, in full sunshine.

But too often in recent years there is a lack of transparency in our political campaigns, largely because of money. All aspects of a campaign that deal with money—hard and soft donations, in-kind contributions, whatever—*must* be in full public view, immediately, and at all times. No exceptions can be permitted. No donation of any kind can be "overlooked" or postponed in its reporting. And names *must* be revealed, because the public's business is in question. Whether for national or state and local elections, it is too easy to "omit" a name as an "error" to be later corrected. It is too easy to leave off names on a list of PAC donors. It is too easy also to "create" donors from names in the local cemetery, which amounts to hiding illegal donations coming from elsewhere; indeed, it is fraudulent. Whatever the level of the campaign, hiding the names of donors, including those with very deep pockets, from public view is unacceptable.

It is now a commonplace to point out that both 527 and 501(c)(3), (4), (5), and (6) SuperPacs frequently flout the law and administrative rules of the IRS and FEC, to engage in potentially illegal political activity; one example is in spending more than 50 percent of their budget on political activity, something very easy to hide. Another is in hiding donations which should be made public, but which are hidden because of the technicalities of a non-profit's legal status. They can do so because they have the financial means to hire sharp lawyers and accountants; because the IRS lacks the manpower and other resources, and perhaps the political will, to go after these organizations;[1] and because the FEC is essentially a toothless agency. But this simply underscores how a lack of transparency makes a mockery of laws and regulations.

To argue, for example, that large donors need to remain anonymous to prevent them from "embarrassment" or "retribution" is unworthy of comment.[2] In democratic elections, transparency applies to everybody, including fat cats with deep pockets. If would-be donors fear embarrassment, perhaps they should not be engaged in whatever activity they think is cause for it; if they fear retribution, it's probably because they feel the need to cover up something. Neither is a reason or legitimate excuse to hide or run for cover. Alternatively, if they are engaged in dubious activity and don't want their names made public, perhaps they should forget about making campaign donations, so the issue of publicizing their names never arises.

In any case, the position that wealthy, large donors deserve special treatment is not just silly, it is beside the point. Any time that private individuals—or corporations—enter the public square in the form of campaign donations, their actions must be fully transparent, no matter how rich or powerful or privileged the donor(s) might be. Full transparency of their donations and campaign activity is therefore essential. Everyone's name who enters the public square must come to light.

But non-disclosure of money and names is not the only threat to the transparency of elections. There are a myriad other ways in which campaigns have learned to obfuscate, to cloud over transparency. We need only summarize them here: deliberately distorting facts; deliberately making misstatements and misrepresentations and boldly asserting lies as truth; and manipulating the 24-hour news cycle to promote and then "lose" stories the campaign wants "out there," are just a few of the ways in which campaigns and candidates can create smokescreens where clarity and transparency are needed. It may well be, of course, that lying and obfuscation cannot be waved away by legislative fiat or even court decisions; basic human instincts for self-preservation are more powerful than either. But voters can demand truth and transparency from candidates and campaigns, and punish them when they are found wanting.

---

### The Fate of Candidates Who Hide and Obfuscate

The failed campaign of the disgraced Anthony Weiner for Mayor of New York in 2013 is an example of how the public reacts when the candidate is found to be lying or obscuring or hiding the truth. Weiner finished last in a field of five in the Democratic mayoral primary, winning only 31,000+ votes, or 4.9 percent of the total.[3] Another example is the failed effort of sullied former New York Governor Eliot Spitzer to become Comptroller of New York City.[4] A counter-example might appear to be former Governor Mark Sanford of South Carolina, whose lies to cover up an extra-marital affair reached epic proportions but who went on to win a seat in the U.S. House of Representatives. But it took considerable time, a monumental effort to "rebuild" his reputation, and a lot of money to do so.[5]

---

### Accountability

Accountability complements transparency. It is the report which a public body or agency or official or even public activity (like a political campaign) makes to the public about what it is doing. How much money did it collect? Where, and from whom, did it come, and in what quantities? What did it do with the money?

How does accountability apply to political campaigns? There are essentially two levels on which it does. The first is its obligation of accountability to the donors. This is the easy part. Assuming the campaign follows the rules and reports both donations and expenditures honestly (there are very few restrictions on the latter, thanks to *Buckley vs. Valeo* [1976]), then the donors can know who are the other contributors and how the campaign spent its money.

---

### Accountability to the Donor

As anyone experienced in political campaigns knows, it is generally easier to persuade a potential donor to contribute for a specific purpose—5 TV ads, extra cartridges for the campaign printer, a mailing list or digital list serve—than for vague, "we need the money" pitches. If the donor then presses the matter, the campaign bookkeeper or treasurer can even show receipts that the money was indeed used for the intended purpose and was so reported.

---

The problem arises when the campaign does not report promptly, fully, accurately, and honestly. It then fools its own contributors, but it also deceives the public. This is the second level of campaign accountability. To be sure, federal and state authorities (and local ones) have become adept at sniffing out "fishy" looking donations. But they usually leave expenditures alone, unless the campaign has used money illegally, like buying drugs or hiring prostitutes. When they find questionable donations, they are empowered to levy fines; but, as we noted earlier in the book, the campaign can long be over by the time this happens.

The more serious problem in accountability to the public, as one might expect, comes when names are not revealed. Not only is there a violation of transparency, but there is also a violation of accountability. There is no need to plow this row again, because the same arguments about secrecy apply to accountability as well as to transparency. It is not only unfortunate, but more importantly a body blow to accountability, that the U.S. Supreme Court, the IRS, and many states, have provided loopholes to avoid this essential requirement of democratic elections.

### Fairness and Responsiveness

It should be abundantly clear to readers of the previous two sections, and much of the prior text in the book, that increasingly our elections are not fair. Too few people with too much money have a decided advantage in the electoral arena. The voices of a vast number of Americans now count for very little, because the campaign playing field is so tilted against them. It is not even clear that their votes count for much, because they have been overwhelmed by avalanches of money that inappropriately influence the outcome. In short, our elections are rapidly becoming unfair, ones in which money counts for more than voters.

But there is another side to fairness in campaigns and electoral politics—responsiveness. When the electoral system responds to money more than votes, it is not only unfair, it is not being responsive. In a democracy, those engaged in the public's business—absolutely including running political campaigns—have an obligation to be responsive to the public. What does responsiveness mean? It means that those carrying out public functions must be aware of public sentiment, public norms, and public wishes. Put simply, campaigns do not exist in a political and social vacuum. Like any other public activity, campaigns need to be aware, and remind themselves, that the public eye is always on them, and the public—even the non-voting public—has an interest in what they do and how they go about doing it.

We leave out the interesting but, for our purposes, irrelevant questions of how the public presence is made known or how the public voice is expressed. But we can and should ask, How is a political campaign to be responsive? It must of course follow the law; when it does not, it is being unresponsive to the public and should be fined. More than that, the law is only part of the public's interest to which it must respond. The public sets standards of decency and fairness. We noted earlier, and need to re-emphasize here, that the public generally cuts some slack for campaigns when it comes to issues of fairness and decency: "That's politics, son" or "What did you expect from these people?," followed by a shrug or rolling of the eyes. But the norm of responsiveness does not allow a complete waving away of issues of decency and fairness.

There are at least two ways in which modern political campaigns ignore issues of decency and fairness: negative campaigning and avalanches of money used to buy elections.

The public has, over the years, repeatedly demonstrated that it dislikes negative campaigning.[6] According to research done for the Institute for Global Ethics at The Bliss Institute, University of Akron:

- More than eight in 10 voters say attack-oriented campaigning is unethical, undermines democracy, lowers voter turnout, and produces less ethical elected officials.
- Seventy-six percent of voters think that negative campaigning produces less ethical and less trustworthy leaders.
- More than 80 percent of voters think that this type of campaigning makes people less likely to vote.

These are damning percentages. The public clearly feels that attack ads and negative campaigns are injurious to the quality of our elections, perhaps to democracy itself. And yet, as the discussion earlier in the book demonstrates, attack ads are not decreasing in number, nor is their level of viciousness and vituperation.

Critics could say that this research—the results of which parallel other studies—is merely a reflection of people's attitudes and opinions. The actual "impact" of attack ads and negative campaigning might be far different.

This view might be true, but it is beside the point. What holds our democratic elections together is the faith that people have in them. If the public is fearful that campaign practices are undermining it, then that faith will be shaken, and the public's confidence in them reduced. Indeed, it is clear that architects of attack ads and negative campaigns don't worry about the health or quality of democratic elections; if they did, they would not design and carry out the campaigns that they do. Their concern is solely with winning elections, and if the "democratic" part of them is bruised along the way, well (they might say), that's just collateral damage. A more honest response might be, "The public be damned."

The public is just as concerned about the amount of money in politics generally and campaigns in particular.[7] They are concerned that there is too much of it and that it is potentially corrupting. It undermines the "responsiveness" of the campaign to the wishes of voters in favor of the interest of fat cats. The message of the avalanche of funds is that elections can be bought. The result serves further to undermine trust and confidence in democratic political institutions, including campaigns. And, as is the case with attack ads and negative campaigns, there is nothing on the horizon to suggest that less money, including from anonymous donors, will be spent in the future on campaigning.[8]

Matters of course are compounded when the donors to soft money campaigns are anonymous. Then, the hard money donors, and the public at large—voters and non-voters alike—are left scratching their heads: Who's pulling the strings? Why is this happening? Where did the ads come from? And even if significant elements of the public feel that the soft money campaign is odious, in bad taste, ethically questionable—where can they point the finger?

It is of interest that in recent years reports have come forward that some candidates have insisted that the names of donors for independent ads be made public, or they would reject or repudiate them. It is not yet clear if this type of attitude represents the *avant garde* of a new attitude towards transparency, accountability, and fairness/responsiveness by campaigns, or is just the eccentric twitchings of a few do-gooder candidates trying to seize the moral and political high ground. The proof of the pudding will be found during the 2016 campaign cycle and beyond, by observing how many candidates, including presidential candidates but by no means limited to them, require that names of all donors be made public.

## Have Our Political Campaigns Become Corrupted?

Where does this discussion leave us? Unfortunately not in a very happy place, because it forces us to ask a very unpleasant question: Have our political campaigns become corrupted?

To address this question successfully, we need to remind ourselves that too often corruption is viewed narrowly: a public official accepting bribes; government contracts that allow public officials, or relatives of public officials, to benefit at public expense; sweetheart contracts; kickback schemes; pay-to-play tactics forcing would-be contractors and even candidates into impossible ethical binds;[9] shakedown and extortion tactics that allow public officials to take advantage of their positions: when a public official, or body, uses its authority to benefit private interests, it is possible to say that corruption has taken place.[10]

But political corruption involves much more than the use of public office for private gain, important as that is. Anything that undermines public confidence and trust in democratic political institutions can also be considered corruption.[11] Even the *appearance* that officials are ignoring the public interest in favor of private interests can undermine faith in democratic governance. Viewed in this way, one is forced to swallow hard and conclude that yes, much of what has happened, and is happening, in American political campaigns represents potential, and too often actual, corruption of our democratic elections.

We have seen throughout this book that the public is not happy with modern campaigns: too much money and too much of it unaccounted for; attack ads and negative campaigning that are more concerned with vilifying opponents than addressing public needs; and more. An important consequence of this development is to force voters, and perhaps the citizenry generally, to wonder what has happened to us, why we flounder and avoid serious political debate on the problems facing us in favor of perpetuating campaign circuses.

When it becomes clear that the self-interested dollars of fat cats are paying for soft money campaigns whose sole purpose is to lambast, demonize, and villify, and that the media are active participants—indeed, actually collude—in ensuring that the campaign agenda consists mainly of smokescreens and sideshows and deceptions, and does not include any attention to what needs serious attending to, public disillusionment and disgust of course will increase. Is there any reason to think otherwise?[12]

## Can the Media Come to the Rescue?

But what about the media? Are they not a countervailing force against those undermining transparency, accountability, and fairness and responsiveness? Do the media not, often in a self-congratulatory way, like to portray themselves as the protectors of democracy? But, regrettably, there is little reason to hope for help from this quarter, essentially for two reasons discussed earlier in the book.

First, the media are not neutral in political campaigns. It's not just that they might favor one candidate over others; in fact, the media work assiduously to define who are the legitimate, serious candidates, and who are the also rans and losers. The media do this by choosing on which candidate(s) to focus, by the kind of stories (and photos) that they run, and by the very language that they use. It is worth remembering that the media have full power to decide which stories to run, when, and how.

Similarly, the media very much define the agenda, even the discourse, of the campaigns. By choosing, for example, to focus on the horserace and circus/operatic aspects of candidates and campaigns, the media omit discussion of "issues" and public questions with which they are uncomfortable, or hesitant. Far easier, far more palatable, far better for enticing readers and viewers (and hence improving advertising revenues) to talk about campaign antics and relatively meaningless daily tracking polls than serious ideas to restart a flagging economy, or proposals to reduce income and wealth inequities, or the dangers of pollution and global warming, or the continuing levels of racial discrimination in America, or any of the other myriad serious public questions staring us in the face.

Why do the media operate in this manner? Because, as noted in a previous chapter, the media have a vested interest in the outcome of campaigns. As part of corporate America, their focus needs to be on their bottom line, not informing the public.[13] And as part of Big Money in this country, the media are not interested in rocking the boat, or in conveying legitimacy to an unorthodox, even heretical candidate who might espouse ideas antithetical to the interests of corporate America. Better to de-legitimize him or her, demonize him or her if necessary, or emphasize the clown-like behavior of him or her to ensure that the voting public does not take such a candidate seriously.[14] And in the end, the media can choose simply to ignore candidates they do not favor, in which case the campaign would likely atrophy and disappear, *à la* Jon Huntsman in 2012.

The other reason why we should not expect the media to act as a countervailing force against the growing corruption of our campaigns is that increasingly the media are ignorant of what campaigns are actually doing. As campaigns become ever more digitally based and technologically sophisticated, the media are increasingly shut out of what the campaign is up to, what its strategy is, how it seeks out and appeals to its likely voters. All of this is now based on statistical modeling, which campaigns guard jealously. In addition, as discussed in an earlier chapter, political campaigns studiously guard media access to the candidate, key operatives, and information; reporters are only allowed in when the campaign wants them in and usually then only under very structured, controlled conditions. As a result, all the media know is what the campaign wants them to know.

But what about digital media, specifically the Internet and social media? Could they not serve as a countervailing force, and provide alternative sources of information about political campaigns that could bring to light some of the practices that are serving to corrupt them? The answer is: possibly.

There is no doubt that the Internet serves as a democratizing force in the spread of information. Now anyone who cares to look can find in the blogosphere vast amounts of it, and opinions as accompaniment. The problem is really not where to look, but how to avoid being inundated by the huge quantity of "stuff" that search engines turn up.

It is well known that too much of the information available on the Internet is unpoliced, essentially unregulated. What this means is that information gathered on the Internet must always be checked and double-checked, because so much of it is suspect and potentially unreliable. But an even deeper, and potentially more serious, matter is that of net neutrality, that is, ready, equal, and open access by one and all to the Internet. Recent decisions by the FCC have called net neutrality into question, possibly favoring large corporate conglomerates, which might make open access by "the little guy" more difficult. To the extent that this happens, and the Internet essentially becomes another handmaiden of what amounts to near corporate monopoly of our media, then its utility as a countervailing force, one that expands the flow of information to the public, will be compromised.[15]

But what about the social media, outlets such as Facebook, Twitter, tumblr, Pinterest, Flickr, InstaGram, YouTube, and all the rest? Can they provide alternative sources of information to subscribers? The answer is that they do indeed, something upon which political campaigns have capitalized, beginning in earnest in 2004.[16] Social media outlets have revolutionized the way in which political campaigns reach their supporters and base, and even broaden them. They have the capacity to reach, in a very personal way, scores of thousands of people, even millions, virtually instantaneously, and, depending on the content, to inform them and mobilize them into action. This is an unprecedented development in the history of mass communications.

But again, the quality of content of the messages being zipped at light speed to social media subscribers determines the degree to which it informs, or misinforms, those who read what comes through their electronic devices. Matters are compounded by the rules that the SEC and FCC impose that influence what can, and cannot, be transmitted. And, finally, there is the increasing interest that corporate media giants are showing in social media outlets. To the extent that they, too, become extensions of conglomerate octopus corporate ownership, so will they limit the ability of subscribers to access alternative sources of information beyond what the "mainstream" media provide.[17]

## Slicing and Dicing the Electorate

There is another potential source of corruption of democratic elections that comes not from outside campaigns, like money, but from the inside.

It is the increasing use of statistical models to target individual groups of voters, and potential voters, to appeal to their interests and not others. Indeed, the propensity of modern campaigns to "slice and dice" the electorate into ever finer segments means that they view voters not as a whole or in large blocs of groups, but as a kaleidoscope of very different shapes and sizes.

Campaigns by their very nature are divisive; they force voters and potential voters to take sides, to choose one candidate or cause over another, or indeed to decide whether or not even to vote. On the other hand, in the past candidates had to think in terms of blocs of voters—how large depended on the office being sought—as they made their appeals. While it was possible to send different messages to different blocs, it had to be done carefully, because the media could be quick to point out inconsistencies in the message. And to try to create a minimum winning electoral coalition, the candidate had to stress common themes, ones that appealed across a range of voting blocs, in order not to rend the coalition asunder.

Also, in the past, campaigns were an opportunity for voters—citizens—to come together, to think about their collective responsibility to preserve and strengthen democratic processes and institutions. The very act of voting represented an affirmation of "*e pluribus unum*"—yes, voters might disagree about which candidate or which course of action is best, but in the end the conduct of elections through democratic procedures meant that everyone was engaged in a common enterprise, a process that was more important than the fragmentation and divisiveness that vigorous, robust campaigns inevitably created. There is evidence, both anecdotal and data-driven, that voters who cast ballots have more positive feelings about democratic elections than those who did not, even if their candidates-of-choice lost.[18]

But, one has to ask, if campaigns now simply view voters as small pieces that must be identified and culled out through appeals to their narrow, even individual, interests, what happens to the sense of collective purpose and commonalty that campaigns in the past could engender? Where is the big picture? How do modern campaign strategies ensure that in the end the mess of jigsaw pieces on the table will result in a coherent finished picture, or a well-designed stained glass window? The answer is that they don't, because nowadays winning political campaign strategies are based on slicing and dicing to build a winning electoral coalition, not on how the picture, or the window, will look the day after the election. "*Unum*" gets lost, as "*e pluribus*" becomes more and more finely and narrowly defined. The potential danger to democratic elections is apparent: appeals to narrow self-interests undercut the sense of community and common purpose that participation in democratic elections can create, and perhaps is supposed to create.

## The Campaign Industry

In what surely can be viewed as irony, it appears to be the case that our own campaigns, specifically the people who run them—the consultants, indeed, the whole panoply of campaign people, techniques, firms, agencies, and organizations that we call the Campaign Industry—may be undermining our democratic elections. We saw in Chapter 4 how big the Industry has become—if it were a single corporation, it would occupy a position of pride on the *Fortune 500* list of prominent firms. And we know, too, that it has become part and parcel of Big Money that so influences our politics, including campaigns, in the United States.

Indeed, it is this last point that needs underscoring. Political consultants helped drive money, big money, into political campaigns. Once PACs became a central part of the campaign scene, and once *Buckley vs. Valeo* (1976) allowed essentially unlimited campaign expenditures, it was the membership of the Campaign Industry that was instrumental in finding ways to funnel huge amounts of cash into our campaigns. Later, of course, with *Citizens United* (2010) and *McCutcheon* (2014), the Supreme Court opened the door to essentially unlimited donations, but it was the Campaign Industry that found the way to spend the money.

And, as we saw, the Industry has been more than complicit in raising the ugliness of our campaigns—negativity, character assassination, the abandonment of any kind of moral compass in designing and running campaigns—and actually engaging in undemocratic practices—dirty tricks, voter suppression, and disenfranchisement. These matters are compounded by the fact that political consultants bring these same practices, and the attitudes which brought them about, abroad when they travel to foreign lands to bring American-style campaigns to other countries. When such things happen, it can hardly be said that the Campaign Industry is helping to build democracy abroad.

## The Big Money Candidate and Undermining Trust in Campaigns

There is another way in which campaigns nowadays can serve to corrupt democratic elections: the emergence of the Big Money Candidate. Readers will recall the full discussion of this new type of candidate in Chapter 3. Here we need only remind ourselves that the Money Candidate has no allegiance to anyone but himself and the campaign's financial backers; to the extent that the campaign's major financial backer is, as we saw, a single wealthy individual, does not the issue of the candidate's true allegiance come into even starker relief? As a result, one can legitimately ask, How, and to what extent, does the Money Candidate possibly serve the public interest? Does this not, in and of itself, potentially contribute to declining public trust and confidence in our political campaigns, and perhaps in government itself, given that their allegiances are based not on public commonalties and a spirit of collective action, or a desire to rebuild political parties so that they could once again serve as the kind of mediating institutions they used to be, or a wish to strengthen the very institutions of government (legislative, executive, or judicial) in which they wish to participate, but on private interests and wealth? Whether or not one can point to "Money Candidates" (and office holders) currently on the political stage who represent the dangers outlined here is not the point: the point is that Big Money candidates are becoming more numerous throughout the political landscape, and they represent a potential corrupting influence to democratic campaigns and elections.

## A (Probably) Futile Suggestion and Several (Possible) Ways Out

Are we stuck? Is there nothing we can do about any of this? Will our democratic elections continue to erode away as more and more of our campaigns are put up for sale to the wealthy, or any of these other dangers—real and potential—become more widespread? Only if We the People allow it.

There is one step we should promptly take about our campaigns that would help shore up our democratic elections and even restore some of what has been eroded away. But its realization, its actualization, is virtually impossible in today's political and legal climate. Nonetheless it should be put forward for public discussion.

Readers will recall that a major danger to democratic elections occurs when private money, and the interest(s) that it represents, enter the public square, in this case political campaigns. The solution: get rid of the private dollars. The only way to save our campaigns and elections from becoming contests over who can throw the most money at them instead of allowing candidates—no matter how flawed they may be or how cockamamie their politics—to duke it out fairly through their campaigns, is to keep private resources out of the whole business. Our campaigns and elections must be funded *solely* by public money. Because private resources—money—are unequally (and, many believe, unfairly) distributed across the population, they are ultimately corrupting of democratic elections. There is no getting around this crucial point.

The author is well aware that the idea of moving exclusively to public funding of campaigns will be sneered at, if it is noted at all. And in the event that anyone pays attention and chooses to rejoin, he is prepared to endure the slings and arrows, verbal at least, of those who would criticize.

On the other hand, the idea is not as outrageous as it might sound. Serious proposals have been floated in which actual public funding—not the optional, basically flim-flam, deceptive, half-hearted "public financing" schemes that are claimed to be available for paying for campaigns—is a reality. For example, two law professors, Bruce Ackerman and Ian Ayres, have advanced an attractive idea called "Voting with Dollars."[19] The basic idea is that voters would receive a voucher of $50 ("Patriot Dollars") to donate to federal campaigns of their choice; any separate private donations would have to be made through the FEC, not directly to candidates or campaigns.

Another reform idea is called "Clean Money."[20] Essentially it provides public money for qualifying candidates (they must reach a certain threshold of "seriousness" by collecting a specified number of small—$5 is the amount often mentioned—donations) for both primary and general elections. Unlike "Voting with Dollars," it can be used at both federal and state/local levels; enabling legislation has already been passed in Maine and Vermont.

Both of these proposals are appealing. "Voting with Dollars" could be adapted to the state/local level as well as for federal offices. It would require that the FEC acquire actual enforcement powers with teeth in them, something it now lacks. And it presumes a level of non-partisanship and fairness that state elections offices—notorious for playing hardball partisan politics—have not in the past always demonstrated.

But "Voting with Dollars" would find favor among those who, recognizing the need to remove private money from campaigns, still want voters to have the ability to make individual contribution choices. Clean Money allows for such choice also; voters would have to ante up $5 or so, to help reach a threshold so that their favored candidate could receive public funding.

Neither of these plans would work if full disclosure of names were not part of the deal. Nor would they work if unlimited, independent soft money expenditures were still part of the campaign scene.

Indeed, even if neither of these and similar ideas received the public attention and approval they deserve, and at most elected public officials (who obviously like the system as it now exists, since it worked for them) agreed to tinker with present practices, the public interest would still be mightily served by limiting the amount of independent money that could be raised and spent, or by eliminating it altogether, and insisting on full public disclosure of any—ANY—campaign donation, of whatever kind. To do this, either a Constitutional Amendment would have to be proposed and adopted (as of this writing, there is one in the works, but pushing Amendments onto the public agenda and successfully passing them has a Sisyphusian difficulty to it), or the U.S. Supreme Court would have to change its mind and overturn *Citizens United* and the decisions it spawned, or the Congress and state legislatures would have to pass necessary legislation limiting the kind of donations that are possible. The author is not in the least bit optimistic about the prospects for any of this happening.

There is another possibility, one which it is recognized might not be feasible (because of First Amendment issues, not merely because of *Citizens United*), to abolish private donations—soft or hard—to political campaigns. If that proves to be the case, then serious consideration should be given to taxing private contributions—all of them, no matter how big or small, whether hard money or soft money. And the tax should be substantial—nay, confiscatory—probably a minimum of 100 percent (although something more draconian would be desirable). In other words, at 100 percent, a donation of $1.00 would carry with it a tax of $1.00. A soft money donation of $500,000 would carry with it a tax of equal amount, but there is absolutely no reason why soft money donations could not be taxed at a higher rate than hard money contributions. A 500 percent tax, for example, on soft money might put a serious damper on the amount of soft money that anyone—individuals or corporations or SuperPacs—would be willing to put up.

The tax would be levied by election officials in the relevant jurisdiction of the campaign. In other words, a donation for a presidential, senatorial, or U.S. House of Representatives campaign would be levied by the FEC. A donation for a County Commission candidate would be taxed by the local county Supervisor of Elections or the equivalent official. The donation to the actual campaign, or the soft money equivalent, could not be accepted until the tax was paid in full. The result would be that the donor would end up paying much more than anticipated, and the relevant administrative unit for the election would have a supplement to its "regular" budget.

Does this proposal "solve" the problem of private money entering a public enterprise, the political campaign? No. But it might put a brake on the amount of money raised on behalf of a candidate, and it might force candidates to seek more and smaller private money donations, since it would be to the financial advantage of the donor to give less, not more.

And there is a final consideration. Roger Austin, an attorney and long-time Republican political consultant in Florida, argued in his doctoral dissertation that if we really want to engage in serious reform of campaign finance, we have to stop the internally contradictory ways in which we have been going about doing it.[21] In particular, he notes, most campaign finance reforms (which began early in the twentieth century) involved both disclosure requirements and regulations of one kind or another. These actually worked in opposite ways, the result of which is that the reforms were doomed to failure. Disclosure, as we have noted at several points in this book, forces openness and transparency. Regulations involve the opposite—because, as Austin observes, the moment regulations are imposed, lawyers and politicians and other political operatives will work assiduously to find ways around them, or to avoid them, which is the opposite of transparency.

Recognizing that it would be both impossible and wrong-headed to abandon all regulations, but recognizing further that they can and should be more sharply, even narrowly, tailored, Austin's recommendation is that we put much more emphasis on full disclosure if we expect to improve campaign finance laws. His suggestion parallels the one made earlier in this book and this chapter: any private moneys donated to political campaigns, assuming we cannot get rid of them altogether, must be fully and immediately and publicly disclosed. Anything less will further undermine public confidence in the integrity of our democratic elections.

## We the People

As is so often the case, the outcome of proposals about how political campaigns are run and paid for is up to We the People.

The truth of the matter is that we, as a nation, could do much better at preserving our democratic elections than we have. In the present instance, we are rapidly in the business of selling our campaigns and elections to massive corporate conglomerates and plutocrats, the 1 percent or so of the population who have a decidedly mal-proportioned share of the wealth. Their interests—their class interest as well as their private individual interests—are not those of the other 99 percent. And we have turned the design and execution of our campaigns to a Campaign Industry that has not only created and perpetuated some of its least democratic qualities, but is itself so gigantic as to ally itself with Big Money, not the everyday voters whom it is trying to attract for its candidates.

Indeed, in one sense the Tea Partyers are right. We need to take back our political campaigns and stop the selfish, destructive, corrosive, unfair practices that have been allowed to pollute them. We need to take back our campaigns and elections, not sell them to wealthy individuals and corporations, so that we can tell ourselves, and both our friends and adversaries abroad, that we do practice democracy when we campaign and vote. But doing so is up to We the People. There is no other way.

## Notes

1  A helpful overview of a controversy created when the IRS began to investigate some Tea Party organizations, but not big time SuperPacs, can be found at Dylan Matthews, "Everything You Need to Know about the IRS Scandal in One FAQ," *Washington Post*, May 14, 2013, viewed online at www.washingtonpost.com/blogs/wonkblog/wp/2013/05/14/everything-you-need-to-know-about-the-irs-scandal-in-one-faq, June 30, 2014. See also, Editorial Board, "The Real Internal Revenue Scandal," *New York Times*, July 5, 2014, viewed online at www.nytimes.com/2014/07/06/opinion/sunday/the-real-internal-revenue-scandal.html?hp&action=click&pgtype=Homepage&module=c-column-top-span-region&region=c-column-top-span-region&WT.nav=c-column-top-span-region, July 6, 2014.

2  *Citizens United* actually rejected this allegation, saying that no evidence had been presented that any donors were harmed because names came forward.

3  See, for example, Jon Terbush, "Anthony Weiner May Just Have Destroyed His Mayoral Campaign," *The Week*, July 23, 2013, viewed online at http://theweek.com/article/index/247262/anthony-weiner-may-have-just-destroyed-his-mayoral-campaign#, September 9, 2013. Weiner finished last in a field of five in the Democratic mayoral primary, winning only 31,000+ votes, or 4.9 percent of the total. See *New York Times*, September 11, 2013, viewed online at http://projects.nytimes.com/live-dashboard/nyc-primary#sha= 10cdce997, September 11, 2013. See also Michael M. Grynbaum, "Forgive? No, a Night to Forget for Scandal-Tarred Candidates," *New York Times*, September 11, 2013, viewed online at www.nytimes.com/2013/09/12/ nyregion/forgive-no-a-night-to-forget-for-scandal-tarred-candidates.html?hp, September 13, 2013.

4  Kate Taylor, "Stringer Defeats Spitzer in Comptroller Primary," *New York Times*, September 10, 2013, viewed online at www.nytimes.com/2013/ 09/11/nyregion/stringer-defeats-spitzer-in-comptroller-primary.html, August 16, 2014.

5  See Corey Hutchins, "You Can Always Go Home Again," Slate.com, March 20, 2013, viewed online at www.slate.com/articles/news_and_politics/ politics/2013/03/mark_sanford_in_republican_primary_runoff_the_former_ south_carolina_governor.html, August 7, 2014. See also the Chronicle of Coverage of Mark Sanford, *New York Times*, online at http://topics. nytimes.com/top/reference/timestopics/people/s/mark_sanford/index.html.

6  See, most prominently, John C. Green, "The Dimensions of Disgust: Citizen Attitudes and Codes of Campaign Conduct," a white paper from the Institute for Global Ethics, Bliss Institute, University of Akron, n.d., viewed online at www.google.com/url?sa=t&rct=j&q=&esrc=s&source=web&cd=5&ved=0CF MQFjAE&url=http%3A%2F%2Fwww.globalethics.org%2Ffiles%2Fwp_dis gust_1222959853.pdf%2F19%2F&ei=0rUwUqmAAorj2wXuw4GYAw&usg =AFQjCNETiJoEg7diwJb_JnTLuJg7IcFiKQ&sig2=NGPGwnQe9n14jpz9H- 9I_g&bvm=bv.52109249,d.aWM, September 11, 2013.

7  See for example Nathaniel Persily and Kelli Lamie, "Perceptions of Corruption and Campaign Finance," *University Of Pennsylvania Law Review*, Vol. 153, No. 1, p. 119 (November 2004); viewed online at www.pennlawreview.com/ print/old/Persily_Lammie.pdf; See also Robert Weissberg, "Why There Is 'Too Much' Money In Elections," *American Thinker*, February 2, 2012, viewed online at www.americanthinker.com/2012/02/why_there_is_too_much_ money_in_elections.html; both viewed September 11, 2013.

8  See for example Daniel Fisher, "Inside the Koch Empire: How the Brothers Plan to Reshape America," *Forbes*, December 24, 2012, viewed online at www.forbes.com/sites/danielfisher/2012/12/05/inside-the-koch-empire-how- the-brothers-plan-to-reshape-america; see also Dave Levinthal, "Koch Industries PAC Spending Significantly More Compared to Recent Election Cycles," Truth-Out, The Center for Public Integrity, June 23, 2013, viewed online at www.truth-out.org/news/item/17152-koch-industries-pac-spending- significantly-more-compared-to-recent-election-cycles; both viewed September 11, 2013.

9  A recent example of pay-to-play, which has become a classic, took place in Illinois, ensnaring Governor Rod Blagojevich, for which he went to prison. See Dan Spencer, "Gov. Blagojevitch Arrested, Pay to Play Scandal Now Includes Obama's Vacant Seat," examiner.com, December 9, 2008, viewed

online at www.examiner.com/article/gov-blagojevich-arrested-pay-to-play-scandal-now-includes-obama-s-vacant-seat; and Janan Hanna, "Rod Blagojevitch Trial: Ali Ata's Testimony Details Pay-To-Play Schemes but Says He Was Not Promised State Job, Huffingtonpost.com, May 25, 2011, viewed online at www.huffingtonpost.com/2010/06/18/rod-blagojevich-trial-ali_n_ 617103.html; both viewed September 13, 2013.

10  See, for example, Mark Grossman, *Political Corruption in America* (Santa Barbara, CA: ABC-CLIO, 2003); Michael Johnston, *Syndromes of Corruption* (Cambridge: Cambridge University Press, 2005); Edward L. Glaeser and Claudia Goldin (eds.), *Corruption and Reform* (Chicago: The University of Chicago Press, 2006); Kim Long, *The Almanac of Political Corruption, Scandals, and Dirty Politics* (New York: The Delacorte Press, 2007); and Michael A. Genovese and Victoria A. Farrar-Myers (eds.), CORRUPTION And AMERICAN POLITICS (Amherst, N.Y: Cambria Press, 2010).

11  See Michael Johnston, "Democracy without Politics? Hidden Costs of Corruption and Reform in America," in Genovese and Farrar-Myers (eds.), *Corruption and American Politics* (2010), Chapter 1, pp. 9–35.

12  See, most recently, Pew Research Center for the People and the Press, "Public Trust in Government 1958–2013," January 31, 2013, viewed online at www.people-press.org/2013/01/31/trust-in-government-interactive, September 13, 2013. This Pew Report claims that public trust in government was, as 2013 dawned, near all-time historical lows.

13  There is little on the political or legal horizon to suggest that corporate consolidation of media ownership will not continue. See for example Edward S. Herman and Robert McChesney, *The Global Media* (London: Cassell, 1998); Edward S. Herman and Noam Chomsky, *Manufacturing Consent* (New York: Pantheon, 2002); and Patricia Landis, "The Ethical Implications of Monopoly Media Ownership," Ohio University, Institute for Applied and Professional Ethics, July 27, 2009, viewed online at www.ohio.edu/ethics/2001-conferences/the-ethical-implications-of-monopoly-media-ownership/index.htm l, June 27, 2014.

14  The media coverage of Donald Trump's presidential candidacy in the summer, 2015, made him seem like a buffoon. See, for example, Harry Enten, "Two Good Reasons Not To Take the Donald Trump 'Surge' Seriously," fivethirtyeight.com, July 16, 2015, viewed online at http://fivethirtyeight.com/datalab/two-good-reasons-not-to-take-the-donald-trump-surge-seriously; Bossip, "Huffington Post Refuses to Recognize Donald Trump's Presidential Bid As a Real Candidacy," Bossip.com, July 17, 2015, viewed online at http://bossip.com/1192997/huffington-post-refuses-to-recognize-donald-trumps-presidential-bid-as-a-real-candidacy; and Sara Murray, "Why Donald Trump is Surging in the Polls," CNN, July 17, 2015, viewed online at www.cnn.com/2015/07/17/politics/donald-trump-summer-surge; all viewed July 18, 2015. Huffingtonpost.com actually announced in mid-July, 2015 that it would not cover the Trump campaign in its politics section, but rather in its entertainment section. See, for example, Jesse Byrnes, "Huffington Post to Cover Trump as Entertainment News, not Politics," *The Hill*, July 17, 2015, viewed online at http://thehill.com/blogs/ballot-box/presidential-races/248314-huffington-post-to-cover-trump-as-entertainment-news-not; and Megan Garner, "Is Donald Trump's Campaign 'News" or 'Entertainment?'", n.d., viewed online at www.theatlantic.com/politics/archive/2015/07/does-donald-trump-deserve-news-coverage/398876/; both viewed July 18, 2015.

15  See the postings of Electronic Frontier Foundation (EFF), "Net Neutrality,"

May and June, 2014, viewed online at www.eff.org/issues/net-neutrality; and American Civil Liberties Union (ACLU), "What is Net Neutrality," n.d., viewed online at www.eff.org/issues/net-neutrality, both viewed June 27, 2014.

16　Readers are invited to review the discussion of social media, including sources and citations, in Chapter 5.

17　See for example, Leslie Kaufman, "News Corp. Buys a Media Start-Up for \$25 Million," *New York Times*, December 20, 2013, viewed online at www.nytimes.com/2013/12/21/business/media/news-corp-acquires-storyful.html?_r=0, June 27, 2014.

18　See for example Susan Page, "Why 90 Million Americans Won't Vote in November," *USA Today*, August 15, 2012, viewed online at http://usatoday30.usatoday.com/news/politics/story/2012-08-15/non-voters-obama-romney/57055184/1; a 2002 survey of voters and non-voters in New Zealand found very much the same results as mentioned in the text. See "Voter and Non-Voter Satisfaction Survey, 2002," New Zealand Chief Electoral Office, Ministry of Justice, 2002, viewed online at www.elections.org.nz/events/past-events-0/general-elections-1996-2005/general-elections-1996-2005/voter-and-non-voter-0, both viewed August 16, 2014. There is also an abundance of scholarship supporting the view expressed in the text. Three representative sources are Sarah Birch, "Perceptions of Electoral Fairness and Voter Turnout," *Comparative Political Studies*, Vol. 43, pp. 1601–1622 (2010); Alan S. Gerber, Gregory A. Huber, David Doherty, Conor M. Dowling, and Seth J. Hill, "Do Perceptions of Ballot Secrecy Influence Turnout? Results from a Field Experiment." *American Journal of Political Science*, Vol. 57, pp. 537–551 (2013); and Matthew R. Miles, "Turnout as Consent: How Fair Governance Encourages Voter Participation." *Political Research Quarterly*, vVl. 68, pp. 363–376 (2015).

19　Bruce Ackerman and Ian Ayres, *Voting With Dollars*: A New Paradigm for Campaign Finance (New Haven, CT: Yale University Press, 2004).

20　Third World Traveler, "Frequently Asked Questions About Clean Money Campaign Reform," n.d., viewed online at www.thirdworldtraveler.com/Political/FAQsCleanMoney_PublCamp.html, May 31, 2012.

21　Roger Austin, *Patterns Of Failure—Rethinking Campaign Finance Reform: What Went Wrong?*, Ph.D. dissertation, Department of Political Science, University of Florida, 2015. As of this writing, Mr. Austin's dissertation has tentatively been accepted; the final defense is scheduled for early fall, 2015.

# Index